GREAT BIRDS
OF THE
GALAXY

GENE RODDENBERRY
& THE CREATORS OF TREK
EDWARD GROSS AND MARK A. ALTMAN

BⓄXTREE

First published in the UK 1994
by BOXTREE LIMITED, Broadwall House
21 Broadwall, London SE1 9PL

10 9 8 7 6 5 4 3 2 1

Some photographs courtesy Foto Fantasies

ISBN: 0 7522 0968 X

Book design by Paul Nicosia
Cover design by Bridgewater Books

Printed and bound in Great Britain by
Redwood Books, Trowbridge, Wiltshire.

C O N T E N T S

It's been 30 years since *Star Trek*'s first pilot, "The Cage," was filmed, and today Gene Roddenberry's universe is more popular than it has ever been. With the original series still telecast around the world, *The Next Generation* effortlessly making the transition from television to movie screens, and the phenomenal syndicated success of *Deep Space Nine* and *Voyager*, *Star Trek* continues to defy the odds as it becomes an even more familiar fixture in our daily lives.

The feature film *Star Trek: Generations* unites the centuries as captains James T. Kirk (William Shatner) and Jean Luc Picard (Patrick Stewart) are brought together for the first time to combat a common adversary. This is an historic moment for a couple of reasons. First, it quite literally represents the passing of the torch from one generation to the other. Second, and perhaps more importantly, it serves as final proof that *Star Trek* is bigger than its creator; that this science fiction universe, if placed in the proper creative hands, will live long and prosper far beyond anyone's imagination.

The late Roddenberry, who had been affectionately known as the Great Bird of the Galaxy, had seen many successors — some approved, some not — over the years who have successfully cultivated the territory he initially pioneered. As early as 1967, in the middle of the original *Star Trek*'s first season, Gene L. Coon, the brilliant writer/producer, guided — and some say defined — the series and wrote many of its most remarkable episodes. In 1968, Roddenberry officially bid adieu to *Star Trek*, choosing Fred Freiberger as his replacement. It was Freiberger who was given the task of piloting *Star Trek* through its stormy third and final season on NBC.

After the critical and near fiscal failure of *Star Trek: The Motion Picture*, which had been shepherded through production by Roddenberry, producer Harve Bennett took over the film series and steered it for four installments. Both series stars Leonard Nimoy and William Shatner got "a piece of the action" as directors and co-writers of their own missions after Nicholas Meyer saved the series with his critically acclaimed sequel, the bargain basement budgeted *Star Trek II: The Wrath of Khan*. Shatner and Nimoy, who had long exerted influence on the original series and in long story conferences on the feature films, each had a chance to shape a *Star Trek* adventure.

Meanwhile, new territory in the *Star Trek* universe was being charted by Roddenberry, who had once again found himself producing a weekly episodic *Trek* series, *Star Trek: The Next Generation*. After controversy early in the show's run and personal illness forced him to relinquish his heavy-handed control over the series, new great birds rose to the task of shaping the latest *Trek*.

Executive Producer Rick Berman, along with first and second season producer Maurice Hurley, helped shape the early voyages of the Enterprise-D. Michael Piller sent the starship spiraling into orbit in its latter years while also joining Berman to create *Deep Space Nine* and *Voyager*. In terms of the latter, the producing duo collaborated with co-creator Jeri Taylor, who had succeeded Piller as executive producer of *The Next Generation* when he had gone on to *DS9*.

In light of Roddenberry's death, many of his most virulent detractors have subsequently tempered their comments with praise in respect, but it is important to note that film and television is a collaborative medium. While critics like Andrew Sarris and the late Francois Truffaut may live and die by the auteur theory, it was not one man that gave *Star Trek* life, but a group of creative and talented writers, producers and actors who contributed to its incredible popularity and endurance.

In the looming shadow of Gene Roddenberry, the passionate and strong-spirited creator, the accomplishments of many of those who gave his creation life have been obscured. Whether this was by design or merely omission resulting from the subsequent deification of Roddenberry by fervent fans, we may never know. When approached for comment, Roddenberry was already very ill and died several weeks later. In this book, we attempt to remedy the oversight which has kept many of the other deserving beneficiaries from the *Star Trek* Spotlight and put them center stage.

"When they dedicated the Gene Roddenberry building, it was clear from people like Leonard and Bill Shatner that they were going to talk about people like Harve Bennett and Gene Coon who have made this thing successful," says former *Trek* film producer Ralph Winter. "There were so many times when there were problems and someone didn't know how we would get by the obstacle, and it would fall on Harve to solve it. Harve is absolutely the unheralded guy to save the series of films. The second name I would put in there would be Nick Meyer in terms of writing and directing on *Star Trek II* and *VI* and having done a significant part of the writing on *Star Trek IV*."

But for many it will not be the frail, elderly man in the wheelchair they remember as *Star Trek*'s creator and original great bird, but the stubborn, obstinate and imaginative captain of the continuing *Star Trek* saga. The man whose boundless energy and imagination gave birth to a universe which often brought him into conflict with others and resulted in one of the most memorable pop culture phenomenons of the 20th century. Without conflict, there would be no art and despite many of the more vehement arguments, fights and disputes Roddenberry had over the years with a myriad of his peers — including the battles that typified the early genesis of *The Next Generation* — his vision lives on and will continue to be carried forth by great birds like Rick Berman, Michael Piller and Jeri Taylor, who have captured the spirit of his creation and continue to explore brave new worlds and civilizations, as well as those who are closing the log book on the voyages of the original starship Enterprise.

Mark A. Altman
Edward Gross

August 1994

It's good to be Great Bird! Gene Roddenberry and friends on the set of the telefilm, Spectre (photo copyright ©1975 20th Century-Fox)

GENE RODDENBERRY
FIRST GREAT BIRD OF THE GALAXY

The universe was supposedly created via a big bang eons ago, at a time beyond imagining. Determining the birthdate of the final frontier is a considerably easier task.

Flash back. El, Paso Texas, 1921. The birth of Gene Roddenberry, the infant destined to become Great Bird of the Galaxy, and the person who would grow up to—quite unwittingly—trigger a cultural phenomenon whose impact continues to be felt today.

Growing up in Los Angeles, Roddenberry eventually pursued a potential career in aeronautical engineering in college, and was an Army pilot during World War II. Following that stint, he became a pilot for Pan Am and a police officer for the LAPD, where he wrote speeches for Chief William Parker. In some ways, the latter played a role in helping him achieve the self-proclaimed position of humanist.

"I was Parker's speech writer," Roddenberry told his official biographer, David Alexander, "writing his philosophical beliefs. I had to justify for him many of the things he did. These were things of rare honesty. I was close to him in the days when he dreamed of building a better police department and when he was engaged in putting his dreams into action. We exchanged a lot of confidences as our relationship went beyond that of a chief of police and one of his sergeants. He used me as a philosophical sounding board, and I used him the same way. Our relationship was such that we were capable of intimate thought and philosophical exchanges. After he and I left the department and went our separate ways, it was difficult to maintain that former closeness. Some time later, I learned he was giving a speech and slipped into the back of the audience to hear him. After the speech, he saw me, came up, and gripped my arm in a gesture of friendship. A week later he died."

While serving as a police officer, Roddenberry also pursued his dream of becoming a writer. Between 1954 and 1959 he wrote for *Mr. Ditrict Attorney* (five episodes), *Highway Patrol* (four episodes), *I Led Three Lives* (three episodes), *West Point Story* (twelve episodes), *Dr. Christian* (one episode), *Kaiser Aluminum Hour* (one episode), *Jane Wyman's Fireside* (one episode), *Boots & Saddles* (five episodes), *Harbor Command* (one episode), *Jefferson Drum* (three episodes), *The Night Stick* (one episode), and *Have Gun Will Travel* (which he became head writer of and ultimately wrote 18 episodes for between the years 1957 and 1962). During these years, he also made his first attempt at science fiction: "The Secret Defense of 117" (starring Ricardo Montalban) for the *Chevron Hall of Stars*.

Between 1960 and 1962 he free-lanced for *The Detectives* (two episodes), *The June Allyson Show* (one episode), *Two Faces West* (one episode), *Shannon* (two episodes), and one episode each for *Target: The Corruptors, Dr. Kildare, Naked City* and *G.E. True*. He also began to investigate the possibility of creating his own series by writing such original pilots as *333 Montgomery* (starring DeForest Kelley), a World War II adventure entitled *APO-923*, and essentially a remake of *333 Montgomery* called *Defiance Country*. None of them went to series, though they certainly whet Roddenberry's appetite in terms of becoming a producer.

"[These pilots] were produced by other people," Roddenberry explained, "and none of them sold. I began to see that to create a program idea and write a script simply wasn't enough. The story is not 'told' until it's on celluloid. Telling that final story involved sound, music, casting, costumes, sets and all the things that a producer is responsible for. Therefore it became apparent to me that if you want the film to reflect accurately what you felt when you wrote the script, then you have to produce it, too. This is why television writers tend to become producers.

"Producing in television is like storytelling," he said. "The choice of the actor, picking the right costumes, getting the right flavor, the right pace—these are as much a part of storytelling as writing out that same description of a character in a novel. Although the director plays an important role in this, the director in television comes on a show to prepare for a week, shoots for a week, and then goes on to another show. Unlike the producer, he is neither there at the beginning of the script nor rarely there for long after you end up with some 25,000 feet of film which now has to be cut and pasted into something unified. There is immense creative challenge and pleasure in taking all of these things and putting them together into something that works."

"Writing for the television audi-

Richard Boone as Paladin in Have Gun Will Travel, *the series on which Roddenberry made his most important advancement as a writer prior to* Star Trek.

ence," he explained in 1988, "does the same thing as the great sculptors and painters and composers also do. What you do is say to the world, 'Hey, these are things as I see it! These are my comments. This is how I see the world.' And you do this with utter selfishness, which is what an artist should always do. All writers should be selfish and say, 'This is the way that I see it,' and under the voice should say, 'Screw you! If you want yours, you can do it too.'"

It was with this attitude that Roddenberry approached his first television producing assignment: 1963's *The Lieutenant*, which starred Gary Lockwood, who would, incidentally, go on to guest star in *Star Trek*'s second pilot, "Where No Man Has Gone Before." In the series, Lockwood portrayed Lt. William Rice, and the essential thrust was an emphasis on the life of a newly commissioned officer in the Marine Corps during peacetime.

Of the series, Roddenberry himself has explained, "*The Lieutenant* was not a Marine Corps picture, although the Marine Corps thought so. It was a story of a young man growing up. I just picked

Gary Lockwood, seen here on the set of Stanley Kubrick's 2001, starred in the Roddenberry-produced series, The Lieutenant (photo copyright ©1968 MGM)

the Marine Corps because a lot of the decisions he has to make are very dramatic. He's in charge of a platoon of men and all that, but I could have easily put him in a stockbroker's office and told the same stories. We did stories about his first unfair boss. His first ideals, which were shattered. His first designing woman. All of the firsts that happen in a young man's life, and his growths as he does those thing and deals with those things. And his first moral thing that he has to stand up for even though it may cost him something. It was kind of a fun show to do.

"The thing I remember best about *The Lieutenant*, was an episode we did which had Dennis Hopper, who was still unknown then, and a young black actor, whom I haven't seen in years [Note: Don Marshall, later to star in *Land of the Giants*]. Lieutenants have platoons in the military and my lieutenant's platoon had a black Marine who rather disliked this white Marine. Those were the days when television was finally allowed to show its first blacks on screen. Until then, it hadn't happened. I remember being invited to write an episode of a show called *Riverboat*, which I proudly

turned down on the basis that it was life on the Mississippi in the 1800's and one rule in it was *no blacks*! So we were sort of pushing the envelope [with *The Lieutenant*]. We had this black Marine at a time in which [on TV] a shoeshine boy had to be white. The preferred occupation for a black was brain surgeon because the networks were so overcome with this idea, 'Aren't we brave, but we don't want to be *too* brave.' But I thought it was a great thing, because it was the black who was prejudiced, and so we made the show. My problem was not the Marine Corps, it was NBC, who turned down the show flat. The studio, MGM, said, 'You've spent $117,000 which we won't be able to recover, and we take this very seriously.' And $117,000 in those days was very serious! Today, the television budgets are a million plus.

"So there was only one thing I could do," he elaborated. "I went out to the NAACP and they lowered the boom on NBC, and they said prejudice is prejudice whatever the color and it's a perfectly legitimate theme to have. And so we were able to show it. One thing I remember about that show particularly, though, was after the Lieutenant had tried to bring about tolerance in his platoon through common sense, and failed miserably, his captain called him in. His captain was played by Robert Vaughn. Brilliantly played. The captain pointed out that he had failed, but he said, 'I'm curious about one thing, Lieutenant. Had you succeeded, what would your next move have been? [Would] you walk on water?'

"Also, I learned tolerance for Marines. Some of them hated the show. They believed the Marines could only be done well by John Wayne coming over the hill with a machine-gun. But a kind of surprising number of people, both enlisted men and higher ups, said that this young man growing up is a valid symbol for young men in the service, too, and we should have soldiers like that. We never resolved that, because about this time a war in Asia began

shaping up and we made some early protests about this. But we didn't get a second year on the air, although I think this was more NBC than the United States Marine Corps."

Things weren't always peaceful, as Roddenberry pointed out, particularly due to a script that was submitted for approval. "The Marine Corps got mad at us finally because we insisted on doing this script, based on a true story, where a young sergeant was up for officer candidate school [and] he was denied because is mother was in the Communist Party. They didn't want us to do that, but we insisted on doing it."

The Lieutenant only lasted 29 episodes, but it was significant for several reasons. First off, it created a working relationship between Roddenberry and a great many people who would eventually work on *Star Trek*, including Leonard Nimoy, Nichelle Nichols, director Marc Daniels, Lockwood, Walter Koenig and director Robert Butler. Additionally, it was during the production of this series that he developed his initial concepts for what would eventually become *Star Trek*.

THE TREK BEGINS

Roddenberry's interest in science fiction can be traced back to his childhood. "I was 11 years old," he recalled, "and there was a boy in my class who life had treated badly. He limped, he wheezed, I don't know all the things that were wrong with him, but he was a charming, lovely, intelligent person. He, because of being unable to get on the athletic field and do many of the things that others were able to do, had sort of gone into his own world of fantasy and science fiction. He had been collecting the old *Amazing* and *Astounding* magazines from those great old days and he introduced me to science fiction. I was not very healthy as a young boy and science fiction offered me an escape [as well]. You could travel to strange worlds, meeting interesting creatures and, regardless of your disability, were able to travel anywhere. I remember listening to some of those old science fiction radio shows and being fascinated by them—they really encouraged your imagination. In fact, the radio itself was science fiction to me. But science fiction challenged the imagination and as a young boy that appealed to me greatly. The funny thing is that everything is science fiction at one time or another. The time we're living in right now would be science fiction to people living 100 years ago.

"[So] I started to read them [*Amazing, Astounding*] and then discovered, in our neighborhood, living above a garage was an ex-con who had come into science fiction when he was in prison. He introduced me to *John Carter* and those wonderful Burroughs things. By the time I was 12 or 13, I had been very much into the whole science fiction field."

Which is not to say that when he got into writing, he saw science fiction as the primary creative vehicle to express himself.

"Although I suppose you could have called me a science fiction fan, this certainly was not the Alpha-Omega of my reading," related Roddenberry. "I think all writers are omnivorous in their reading. I know few writers that I respect that read only science fiction. Isaac Asimov, for example, I know reads broadly on history, economics, sociology, everything. As a result, when I decided to become a writer, I decided to become a *writer*, not just a science fiction writer."

Like Rod Serling before him, Roddenberry saw science fiction (with *Star Trek* as the particular mode of communication) as an opportunity to explore some of life's "larger" themes, while continuing a tradition of literary creativity begun centuries earlier.

"I had been a freelance writer for about a dozen years and was chafing increasingly at the commercial censorship on television, which was very strong in those days," he said. "You really couldn't talk about anything you cared to talk about [and] I decided I was going to leave TV unless I could find some way to write what I wanted to. A writer is an artist who's very job is about opening his mind to things.

"I once wrote into a script that the newspapers on the corner were held down in the wind by a tire iron. I needed that because someone was going to grab a heavy object there as a weapon in a scene. I was called in and they said, 'Please take the tire iron out and make it a brick.' I said I sort of like the tire iron. And they said, 'Yes, but it really conjures up the failure of an advertised product—tires—and we'd rather not have that. It actually reached that far. In those days, you couldn't, in a Western, have your people 'ford' a river because you might be trying to get Chevrolet as sponsor.

"I couldn't get a show on television questioning whether or not the United States was a mistake," Roddenberry continued. "I cannot write a television drama commenting seriously on unions or management, or on the armament sales that we're involved in. I couldn't write, assuming I wanted to, a pro-Arab, anti-Israel drama. Now, the answers you get are that, 'Yes, but we do brave things in news and public affairs programming.' What they miss is the fact that fiction affects people more strongly than news and public affairs. Drama makes you identify with what's happening. If a good writer, or many good writers, during the Vietnam conflict had been permitted to write fictional tales of what was happening in Vietnam, making you identify and become a Vietnamese peasant whose daughter has just been burned to death by napalm; or had we been able to write fiction so you could feel the horrible changing of a man that produced a Calley and made you become that man and wrench your guts as it happened, I'm absolutely certain that the war would have been over two years earlier.

"I recalled that when Jonathan Swift was writing *Gulliver's Travels*, he wanted to write satire on his time and went to Lilliput in his story to do just that, [and] then he could talk about insane prime ministers and crooked kings and all of that. It was sort of this wonderful thing. Children could read it as a fairy tale, an adventure, and as they got older they'd recognize it for what it really is. It seemed to me that perhaps if I wanted to talk about sex, religion, politics, make some comments against Vietnam and so on, that if I had similar situations involving these subjects happening on other planets to little green people, indeed it might get by and it did.

"I apparently went right over the censors' heads, but all the fourteen year olds in our audience knew exactly what we were talking about. Also, I had watched science fiction. I was not a science fiction writer, though. I had written all sorts of things. I had said, 'Gee, too much of science fiction is about gadgetry and not about people. And drama is people. If I ever get the chance to write science fiction, I'm going to try to make it scientifically accurate as possible and write them the way we wrote the old *Playhouse 90*. And it worked. I thought that [*Star Trek*] might be a way I could infiltrate my ideas, and that's what it's been all the time. It's difficult for people to understand that even in the barren vineyards of television you might do these things. Actually, you can do them better there because you reach more people with more impact. You don't do it by each of your episodes being a fine *Hallmark Hall of Fame*, or those great shows that are meaningful and deep and advertised as such. The power you have is in a show like *Star Trek*, which is considered by many people to be a frothy little action-adventure; unimportant, unbelievable and yet watched by a lot of people. You just slip ideas into it."

Morality plays had been a staple of his writing efforts for television, and it was a form which was given the opportunity to bloom fully in the *Star Trek* format. "I have always written that way," he detailed, "and, again, I think all writers who care about their writing *do* write that way. For example, right now I am thinking of *Have Gun Will Travel*, a nice shoot 'em up western. I wrote a script in which the basic theme was the story of a Protestant pastor who was the reverend in a large penitentiary and it was really a story of how could he equate his feelings of 'Thou shall not kill' with the fact that he had to march with a prisoner into death row and participate in a man being executed. He had to ask himself, 'If I believe in Christ,' or his particular messiah, 'what would he have done? Would he have gone along with it because it's easier within the system? Or would he have said, "Stop, you've got to take me first?"'

"So, yes, I think all writers who care about their writing write that way. Now the reason it was more obvious in *Star Trek* is, as you know, science fiction is one of the most marvelous vehicles in the world for making comment. I agree with Ray Bradbury who said some years ago that science fiction is really one of the last places we've got where the philosopher can operate and roam as freely as he wishes. This is certainly true of all science fiction classics. I don't know how you could make a stronger statement against letting our society become a police state than George Orwell made in 1984. Powerful statement. Science fiction *lends* itself to these things and this is why it is a little more obvious on a *Star Trek* than maybe on a series like *Have Gun Will Travel*, or some other thing. I think that this is why SF has become so much a favorite type of reading of colleges and just generally bright people across the land, because SF makes comments: Who are we? Where are we going? What is it all about?"

Roddenberry's initial concept for *Star Trek* concerned a starship of the Federation of Planets whose mission would be to —if you'll pardon the cliché —"explore strange new worlds, seek out new lives and new civilizations...to boldly go where no man has gone before." Interestingly, many people have

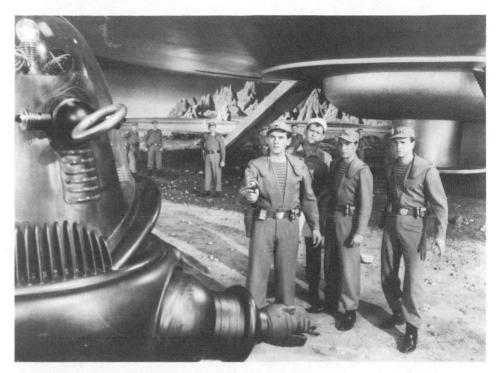

Although Roddenberry denied it, Forbidden Planet *was seen by many as an influence on the creation of* Star Trek *(photo copyright ©1994 Turner Entertainment).*

expressed their feeling that the concept was heavily influenced by the classic science fiction film, *Forbidden Planet*.

"Definitely not," differed Roddenberry in the 1970s. "The only time I ever thought of *Forbidden Planet* specifically when I was laying *Star Trek* out was when I said to myself that here were some mistakes they made in the film that I did not want to repeat. I think one of the obvious mistakes, and one that amazed me when I saw the show, although I generally liked [it], was the fact that you had a ship capable of interstellar travel and you had a cook aboard who scrubbed pots and pans by hand, and I said, 'Hey, come on, it just doesn't fit.' At least they would have had a radar range oven or something if they had interstellar capacity! But, no, I cannot remember a single time during the planning of *Star Trek* that I looked at another show and said, 'I will borrow this.' On the other hand, of course, you have this marvelous thing called a brain that all of your life is storing away information and sometimes you pull it out and say, 'This is Heinlein in such and such.' Or even

probably what happens more often is your brain, being the marvelous thing it will, will take bits and pieces from three or four things and then meld them together in something you need for a particular show. Most writers who are good writers, or at least *care*, very seldom borrow things specifically. *Hacks* do that. On the other hand, most good writers do write things where people can go to them and say, 'Ah, this is a bit of this from this and this a bit of that from that,' but they don't write it that way."

In 1991 the world celebrated *Star Trek*'s 25th Anniversary, but in 1963 its basic premise was unlike anything that had been seen on television before. As stated previously, Gene Roddenberry had developed his initial thoughts for the series while producing *The Lieutenant* and failing to get series interest in his cop (*Police Story*) and western (*The Long Hunt of April Savage*) pilots. Roddenberry's original series presentation, dated March 11, 1964, described *Star Trek* as "a one-hour dramatic television series; action-adventure-science fiction; the first such concept with strong central lead characters plus other continuing regulars; and while maintaining a familiar central location and regular cast, explores an anthology-like range of exciting human experience."

He went on to describe the series premise as one akin to the then enormously popular *Wagon Train*, with regular characters traveling to distant worlds which bore some similarity to ours. Once there, they would encounter whatever circumstances would lead to action, adventure and drama. Their method of travel would be a "cruiser" named the U.S.S. Yorktown, a vessel enroute on a "well-defined and long-range Exploration-Science-Security mission which helps create our format." The time period is described as being some point in the future, which could mean either 1995, 2995 or some other date. "In other words," Roddenberry wrote, "close enough to our own time for our continuing characters to be fully identifiable as people like us, but far enough into the future for galaxy travel to be thoroughly established (happily eliminating the need to encumber our stories with tiresome scientific explanation)."

The key to the series, he added, was the concept of the Yorktown encountering numerous parallel worlds. In other words, planets whose conditions, both atmospheric and in terms of life forms, would mirror that of Earth. Said Roddenberry, "The 'Parallel Worlds' concept makes production practical by permitting action-adventure science fiction at a practical budget figure via the use of available 'earth' casting, sets, locations and so on. As important (and perhaps even more so in many ways), the 'Parallel Worlds' concept tends to keep even the most imaginative stories within the general audience's frame of reference through such recognizable and identifiable casting, sets and costuming."

The Yorktown, the presentation continued, would be captained by Robert M. April, a role "designated for an actor of top repute and ability. A shorthand sketch of Robert April might be a

'space-age Captain Horatio Hornblower,' lean and capable both mentally and physically." It was conceived that April would be the primary focus of many of the stories, while in other instances he may be the catalyst that launches the story surrounding a guest star. "A colorfully complex personality, he is capable of action and decision which can verge on the heroic — and at the same time lives a   continual battle with self-doubt and the loneliness of command."

Drawing comparisons between April and such people as Drake, Cook, Bougainville and Scott, Roddenberry pointed out that the captain's Achilles heel was his often choosing action over administrative duties, while allowing himself to take the greatest risks they encounter. What differed him from explorers of the past   was the compassion he felt for others, be they human or alien, and the temptation he would constantly have to fight to risk the lives of many to save one.

April's executive officer was a female referred to only as "Number One," and she is described as being "almost mysteriously female, in fact— slim and dark in a Nile Valley way, age uncertain, one of those women who will always look the same between years twenty and fifty....expressionless, cool." Number One, it was proposed, might even surpass April in terms of her knowledge of the Yorktown and its various capabilities.

Ship's navigator was supposed to be the Latin Jose Ortegas, a brilliant 25-year old described as being in the process of maturing. Roddenberry writes, "He fights a perpetual and highly-personal battle with his instruments and calculators, suspecting that space, and probably God too, are engaged in a giant conspiracy to make his professional and personal life as difficult and uncomfortable as possible."

Phillip Boyce was ship's doctor, and considered to be April's only confidant; the person the captain could turn to in moments of personal confusion or

An early NBC publicity photo featuring Leonard Nimoy as Mr. Spock (photo copyright ©1966 NBC).

crisis. Boyce, we're told, views each landing "in terms of relative annoyance, rather than excitement."

Mr. Spock was the only *Star Trek* character to appear in this proposal that would eventually be brought to celluloid life. Here he is deemed the first lieutenant and the captain's right-hand man. As Roddenberry explained it, "The first view of him can be almost frightening—a face so heavy-lidded and satanic you might almost expect him to have a forked tail." Spock was considered to "probably" be at least half-Martian. He is described as having a reddish complexion with semi-pointed ears. Spock's "quiet temperament is in dramatic contrast to his satanic look....His primary weakness is an almost cat-like curiosity over anything the slightest 'alien.'"

The final "regular" of the format was Colt, the Captain's Yeoman, a "blonde with a shape even a uniform could not hide." There to help April in whatever way may be necessary, Colt would have been his secretary, reporter, bookkeeper and "undoubtedly wishes she could also serve him in more personal departments."

From there, the proposal went

into the series format, with an emphasis on budget considerations, and was broken into nine sections:

"Sets": Since the Yorktown would go to "Class M" planets (those whose atmospheric conditions would be similar to Earth's) and, taking into account the parallel worlds approach, stage sets, backlots and other locations to be utilized in the creation of alien worlds would be simple to accomplish.

"Stages": As Roddenberry explained it, the sheer latitude of STAR TREK stories would allow the production to adapt their scripts to fit ongoing studio construction.

"Set and Locale Carry-Over": An interesting concept, and one that would never quite make it to the produced version. Roddenberry wrote, "Where particularly advantageous set or location conditions occur, or where a particularly exciting 'world' is created, *Star Trek* may do three or four stories there." In a sense, this would have created a "story arc," allowing for more complex thematic material and character development. Unfortunately the idea was never used, not even in *Star Trek*'s 24th Century descendent, *The Next Generation*. On the other hand, it is a form that the second spin-off series, *Star Trek: Deep Space Nine*, has toyed with.

"The Cruiser": The idea was that the Yorktown would be a standing set, its various aspects being able to be redressed as deemed necessary, thus allowing for further elaboration of the vessel itself with a minimum budget expenditure.

"Landings": "The Cruiser will stay in space orbit, will rarely land on a planet. Landings are made via a small—and transportable—recon rocket vehicle. Generally, audience view of sightings and landings will be that of the control crew, i.e., through instruments or on a 'telescreen'." This was one concept that would most definitely *not* remain with the series. As eventually established, the Yorktown (soon to be renamed Enterprise) was simply too large a vessel

to enter a planet's atmosphere, and the concept of a "recon rocket" was dropped due to the fact that its use would slow down storylines. In its place came the ship's transporter, a device which would instantly "beam" the crew down to a planet's surface.

"Casting": While not ruling out "monster" episodes, Roddenberry emphasized that the majority of the show's casting would be "fairly routine," utilizing paddings, wigs and simpler makeup devices to make a human look like an alien.

"Language": The concept was initially called a "telecommunicator," but was eventually known as the Universal Translator. About the size of a transistor radio, the idea was that this device would convert various languages into English so that our heroes as well as the audience would understand what was going on.

"Weaponry": The Yorktown would have been equipped with defensive-only laser beams, while crewmembers would arm themselves with rifles and pistols. The armament for those weapons would be a choice of either bullets, explosive projectiles or hypodermic pellets which would either stun or tranquilize their target. Aliens, it was added, would be equipped with spears, bows, swords, lances and a variety of firearms. Enterprise weapons would eventually consist of phasers and photon torpedoes.

"Costume": Again relying on the concept of parallel worlds, the "natives" would be adorned in clothing quite similar to those of the Indian or Viking. Uniforms of Yorktown crewmembers would be "naval" in general appearance, "attractively simplified and utilitarian."

Roddenberry follows with some specific information regarding the S.S. Yorktown, most notably: "As with *Gunsmoke*'s Dodge City, *Kildare*'s Blair General Hospital, we may never get around to exploring every cabin, department and cranny of our cruiser. The point being—it is a whole community in which

we can anytime take our camera down a passageway and find a guest star or secondary character (scientist, specialist, ordinary airman, passenger or stowaway) who can propel us into a story."

There would, he pointed out, be instances where an entire episode might take place aboard the Yorktown, which would of course help in terms of budget due to the use of such standing sets as the bridge, communication room (ultimately dropped) and crew quarters.

There is little doubt that Gene Roddenberry had, at times, wanted to put his head through a wall with frustration as he tried to sell the premise of *Star Trek*. In the past he has discussed in length the long battle it was to convince *anyone* that this show could work. Initially, MGM, the studio behind *The Lieutenant*, had expressed interest in the project, but ultimately declined. Finally, he found someone who would listen: Oscar Katz of Desilu (the company created by Desi Arnaz and Lucille Ball). No sooner had the agreement been made, than a meeting was set up with CBS.

During that meeting, as Stephen E. Whitfield reported in *The Making of Star Trek*, "Gene talked for almost two hours, outlining his ideas for the series, explaining ways in which a science-fiction series could be made on budget, and ways it could be made to appeal to a mass audience. They were particularly interested in his ideas on spaceship design, the types of stories to do, how to cut costs, and other technical aspects that Gene had developed. At the end of the two hours, and after having been questioned closely by most of those present, he thought he had sold them. Then they said, 'Thank you very much. We have one of our own that we like better. But we do appreciate your coming in."

In the same book, Roddenberry said, "My attitude was, 'You S.O.B.'s, why didn't you tell me that after the first ten minutes? If you want technical advice and help, hire me and pay me for it!' It's like calling a doctor and having him ana-

Incredible but true: CBS turned down Star Trek *because they had their own science fiction series in the works,* Lost in Space *(photo copyright ©1990 Twentieth Century Fox).*

lyze you for two hours and then telling him, 'Thank you very much for pinpointing what's wrong, and I've decided to go to another doctor for the treatment.'"

That series was *Lost in Space*, which CBS would debut in the 1965 season. In the meantime, Roddenberry and Katz continued to push forward and finally convinced NBC to take the risk and finance the pilot. Deal in hand, they set about putting the production together while Roddenberry turned "The Cage" into a teleplay, simultaneously renaming Captain Robert April Christopher Pike, and the Yorktown the Enterprise. What he ended up with was a teleplay in which the United Space Ship Enterprise arrives at the planet Talos IV to answer a distress signal. Pike is taken prisoner by the telepathic Talosians who want him to mate with another human being named Vina, so that they can repopulate their nearly lifeless world. To accomplish this goal, they use their abilities to plunge Pike from one fantasy into another, attempting to blur his hold on reality and creating a false sense of security. Number One, Mr. Spock and other crewmembers work to free him and, together, they end

the Talosian plan.

Jeffrey Hunter, who had recently played Jesus Christ in *King of Kings* and co-starred with John Wayne in *The Searchers*, was cast as Captain Pike, though other actors had been considered.

"I remember Lloyd Bridges was very much under consideration," Roddenberry recalled, "except when I approached him with it, he said, 'Gene, I like you, I've worked with you before in the past, but I've seen science fiction and I don't want to be within a hundred miles of it. ' I understood what he meant then, because science fiction was usually the monster of the week, the ink blot that gobbled up Tokyo. I tried to convince him that I could do it differently, but at the time I wasn't sure that I would treat it differently. I wasn't sure I could manage it."

Majel Barrett, who would go on to marry Roddenberry and portray Nurse Christine Chapel in the ensuing television series, was cast as Number One, with John Hoyt as Dr. Boyce. One of the most integral roles to fill was that of Mr. Spock. After considering Martin (*Mission: Impossible*) Landau and Michael (*The Wild Wild West*) Dunn, Roddenberry decided to go with Leonard Nimoy,

whose credits included *Zombies of the Stratosphere* and two episodes of *The Outer Limits*.

Roddenberry reflected on working with Nimoy during an episode of *The Lieutenant*, noting, "He had played a Hollywood producer, of all things, in an episode with a gum-chewing, wise-cracking secretary who later became my wife. I looked at him during those days and I thought that if I ever did this science fiction series, I'd use him because of his Slavic face and his high cheekbones. And so I just cast it with a phone call by asking him to come over."

"The Cage" was directed by Robert Butler who had also worked with Roddenberry on *The Lieutenant* and has since gone on to become the "King of the Pilots," having helmed the initial episodes of *Batman, Moonlighting, Remington Steel, Hill Street Blues, Midnight Caller, Lois & Clark: The New Adventures of Superman* and many others.

At a *Star Trek* 20th Anniversary convention in 1986, Roddenberry discussed what happened with "The Cage," as well as the network's motive for rejecting the pilot.

"The reasons were these: too cerebral, not enough action and adventure," he said. "'The Cage' didn't end with a chase and a right cross to the jaw, the way all manly films were supposed to end. There were no female leads then—women in those days were just set dressing. So, another thing they felt was wrong with our film was that we had Majel as a female second-in-command of the vessel. It's nice now, I'm sure, for the ladies to say, 'Well, the men did it,' but in the test reports, the women in the audience were saying, 'Who does she think she is?' They hated her. It is hard to believe that in 20 years, we have gone from a totally sexist society to where we are today—where all intelligent people certainly accept sexual equality. We've made progress.

"We also had what they called a 'childish concept'—an alien with pointy ears from another planet," he added.

"People in those days were not talking about life forms on other worlds. It was generally assumed by most sensible people that this is the place where life occurred and probably nowhere else. It would have been all right if this alien with pointy ears, this 'silly creature,' had the biggest zap gun in existence, or the strength of 100 men, *that* could be exciting. But his only difference from the others was he had an alien perspective on emotion and logic. And that didn't make television executives jump up and yell, 'Yippee!'

"At that time, space travel was considered nonsense. It wasn't until we were off the air three months that man landed on the Moon and minds were changed all over. The Talosian planet's 'ridiculous' premise of mind control annoyed a great many people and the objection, of course, overlooks the fact that the most serious threat we face today in our world is mind control—such as not too long ago exercised by Hitler, and what's now exercised by fanatical religions all over the world and even here in our own country. Mind control is a dangerous subject for TV to discuss, because the yuppies may wake up someday and be discussing it and say, 'Well, wait a minute, television may be the most powerful mind control force of all,' and may begin taking a very close look at television. And so most executives would like to avoid that *possibility*.

"Looking back," he added elsewhere, "they probably felt that I had broken my word. In the series format I had promised to deliver a 'Wagon Train to the Stars'...action/adventure, science-fiction style. But, instead, ['The Cage'] was a beautiful story, in the opinion of many the best science fiction film ever made up to that time. But it wasn't action/adventure. It wasn't what I had promised it would be. Clearly the problem with the first pilot was easily traced back to me. I got too close to it and lost perspective. I had known the only way to tell STAR TREK was with an action/adventure plot. But I forgot my plan and tried for something proud."

Although rejecting 'The Cage,' NBC did give Roddenberry the okay to go forward with a second pilot, although they did make several "suggestions," including the removal of Mr. Spock.

"They rejected most of the cast and asked that Spock be dropped too," Roddenberry concurred. "In fact, they particularly asked that Spock be dropped. This is one of those cases where you go home at night and pound your head against a wall and say, 'How come I am the only one in the world that believes in it?' But I said I would not do a second pilot without Spock because I felt we had to have him for many reasons. I felt we couldn't do a space show without at least one person on board who constantly reminded you that you were out in space and in a world of the future. NBC finally agreed to do the second pilot with Spock in it, saying, 'Well, kind of keep him in the background.'"

This was particularly ironic when one considers that Spock would eventually go on to become one of the most popular characters on the show. In fact, the constant struggle between logic and emotion that waged through the half-Vulcan/half-human touched a generation searching for direction.

Of Jeffrey Hunter's departure, Roddenberry said, "I thought highly of him and he would have made a grand captain, except his family convinced him, or his wife or someone, that science fiction was really beneath him."

Taking over the center seat would be Canadian-born actor William Shatner, whose career had included highly acclaimed roles on stage (*The World of Suzie Wong, A Shot in the Dark*), screen (*The Brothers Karamazov*) and television (*Twilight Zone, The Outer Limits, For the People* and the pilot for an unsold series, *Alexander the Great*).

"Where No Man Has Gone Before" went into production soon thereafter. Joining Shatner, Nimoy and Gary Lockwood was Paul Fix as Dr. Mark Piper, George Takei as Physicist Sulu, James Doohan as Chief Engineer Montgomery Scott, Lloyd Haynes as Communications Officer Alden and Andrea Dromm as Yeoman Smith, with Sally Kellerman "guest starring" as Dr. Elizabeth Dehner. As fans of the show recognize, the final *Star Trek* cast was slowly taking shape.

At a convention appearance, Roddenberry expressed, "The second pilot seemed to have great concepts: humans turning into gods. But they were nice safe gods, gods who go 'Zap! You're punished.' Kind of like the guys you see on those Sunday morning shows...The biggest factor in selling the second pilot was that it ended up in a hell of a fist fight with the villain suffering a painful death. Then, once we got *Star Trek* on the air, we began infiltrating a few of our ideas, the ideas you folks have all celebrated. *Star Trek* fans are people who are ready for the 23rd century dreams now. And I wish to God our leaders could catch up with them."

Elsewhere, he expressed his satisfaction over having been given the opportunity to do a second pilot. "Science fiction pilots are difficult things to do," he said. "You know, if you are going to do a pilot on a police show, let's say mid-town robbery squad, the network can reasonably expect you to get 95% of everything right and it's easy to do because you know what cops wear, you know how to catch a taxi, how to use a telephone and how to work a .38. When you get into SF you're very lucky if 75% of your pilot is believable because you're creating, in space science fiction, everything new. It was very helpful to be able to do one pilot, stand off, take a look at it and then do a second. The second pilot was really better in many ways because we had a chance to look at the costume work, how the gadgets worked and all that."

The public's first view of *Star Trek* came at the Cleveland, Ohio Tricon on Labor Day weekend in 1966. There, 20th Century Fox screened their upcoming special effects extravaganza,

Fantastic Voyage; Irwin Allen, the man behind such series as *Lost in Space* and *Voyage to the Bottom of the Sea*, presented the pilot episode of his latest effort, *The Time Tunnel*; and Gene Roddenberry unspooled "Where No Man's Gone Before," later adding "The Cage" due to public demand.

In the pages of *The Star Trek Compendium*, author Allan Asherman, who had been at Tricon, wrote, "...There was nothing childish about the episode, 'Where No Man Has Gone Before.' We waited for a kid or a wisecracking robot to enter the picture, but they never arrived. Even the music was somber, serious and spectacular....Then the whispers started, 'He did say this was for television, didn't he?' Maybe we'd misunderstood ....The audience continued to watch the episode intently. A very human captain was attempting to avoid killing a close friend. A satanic-looking first officer was pressuring the captain to liquidate the mutating individual. Someone noticed that Gary Mitchell's hair was gradually turning gray—one of the episode's many subtle touches. We noticed people of varied race, genders and planetary origins working together. Here was a future it did not hurt to imagine. Here was a constructive tomorrow for mankind, emphasizing exploration and expansion. This was the science fiction television series we all wanted to see. We were all extremely impressed.... After the film [Gene Roddenberry] asked for the audience's opinion; we gave him a standing ovation."

In the same author's *Star Trek Interview Book*, Roddenberry reflected, "I was nervous [at Tricon], particularly when I saw them watching other films that were shown before, and booing, and stomping, and laughing at things. I walked out there thinking, 'They're finally going to show this one.' There was a rather loud gentleman surrounded by other people discussing something at the time my show was starting, and upset already, I turned on him: 'For Christ's sake, could you be quiet? My

show is on now.' And Isaac Asimov said, 'Yes, you're perfectly right. We will tone it down.' And someone said, 'You're dead, you just insulted Isaac Asimov.' Well, it turned out that I had not, and over the years we became fast friends. He understood. Then I watched how they accepted this show. I said to myself, 'Yes, there *are* people, if we go this way and try these things, who are going to appreciate them.' I realized then that we would have fans of some sort and, of course, where that went is insanity. I thought we had a show that some people would remember. I thought it would be nice in future years if someone would stop me and say, 'Hey, I saw that thing called *Star Trek* you did and I liked it!' That was the most I had hoped for and that would've been nice. But the phenomenon I was not prepared for. You can't be prepared for those things. What kind of an idiot is going to sit down one afternoon and say, 'Well, let's see, what will I do today? I think I'll create a phenomenon!'"

In 1967, Roddenberry expressed his enthusiasm for the cast that had been gathered. "*Star Trek* is blessed with the finest group of professional actors I've ever worked with," he stated. "I'll never forget Bill Shatner coming into my office, holding a copy of our first script, saying he had some suggestions. I was understandably apprehensive — I had never worked with Bill before and wondered if this would be an ego-centered list of selfish demands. I was delighted, pleased, then admiring, when his observations turned out to be shrewd dramatic points which improved the whole story immeasurably.

"Leonard Nimoy," he added, "same comments. Although I created the basic Spock, the final fleshing out of the character was a joint endeavor in which Leonard and I worked as co-creators. Nimoy is actually a bit like Spock in real life: He's a dignified gentleman with social attitudes and philosophies which I admire greatly.

"DeForest Kelley, long a close

friend, is one of the most accomplished actors I've ever known. For years I was mystified to see the industry using only a small part of his enormous range and talent. One of my principal delights in *Star Trek* has been the opportunity to showcase that talent in a small way, knowing that now his career can only zoom upward. He'll win an Oscar one day and I hope I can be there applauding when he picks it up.

"I could speak for a half hour on the talents of each of the others too. *Star Trek*, among all television shows, is unique in this collection of talent, of which, without the all-too-usual exception, every one of them is an admirable gentleman or a fine lady. The group has become a 'One in a Lifetime' collection of friends."

Of all the characters, it quickly became obvious that the three most prominent would be Kirk, Spock and McCoy. As Roddenberry explained it, deliberately so.

"The three star billing were the ones that you would see a lot of," he said. "Plus science fiction wasn't 'in' in those days and we were going to do a lot of things we knew people might not understand and I wouldn't have stream of consciousness. In novels, stream of consciousness goes inside the hero's head and you can read what he's thinking. You don't have that in television and so I thought that if I took a perfect person and divided him into three parts, I could have the administrative, courageous part that would be the Captain; the logical part who is the Science Officer and the humanistic part with the doctor. Then, when something comes up, the Captain could say, 'I don't know, fellas. We must do it,' and Spock would say, 'However, the logical thing is...', and the doctor would say, 'Yes, but the humanity of it,' and I could have them talk about it without having stream of consciousness, and it worked!"

Shortly before his death, Roddenberry elaborated on his feelings regarding the Kirk/Spock relationship to

From Top-Left: Nichelle Nichols (Lt. Uhura), DeForest Kelley (Dr. Leonard McCoy), William Shatner (Captain James T. Kirk) and Leonard Nimoy (Mr. Spock) (photo copyright ©1966 NBC).

writer Yvonne Fern. In the pages of *Gene Roddenberry: The Last Conversation*, he reflected, "It is a profound relationship. A love relationship. Each has what the other needs, in order to be a complete person. That relationship could be considered the essence of *Star Trek*, if you regard it as almost perfect contact between beings. I hesitate to say this for publication, because I don't want to be regarded as supporting the Kirk-and-Spock show. I don't. The other characters are very important. There is much more to *Star Trek* than Kirk and Spock.

I'm just trying to indicate here that that relationship symbolizes on board the Enterprise what the mission of all the characters is."

With the proper cast in place, Roddenberry turned his attention back to the show's scripts. He knew that theirs was going to be one of television's first intelligent science fiction series, with realistic characters and extrapolations on today's technology. In other words, every aspect of the Enterprise would be based on items being developed in the present. For example, the diagnostic beds in

sickbay, as advanced as they seemed, were studied by one of the U.S. armed forces, who told Roddenberry that they had been developing something along similar lines. Even the weapon system known as phasers was only one step removed from the laser beam.

"We realized that lasers might very well become commonplace by the time the show got on the air," he said, "or at least within the next couple of years. Rather than run the risk of being outdated, we decided to say 'phaser' instead. The reason we picked phaser is the 'phasing' principles in physics by which power can be increased. It was logical and it sounded good, so we used it. We didn't want people saying to us three years from now, 'Oh, come on now, lasers can't do that.'"

Behind the scenes, however, in terms of the writing of the scripts themselves, things didn't seem to be going too smoothly after a while, at least as far as John Black was concerned. As story editor, he was doing whatever he could to bring in top science fiction writers, but they weren't being treated with the respect that he felt they deserved.

Said Roddenberry, "It seems that way, but it wasn't true. I didn't want only science fiction writers, because many of the science fiction writers available to me then talked about objects, about science rather than about people. Over half of them are just good regular writers because I wanted my show to be about people, not objects, and if you think back, the things you remember are the characters. During the first year, I wrote or rewrote everybody, even my best friends because I had this idea in my mind of something that hadn't been done and I wanted to be really there. Once we had enough episodes, then the writers could see where we were going, but it was really building people to write the way I wanted them to write. I lost a lot of friends, writer friends, because writers don't like to be re-written, but the whole thing was in my head, and I [couldn't] say, 'Mr. Spock, write

......like you would write so-and-so,' because there'd never been anyone like that around. So I rewrote them and lost friendships."

When Gene L. Coon joined the *Star Trek* staff as line producer about midway through the first season, Roddenberry became executive producer.

"I had no choice," said Roddenberry. "The only way I could get people like Gene Coon to come in and produce—and I needed a producer, more helping hands—was to become executive producer, actually a supervising producer. Today, it would be different. No one would object to a very complex show having two, three or even four line producers with a supervising producer over them. In those days, it was unheard of, but I just had to get some extra people in any way I could. I had found myself working 12 or 14 hours a day and I could no longer do it. Everyone on our staff was in the hospital at least once during those three years just from total exhaustion. We were doing a half a science-fiction movie every week. Imagine what a burden that is. Science-fiction movies usually take 20 weeks to do. We were doing one every week!"

Star Trek had survived a rejected pilot, network opposition and near-cancellation. Unfortunately, this only represented the first round of an interstellar boxing match that would continue over the next two years.

The second season introduced several changes to the series, among them the addition of actor Walter Koenig as Russian navigator Pavel Chekov. This character made the bridge of the Enterprise a true United Nations-like ensemble in space.

"The Russians were responsible," said Gene Roddenberry. "They put on the Pravda youth paper that, 'Ah, the ugly Americans are at it again. They do a space show, and they forget to include the people who were in space first.' And I said, 'My God, they're right.' Walter Koenig and I had worked together on a show I did earlier, and he's great

and I brought him in. And then I wrote the Russians and told them, 'I'm sorry we did it, and here's the information.' I never heard back from them. But not 'cause they're bad guys. The Air Force announced they had succeeded in phasing a thing and they were gonna call it a 'phaser.' And I wrote them and I said, 'I hope you use it with the respect for life as we did.' They didn't answer that either."

While *Star Trek* continued along its path, touching its primary audience — the youth of America — NBC made the announcement: the series would be canceled at the end of the season. Two major members of fandom, John and Bjo Trimble, initiated a letter writing campaign that spread like fire, inundating NBC with a reported one million letters. The network had no choice but to announce that *Star Trek* would be returning for a third year.

"I was amazed," Gene Roddenberry admitted in the pages of *The Making of Star Trek: The Motion Picture*. "I think you can't write and produce a show without hoping a lot of people out there will like it, but when I had heard they had received something over a million letters, I was stunned and delighted of course that they kept us on. The first reports from NBC were that they were not only going to keep us on, but they were going to put us on at a better time, although I think there were quite a few executives at NBC who felt that I was behind the whole campaign, as if I have a secret telephone somewhere from which I 'manipulate' fans and organizations."

In approaching the proposed third season, Roddenberry had to deal with the fact that Gene L. Coon was gone and would not return, and that his replacement, John Meredyth Lucas, moved over to *Mannix* when NBC had canceled *Star Trek*. He realized that he would have to once again get down in the trenches and produce the series personally. It was a task he apparently gained enthusiasm over, despite the long hours it would require, as he announced

his plans for the approaching season.

"We have a perfect vehicle for adventure, satire and social comment," he said. "Next season, we will travel to a planet which closely parallels earth, with one difference. The police are the best educated, and most highly respected citizens of the land, the equivalent of scientists and educators here. We are using science fiction to show the police as they could or should be if they had support from the public, and scientific support. If this raise any questions about our own society, so be it. Another episode will deal with medical research and brain transplants.

"[We] should deal in even greater depth with drama themes of contemporary meaning to man and his society. Although *Star Trek* will and should remain action-adventure entertainment, they [NBC] have urged us to continue and intensify speculation on any exciting aspect of law, religion, comment on the insanity of warfare, on bacteriological and other horror weapons, on the promises and problems of human organ transplants, on varied or even exotic forms of law enforcement, and on any other matter of current public debate and interest."

Unfortunately, the hopes that the network would get behind *Star Trek* and give it the best possible chance to reach a more wide-spread audience, quickly dissipated. With the broken promises went Roddenberry's full involvement with the show.

"As you know, we had a good fight," Gene Roddenberry told a gathered Berkeley audience in 1968 regarding the letter writing campaign to save *Star Trek*. "NBC was certain I was behind every fan, paying them off. And there was a group from MIT picketing the building and a group in New York and bless MIT, bless CalTech, bless them all. They [the network] had a coterie of junior executives down there buttonholing all of the people saying, 'Listen, did Gene Roddenberry send you?' And they finally call me up. They say, 'Listen, we know you're behind it.' And I said, 'That's very flattering, because if I could start demonstrations around the country from this desk, I'd get the hell out of science fiction and into politics.' From what I've seen of politics lately, they could use a few good science fiction fans.

"At any rate," he continued, "you all know we won the fight and at that time I told them that if they would put us on the air as they were promising—on a weeknight at a decent timeslot, 7:30 or 8:00, I would commit myself to produce *Star Trek* for the third year. Personally produce the show as I had done at the beginning. This was my effort to use what muscle I had. In fighting a network, you must use what muscle you have. They are monolithic, multibillion dollar corporations whose interests are not necessarily in the quality of the drama. Basically, the hard facts of life in television and the one you must understand is that a show is bought or sold on how much toothpaste or underarm deodorant will that show sell. Basically, that is why a show is bought and why and how it is kept on the air.

"If a creator, a writer, were to come along and come up with a bit of significant visual imagery, the finest thing you could think of that could shape the future of our nation, help it, guide it the way it should go, the chances are you could not get it on the air nor could you sustain it there if you got it there because that type of visual imagery does not appeal to Aunt Maude in Peoria...and I do not have anything against any Aunt Maudes here because I have one...but by that I mean it does not appeal to the mass audience who, when the announcer says, 'I want you to run down tomorrow and buy a can of Lifeguard and not leave your family defenseless,' she says, 'By golly, I'll do that first thing.' Unfortunately, science fiction fans are the lousiest audience in the world: they think, which is heresy!

"This may answer a lot of your questions why *Star Trek* has not done certain things that you as fans would like

to see it do or why it has not done certain things more. If we have every fan in the country weathered to us, and we are delighted and honored that so many of them are, if we have every university professor, every college graduate, every professional man in the country watching our show, and this was our audience and it would be an audience of seven or eight million people, and it would be an audience that would honor the creators of any show, we would go off the air after fifteen episodes.

"It is one of the unfortunate curses of television, you can have as high as eleven or twelve million devoted fans, more people than have seen Shakespeare since the beginning, and be a failure, 'cause at a certain time on a certain night you have to pass the magic number of fourteen million. At any rate, you scared the hell out of the network and they decided to keep the show on.

"At that time, I was committed to then produce the show, personally oversee every aspect of it. I received then a week later....Oh, you did another terrible thing to the network, I must tell you this. They phone me up in the middle of this and say, 'Goddamit, Gene, do you realize that it's costing us to answer these letters?' And thanks to you, and thanks to people like Asimov and others they were...you see, they couldn't ignore the letters because they   might have ignored yours and taken a chance on you, but intermixed in the letters were letters from the Executive Vice President of General Motors, you know, people like that who buy air time, so they couldn't take a chance, they had to answer them all.

"So you may remember the famous voice announcement that came on. First time the networks ever did it. One week they finally put it on the air (you remember), "*Star Trek* will be on next season.' Well, I got a call a week later and they say, 'Goddamit! Listen, Gene, we put on the air that you're staying on the air and so far we received 100,000 letters thanking us. Now will you

tell them to stop!'

"I was back there about this time and one of the V.P.s got me in a corner and he says, 'I'm gonna level with you. We've got a committee of six vice presidents working on this and we thought you were guilty, but we know it's Fred Pohl.' And he does share a considerable share of the blame and we're very proud and pleased with him as with many others, of course, but we were delighted to make him a scapegoat of the network and let them hate him for a while.

"But at any rate, about ten days to two weeks later I received a phone call at breakfast and the network executive said, 'Hello, Gene Baby...' Well, I knew I was in trouble right then. Said, 'We have had a group of statistical experts researching your audience, researching youth and youth-oriented people, and we don't want you on a weeknight at an early time. We have picked the *best* youth spot that there is. All of our research confirms this and it's great for the kids and that time is 10:00 on Friday nights.' I said, 'No doubt this is why you had the great kiddie show, *The Bell Telephone Hour* on there last year.'

"Well, I want you to understand some of the politicking, some of the pressures they dropped on me. The only gun I then had was to stand by my original commitment, that I would not personally produce the show unless they returned us to the weeknight time they promised. As a matter of fact, I threatened for a time to walk with the whole show because this was the only possible muscle to say—I don't own any General Motors or anything like that, so I had to threaten them with the one thing I do on the show, which is what I might be able to bring to the show on a line producership level. I wasn't particularly anxious to put in a third year of 14 hours a day, six days a week, but *Star Trek* was my baby and I was willing to risk it if I could have a reasonable shot at a reasonable time. And we talked it over and held fast. We almost swayed them

...ultimately they said, 'No, we will not do it.' And then I had no option, I could not then say, 'Well, I'll produce it anyway,' because from then on with the network any threat or promise or anything I made, once you back down you become the coward and your muscle from then on in any subsequent projects will never mean anything.

"So I had no option but to then drop back and become executive producer of the show, and I did find a producer, Fred Freiberger, who has produced *Slattery's People* and *Ben Casey*, and has impeccable credits and an honest love of science fiction since boyhood. He is backed up, of course, by our regular staff of Bob Justman and the directors, the cameramen, Bill Theiss, costumer; Matt Jeffries, art; so backed up by the regular staff they are now producing *Star Trek* while my function in it is judiciary, is policy administration. I limit myself to reading the scripts, commenting on them and the runs. I foresee a good season if we have a lucky break on the weekend, the shows that come before us, and with your help we ought to be able to maintain our audience and go for a successful year and then to others.

"But I felt I owed it to the fans who did so much for the show to give them the inside story of what happened from the time we won the campaign till I received the 'Gene Baby' call."

Despite his attempts to provide a proper explanation for why he stepped away from the series, there is a widely-held feeling that his doing so was a veritable slap in the face to the people who labored to keep *Star Trek* on the air. In a sense, it was as though their efforts meant nothing.

Over the years, Roddenberry added to the comments he had made at Berkeley, stating, "I think there was a little rationalization in [my decision]. I think also what was affecting me at that time was enormous fatigue; I think maybe I was looking for an excuse to get out from under the fight that I had not just been having for two years, but really for four. I think the fatigue just caught up with me. I think I would come back and produce it the third year myself if I had it to do over. I'm not taking a back-handed slap at the people who did produce it the third year, line produced it. Obviously when you bring a producer in and you're going to let him produce it, you've got to let him do it his way. I think his way, or their way, was somewhat different than our way the first two, so it did look different....As long as the original creator stays with the show, it gives it a certain unity. When other minds become involved, it's not that they are lesser minds or not as clever writers, but you lose the unity of that one driving force."

TARZAN

Star Trek's third season began production under the supervision of the aforementioned Fred Freiberger, while Roddenberry almost completely distanced himself from the series and began focusing on other projects. One of them — and one that has rarely been mentioned — was a modern version of Edgar Rice Burrough's *Tarzan*. In the summer of '68, he discussed the project from his point of view, that of writer and producer. Admittedly those comments, as presented here, are quite indepth for a project that never came to fruition, but it's historically interesting to see Roddenberry's mind at work outside of the science fiction arena.

"Edgar Rice Burrough's original Tarzan character was a fascinating combination of superman, Dr. Doolittle, fearless Western marshal, and mysterious half-alien," said Roddenberry. "The earliest Tarzan motion pictures carried much of this flavor of Burroughs' novels and no one who lived during that era can forget the sensation these films created among adults as well as children."

He noted that he had been screening and studying the various adaptations of the Ape Man, and one of the primary things he noticed was the way that the various projects had tended to move farther and farther away from the source material.

"Although many of the later films were skillfully made and had great production values," Roddenberry offered, "much of the Tarzan mystique is missing from them. As dated as the earliest films now seem, a very special thrill and entertainment value is there when one sees Tarzan leap into the midst of a dozen armed men, his enormous strength and agility sending half of them sprawling and the other half running in fear. Equally exciting in those early films is the way in which Tarzan ruled the jungle, his wild challenge shouted from a tree top turning back a cannibal war party, and so on. And in those early films better than Dr. Doolittle himself, Tarzan communicated with Tantor the elephant and wild beasts of the jungle, was warned by them of danger, used them occasionally as allies. How exciting it is to identify with him as he soars from tree to tree. And how it pleases the small snobbery in all of us that this same man is actually a titled English lord—not to mention the drama potential in this multidimensional half-savage and savage and half-civilized man."

While believing that it would not have been fair to criticize the subsequent motion picture alterations of Burroughs' original concept—due to the fact that such changes were necessary to rationalize new adventures, while continued success at the box office seemed to prove the filmmakers right—the character was becoming a victim of diminishing returns. He felt that the diminishing factors were two fold:

"Until only recently," explained Roddenberry, "Africa retained enough of its 'dark continent' to keep the Tarzan concept credible. But the last few years have seen a rush of African changes, plus broad public knowledge about the new Africa. Even the children in our audience are now rapidly becoming a collection of nations in birth, complete with roads, railways, radio and TV stations, big cities, tourists, luxury resorts, national animal parks and so on. These changes are happening more rapidly, almost by the month now, and credibility of the Tarzan character and concept suffers in direct proportion. We are near the point where it would be almost as easy to establish the credibility of an apeman's living in the wilds of Manhattan's Central Park."

Second, "The spectacular growth rate of modern technology is rapidly making any modern Tarzan more and more unbelievable. The sheer weight and efficiency of modern transportation, weaponry and communications available to almost anyone, makes it more and more incredible that any problem could be solved better, if at all, by a half-naked man armed with knife and vine-lariat."

He felt that the producer of a modern Tarzan would have a two-fold dilemma: ignoring the facts of today's Africa would cause the credibility of the film and character to suffer, while at the same time the use of the current social and political aspects of the country would take away from what would essentially be an escapist action-adventure film.

"Inventive stories which take Tarzan to India and other far off places have helped," he stated. "But there is a limit to exotic places with bizarre customs, and the on rush of technology and the audience's growing knowledge of the world is creating credibility barriers everywhere. Any reappraisal of Tarzan must also take in account current trends in film and television action-adventure. There has been a marked audience trend toward imaginative escapism—witness the detective-spy movement which began with James Bond and has continued strongly since. The new interest in film science fiction indicates this trend is still growing."

These factors, according to Roddenberry, would indicate that there would have to be a considerable alteration in approach to any future Tarzan film or television projects. Perhaps the best way they could address these changes would be to go back to Burroughs' original conceptions of the character.

"Even when writing the first Tarzan novel," said Roddenberry, "Burroughs realized that the shrinking world and growing technology, even of those days, could make an 'apeman' unbelievable. Needing a 'time-cushion' to help him create the necessary suspension of disbelief, his original novel began, '....on a bright May morning in 1888...a sailing vessel The Fuwalda, a barkentine of about one hundred tons....' Burroughs recognized other advantages in going back to the 1880's...it allowed full use of the 'dark continent' mystique in which Africa was a place of vast unexplored areas, and one could more easily believe in blood-thirsty cannibal savages, white renegades, and mist-shrouded high plateaus on which might be found the vestiges of lost civilizations holding incredible treasures."

He believed that the traditional American was a good example of a similar "time cushion," and an idea that worked extremely well on television. Paladin, Matt Dillon or Doc Holiday may have had basic absurdities to their characters, they nonetheless managed to become believable when separated from our current society by a century or so. "The audience is able to accept a James Bond in our century because he uses paraphernalia and problems of our century in his stories. But to state that a present day hero can solve problems with a single-action revolver or a jungle knife....suggests that our hero may be a simpleton. Burroughs realized something else—in a savage unexplored and largely untraveled Africa of the 1880's, brute strength and animal cunning, combined with human intelligence, might logically result in such a man becoming 'Lord of the Jungle.' Although the 1912 audience might reject the current existence of 'great apes' which would adopt and nurture a man-child, they would be more

Roddenberry's intended version of Tarzan resembled the realistic portrayal of Christopher Lambert in Greystoke: The Leged of Tarzan, Lord of the Apes *(photo copyright ©1983 Warner Bros Inc.).*

willing to believe there might have been such anthropoids in the 1880's.

"Every dramatist," Roddenberry emphasized, "knows the audience wants to believe, wants to be entertained...the first and most important task of any imaginative fiction is to create a time, place and situation which makes belief possible."

He did concur with the notion that setting Tarzan in the '20s or '30s might be acceptable to the audience and help in production costs, but these "half modern" time frames would lose the romantic attraction that might draw in a mainstream audience. The 1880's era, he reasoned, would work best for them. "It gives us sufficient civilization for almost any type of story, but without the disadvantages previously listed. And the 1890's have a certain romantic appeal....interesting male and female costumes, horses and carriages, incredibly difficult safari conditions, the jeopardy limitations of single shot firearms, acceptable paternal colonialism, the colorful contrast of the over polite manners and courtesies of 1880 versus our apeman's essential simplicity, the believable existence of Arab slave traders, ad infinitum. The whole new Tarzan spectrum available in Africa, 1880's, will inevitably give a new Tarzan film and television format a completely new look. It has an additional 'extra' — the opening up of totally new story areas for future Tarzan features, ones which no film distributor need fear will be 'retread' of any of the features produced in the past."

The Burroughs novels themselves showed Tarzan continually evolving as a character, from a half-savage unaware of the outside world to being married, having a son, becoming a grandfather and actually learning how to pilot an airplane. In terms of which incarnation of Tarzan to utilize, Roddenberry's feelings were that they should adapt Burroughs' version to their particular needs.

"First," he began, "we need more than the early simple apeman. We should take advantage of the drama potential in a man who is able to wear (and afford) the finest tailored clothing of his times, with high rank and social prestige which makes him welcome in the most civilized of gatherings....and yet who, stripped of his 'civilized veneer,' becomes as strong, wild and dangerous as the most savage jungle beasts. While Tarzan should never become psychological drama, it lends color and depth to the character to have him a man of two worlds, constantly at war with each other. In fact, without ever articulating this theme, it will still exist in the visual contrast and excitement in this young nobleman stripping to his loincloth and reverting to the apeman. In much the same way the comic book audience is delighted to identify with mild mannered Clark Kent who strips down to become Superman. And a surprising large number of adult novels offer the same delight by featuring detectives and undercover agents who use some ordinary cover identity to hide their true adventuring-lover-hero selves. From comics to the classics, dual-identity has been one of the most commercial, exciting, and successful devices in fiction."

He noted that Tarzan's alter ego is a legitimate one. He is actually John Clayton — Lord Greystone — with a most distinguished hereditary title passed on to him from his father. If he had resided in England, he would be highly respected in the most elite circles. "Except for a few very close and intimate friends, no one knows that Greystoke is anything but what he appears to be. Some have heard of a fabled 'Tarzan' said to live in the deep jungle, but few believe the story to be any more than the imagination of ignorant savages or feverish delusions of white hunters."

The essential Tarzan character, the writer/producer emphasized, had too often in the past been "miraculously unencumbered by any sex-drive, [but] also worried almost to the point of tears over a thorn in the foot of a baby elephant, over the level of teaching in local village schools, the rights of natives, and the general unfairness of the world, ad nauseam. Had he taken up a shepherds crook and been followed by ten disciples, he could hardly have been depicted as more gentle, selfless and kind.

"I would enjoy doing a film and format on Africa's Albert Schweitzer, but Tarzan is a whole different character and story. He is an apeman, Lord of the Jungle, raised by Numa the lion, winner of kingship of his tribe over the great ape Kerchak. Tarzan kills Bara, the deer, for food and eats the flesh raw and still prefers that food over the menus from the finest restaurants in Europe. Death is as natural to him as life. A strong-willed, mature, jungle, naturalistic attitude toward all aspects of life is vital to the believability of any new Tarzan, whether motion pictures or television. If the alternatives are Ozzie Nelson and Attila the Hun, we must choose the Hun with the testicles. Those who insist that either feature or television mass audiences respond best to single-dimension, parsonish, over-generous, pabulum-and-syrup eunuchs, have been proven wrong time after time. It is the character of Tarzan himself who will determine the

success of any new film and the 'new look' in any resulting television format."

It was his belief that every Tarzan film, from the first to the last, had their greatest problems in terms of believability. The character's credibility had been weakened or destroyed by writer-director mishandlings of successions of seemingly small and trivial things, which cumulatively made it impossible for an increasingly sophisticated audience to believe in the character or the story.

"Making the basic Tarzan concept believable is the problem which I faced in creating and producing Star Trek with its 23rd century vessel, bizarre planets, aliens and half-aliens," said Roddenberry. "That concept and characters were in danger of being destroyed by a similar succession of minor errors. Such things as running down a spaceship corridor to deliver a message when it is obvious an advanced vessel would have intercom systems....or allowing an alien to come aboard without the basic security safeguards found even now in a 20th century naval vessel....bringing disease aboard when even today's primitive 20th century spacecraft plans include decontamination units. We found we were too often establishing advanced devices which could do this or that in an early scene, then forgot to have our characters use them when faced with jeopardy in later scenes....and so on.

"Why does a Tarzan or a Star Trek make so many simple scene-mechanics errors when the same does not occur in most other films? The answer is so obvious it can be easily missed. A writer or director making an ordinary contemporary film can depend upon his own working knowledge of his own worlds to guide him. He knows that a telephone is the most efficient way of summoning the police. He knows from personal experience all about taxi-cabs and traffic, elevators, restaurants and waiters, currency, all the other simple mechanical details of modern life, and necessary to the believability of his contemporary film. Thus, it is most unlikely he will have a character take an elevator across town or summon a waiter to apprehend robbers.

"In a Tarzan film, as in science fiction and most other imagineering films, it is vital that more than ordinary care be taken in scene mechanics. The care extended in making a contemporary film is simply not sufficient to guarantee believability in an imaginative-escapism film. No one need be too worried over correctly portraying the mechanics of using a taxicab, but the mechanics of crossing a jungle stream must be carefully scrutinized for logic and believability. It must be constantly asked whether Tarzan's established keen hearing would have warned him of the antagonist by now....or would he logically go from here to there by a tree or by foot....or should he travel with the safari or would it be more logical to range out ahead scouting for danger? Whatever the answer, it must make as much visual sense as whether a contemporary hero under given circumstances would or would not wait for a green light at an intersection."

In summary, Roddenberry stated, "I am confident that all this can be accomplished. I believe a Tarzan film can be made which will be entertaining, gratifying to those involved in it, and profitable to the investors."

He was wrong, and Tarzan would be one of numerous disappointments Roddenberry would face over the next few years. As he pointed out in a letter he wrote to the Burroughs fanzine *ERB-dom* in 1969: "The Tarzan feature died at birth. It turned out that National General really never had a serious interest in a motion picture box office Tarzan film, but rather this seemed to be their way of exploring whether or not a new Tarzan television series could get on the air. This was not my interest. I wanted to do a first class motion picture, not a 'television featurette.' When they kept cutting the budget, they eventually reached the point where I could see that

a quality film was impossible and, at that point, I killed the project."

Shortly thereafter, NBC canceled *Star Trek* as well, with no hope of a letter writing campaign possibly saving the show yet again.

Commented Roddenberry, "A fellow from demographics came to NBC and said, 'Congratulations, you've just gotten rid of your most important and successful program.' they did not know what he was talking about. *Star Trek* had a low rating, and they didn't understand what he meant. He told them that, demographically, the people who were watching it were the people who were buying new cars, building new homes, et cetera. With regular ratings points, the network was just counting heads— retired fireman's widows and the like. *Star Trek* was reaching an audience they had never considered important: a narrowly defined group of consumers which accounted for much of the buying power in the country at that time. NBC argued for about a year over bringing the program back but by then it was too late to bring *Star Trek* back.

"I would have appreciated them telling me about all this then. My ego was going downhill after the show was terminated. I needed a boost."

A LIFE BEYOND TREK

Network cancellation was the best thing that could have ever happened to *Star Trek*. Had NBC renewed the show for a fourth or even a fifth year, the series would have undoubtedly continued to chug along. But, with considerable budget cuts each season, there would have a diminishing quality about the whole project and it would have undoubtedly faded into the annals of television history.

Such, as we know, was not the case with *Star Trek*. Instead, the network canceled the show in 1969 and it immediately went into syndication, a.k.a. reruns. Now, syndication has been known

to turn many a show into a sensation, with independent stations "stripping" the series five nights a week and giving viewers a daily dose of whatever show they find most appealing. It is syndication that has allowed Ralph Kramden to threaten Alice with a free trip to the moon for over three decades, provided Lucy with an equal amount of time to get herself out of one mess and right into another, and perpetuated the ongoing sloppy versus neat conflict of Oscar and Felix. It has even allowed the three year mission of the starship Enterprise to extend itself over a period of twenty six years.

In the fall of 1970, Paramount began offering the show to independents, hoping that they would be able to recoup a few lost dollars on this "dog." Despite a slow beginning, the number of stations interested in carrying the series gradually increased, with the audience, in turn, growing as well.

Shortly thereafter, it had become obvious that there was something brewing. With Neil Armstrong's boot gracing the lunar surface the previous July, outer space suddenly became vogue. Space was the place, and *Star Trek* was the ticket to get there.

"*Star Trek* probably came along too early," explained Gene Roddenberry in *The Making of Star Trek: The Motion Picture* [1980, Wallaby Books]. "Had man landed on the moon during our first or second year, the idea of space flight wouldn't have seemed so ludicrous to the mass audience. *Star Trek* probably would have stayed on the air. The eye of the world did not turn to space seriously as a future possibility until we were in our third year, and by then it was too late.

"In the last ten years, the future has suddenly come upon us. People are beginning to realize that the future is happening *now*. Whereas ten or fifteen years ago the future was something a quarter century or half century ahead, the rate of human development is moving so fast now that the future has finally caught up with us. Today you can't risk *not* thinking about the future, because many of the things you take for granted today may not even be here tomorrow."

Of the show's growing popularity, Roddenberry has pointed out three possible explanations.

"First," he's said, "we had real heroes, almost old-fashioned heroes, people who believed in their work, believed in honor, who believed that things must be done even at the cost of great danger and sometimes your life. Second, *Star Trek* was an optimistic show that said, 'There is a future for us humans, the human adventure is just beginning.' In a time when so many people were saying, 'In 20 or 30 years, it's all gonna go boom,' it was a breath of fresh air to turn on the TV and hear them say, 'Hey! We've just begun. Most of our adventures are ahead of us.' It's that spirit of optimism. And third, *Star Trek* stories are *about* something. They aren't inane —running around with sound and fury and bang, bang car chases, things that add to nothing....Every episode makes a statement of some sort. And people are hungry for statements."

So hungry in fact, that they began putting on *Star Trek* conventions, which served as a means for the stars to reunite on stage, and for fans to get together to chat and purchase *Star Trek* merchandise. All throughout the "convention years," the syndicated episodes were breaking all kinds of records, easily equating itself with the most popular shows in reruns, including *I Love Lucy* and *The Honeymooners*. Paramount noted this with interest, and was somewhat more than intrigued when the public began to demand a revival of the show. Rumors abounded, with the general feeling being that *Star Trek* would either come back as a new television series or perhaps even a feature film.

Still, Paramount made no official move. It's likely that they viewed the phenomenon as little more than a fad; that any such revival would, in effect, "miss the boat," and they would stand to lose even more money. While the studio continually second-guessed itself,

Roddenberry attempted to funnel his television years as a producer toward motion pictures. His first effort was 1971's *Pretty Maids All in a Row*, a disastrous black comedy directed by Roger Vadim and starring Rock Hudson, Angie Dickinson, James Doohan and Joanna Cameron. Rapidly discovering that writing and producing for features was quite different than what he had been used to, Roddenberry moved back to television and the genre he had had his greatest success in.

In the meantime, while fandom fl ished, as did the merchandising of the show, animation production companies began to approach Roddenberry and Paramount Pictures with the idea of doing an animated version. Many of these suggestions were turned down, but Filmation came to them with a package that they liked. The idea was to do a series that would air on Saturday mornings, but would also feature the basic ideals of the original show. Both Roddenberry and Paramount agreed that this would be a good idea, and to that end the original cast was signed to provide the vocals to their animated counterparts. Additionally, many of the writers involved with the live-action series were hired to pen scripts. Twenty two episodes were produced in all and, for the most part, the efforts in securing the finest possible talent paid off. The show featured scripts which proved themselves to be quite literate, and certainly a bright spot on the Saturday morning schedule. Unfortunately, like its predecessor, *Star Trek: Animated* was canceled prematurely, with Roddenberry and the original cast once again going their separate ways, apparently forever, though STAR TREK fandom certainly lived on.

For the fans of the little science fiction show that refused to die, it probably seemed as though Gene Roddenberry came out of nowhere when *Star Trek* premiered, and had done nothing from the show's cancellation in 1969 until the release of *Star Trek: The Motion Picture* a decade later. But

Majel Barrett portrays a modern-day witch in the Roddenberry written and produced pilot, Spectre *(copyright ©1975 Twentieth Century Fox).*

nobody can say the guy didn't try.

Roddenberry's supernatural television pilot *Spectre* went nowhere, and a proposed film project with Paul McCartney fell to the wayside when the revival of *Star Trek* seemed to be becoming a reality. He did, however, manage to create a pair of television pilots that came *this* close to becoming weekly series.

GENESIS II

"Our civilization as we know it had been destroyed," said Gene Roddenberry of *Genesis II*. "It had fallen part. It had not been, however, due to nuclear warfare. Really, nuclear warfare is not necessary to cause a breakdown of society. You take large cities like Los Angeles, New York, Chicago—their water supply comes from hundreds of miles away and any interruption of that, or food, or power, for any period of time and you're going to have riots in the streets.

"Our society," he added, "is so fragile, so dependent on the interworking of things to provide us with goods and services, that you don't need nuclear warfare to fragment us any more than the Romans needed it to cause their eventual downfall. It's important to know that I wasn't saying that *Star Trek's* future, which would occur several hundred years after *Genesis II*, never happened; I'm saying that humanity has always progressed by three steps forward and two steps back. The entire history of our civilization has been one society crumbling and a slightly better one, usually, being built on top of it. And on mankind's bumpy way to the *Star Trek* era, we passed through this time, too."

The premise for Gene Roddenberry's *Genesis II* is that the earth is in ruins, with different pockets of society living around the globe, some highly advanced and others more barbaric; looking for a better way of life. Dylan Hunt is a 20th century NASA scientist who is revived from suspended animation by a team of scientists who call themselves PAX, and who have given themselves the task of helping mankind slowly rebuild society and mature as a species. Hunt, with PAX, embarks on this mission via an underground subshuttle system which can move them from one area of the planet to another in a matter of minutes.

"The idea of PAX," detailed Roddenberry, "must have come from *Lost Horizon*. It was a society of people who said, 'Let us preserve the books and knowledge until man is ready to come back.' When Rome fell, there was no one to preserve their society and culture and within a short while, villages a hundred miles apart spoke different languages. Our stories were about how different parts of our country evolved into their own societies....The idea of a subshuttle is based on the fact that if the world does go through another war, surface, air and sea transportation will become impossible. With the massive destruction that would occur, those kinds of transportation certainly would not function the way they do now. The only effective long distance transportation that would be left would be an underground shuttle system. And today, for environmental

and economic reasons, this type of system is being studied. The shuttle travels in a near vacuum in these tunnels and uses electrical power that could come from solar, nuclear or hydro-electric plants. We were talking about things that might become realities just as we were on *Star Trek*."

Genesis II scored highly in the ratings and was close to becoming a weekly series, a point which inspired Roddenberry to do a number of treatments for potential episodes. Unfortunately, at the last minute all plans were canceled. It seemed that Fred Silverman, then head of CBS, had been amazed by the constantly high ratings that the *Planet of the Apes* films continued to draw on the network, and had purchased the rights to adapt the popular films into a weekly series starring Roddy McDowall.

"He thought the monkeys were so cute that he canceled doing *Genesis II*," Roddenberry laughed derisively. "Several of us tried to warn him that it was a one-time joke. He didn't listen and it was a disaster that cost them many millions of dollars. It's a pity, too, because *Genesis II* had the makings of a very exciting show. It had one thing in common with *Star Trek* and that was that you could bring in a good writer and say to him, 'What bothers you about the world?', then go and invent a place in this new world and have it happening there. It's a tragedy that opportunities like this to do exciting things and to talk about exciting things are pulled out by the roots by business executives who have no desire to give writers, directors and actors a chance to explore and elevate the art of film and television. And it could have been more exciting than the monkeys which captured his attention, but he seemed to be incapable of looking beyond and seeing the potential of something new and different."

Ironically, like *Star Trek*, *Genesis II* was given a second chance, this time under the name *Planet Earth*. John Saxon replaced Alex Cort as Dylan Hunt

Alex Cort and Mariette Hartley as seen in the pilot that Roddenberry felt would have made as good a series as Trek, Genesis II *(photo copyright ©1973 Warner Bros Inc.).*

and PAX was moved to the surface, although the subshuttle idea was retained. PAX continued to be a secret organization designed to aid the rebuilding of earth. Unfortunately, the second pilot didn't go over nearly as well as its predecessor. A third version, entitled *Strange New World*, was a spinoff of sorts starring John Saxon but produced without Roddenberry's involvement. It faded even quicker than the first two films. Thus marked the end of the *Genesis II* premise.

However, one of the potential story ideas dreamed up by Roddenberry played a role in the future of *Star Trek*. "Robot's Return," chronicles what happens when a NASA space probe, having acquired consciousness from a machine planet, returns to earth seeking its creator, and believes that Dylan Hunt plays a role in the puzzle. Admittedly the plot has similarities to *Star Trek's* "The Changeling," but it metamorphosized even further into the storyline for *Star Trek: The Motion Picture*, in which V'ger (Voyager 6) was willing to destroy all life on earth if it was not united with its creator.

"I think *Genesis II* should come back," Roddenberry said before his death.

John Saxon replaced Alex Cort in the role of Dylan Hunt in the revised version of Genesis II, Planet Earth (photo copyright ©1974 Warner Bros Inc.).

"Somewhere in there is a marvelous premise for a series. Lots of excitement. You'll never know what we'll encounter from one story to the next. There were as many exciting story ideas at the start of *Genesis II* as there were for *Star Trek*."

THE QUESTOR TAPES

In *The Questor Tapes*, Roddenberry conceived of an alien race that had spent eons helping mankind's progress by placing human-like androids within society to help guide the species. This television pilot presented Dr. Jerry Robinson (Mike Farrell) teaming up with an android named Questor (Robert Foxworth), who is on a quest to meet with his creator, Professor Vaslovic, and discover the truth about himself.

"Vaslovic, who was actually an android himself," Roddenberry explained, "realized that the line of androids who had been helping to guide Earth for thousands of years was about to end. He was unable, because of certain conditions, to complete his replacement: Questor. Instead, he left all of his plans with a five-nation scientific consortium. They begin constructing the android for their own purposes, not really understanding all of the components or systems. However, Vaslovic had left a tape of secret programming that is only partially assimilated by the android. That part instructed the android to escape once it had been completed and go about its work."

In his background for the pilot, Roddenberry pondered the notion that if you "awoke" on the first day of your life with a vast amount of information in your brain on science, mathematics, literature, history and economics, how would you react if you discovered that you had no knowledge of yourself? "*Cogito ergo sum*—I think, therefore I am," wrote Roddenberry. "....You think, you wonder, you move like a living thing. But can a mechanical thing like yourself be called 'alive?' Whatever you are, that question leads inexorably to the enigma which has puzzled and plagued Man himself from his own beginning. It is the most powerful of all dramatic themes. *Who was my architect? For what reason am I placed here?* ....We boldly challenge the audience to identify with an unusual television character who begins as a machine but who may turn out to share more of their own thoughts, doubts, frustrations, loneliness and dreams than many human fictional characters. Questor, in fact, is designed to become *more human than human*."

Jerry Robinson is described as a scientist who "is somewhat graceless in human company and especially with females. But at a lab bench, he displays an incredible 'feel' for machinery and a touch as deft as any skilled surgeon. If Questor had been designed to play a mechanical Sherlock Holmes, Robinson would have been an ideal choice as a 27-year-old Watson. The same affection-annoyance relationship exists between the two. While Robinson would be one of the first men in the world to feel affection for a working android robot, he would also be the quickest to feel annoyed at a mechanical thing beginning to take on human qualities. His mild, unobtrusive manner will see the coolly logical Questor naturally become the dominant half of the relationship."

Questor was supposed to be a weekly series. "We had an office and a production date," said Roddenberry. Unfortunately, both Universal and NBC came to him and announced that they didn't like the Jerry Robinson character. This was the same network, incidentally, which said that they didn't want Mr. Spock. "I thought [Robinson] was vital to Questor," said Roddenberry. "You can't have just an android; you've got to have a partnership between an android and a human."

What was wanted was a chase series, ala *The Fugitive*, in which Questor is being hunted down by a scientific community that wants to dissect him. "I just didn't want to do a chase series," he admitted. "And so, I just let it die. Looking back, maybe I should have found some talented writer/producer who wanted to do the series in that format and just step back and let him do it. The rumor at the time was that Questor was too much like *The Six Million Dollar Man*. That wasn't the reason why the series didn't go. If I had made *Questor* more of a *Six Million Dollar Man*, they would have continued with it. But I just didn't want to do a *Six Million Dollar Man*; it was asking too much."

THE NINE

With these failed pilots behind him and Paramount claiming that the original *Star Trek* had yet to turn a profit (this despite the fact the show was the most popular and successful in syndication), Roddenberry was finding it increasingly difficult to survive financially.

"Paramount is basically the owner of *Star Trek*," he said in 1982, "and I'm supposed to get one-third of the profits. You want to talk about science fiction writing? The greatest science fiction in the world is written in accounting offices! You know, Paramount accountants say that this show that has played all over the world is now half a million dollars in the hole. It's true, but I think they deserve praise. Despite losing money, they have shown *Star Trek* consistently for 16 years all over the world. That's decency."

Having no choice, in the '70s Roddenberry attempted to scratch out an existence for he and his family by doing a college lecture tour.

"I have been through harsh times," he admitted. "My dreams were going downhill because I could not get work after the original series was canceled. I remember I was really devoted to the fans at colleges when they voted that they wanted me to come and lecture. I remember one of my first speeches — I got all of $600 or $700, which included the cost of the trip. I felt lucky to net the $400 or $500 that they paid for me.

"I was stereotyped as a science fiction writer, and sometimes it was tough to pay the mortgage. They said, 'You're a science fiction type.' I said, 'Hey, wait a minute, I used to write Westerns, I wrote police stories,' and they said, 'No, you're now science fiction.' I don't feel bitter about that. That's the way Hollywood is and that's the way mediocre people think. It's an easy way to think and television, like movies, like play, like everything in the world, is staffed by mediocre people with, thank God, a few other people who do make things happen. They make the big changes."

While rumblings had begun that Paramount would be producing a new live-action version of *Star Trek*, Roddenberry still had bills to pay and he attempted another original screenplay. This one was entitled *The Nine*, and it reveals more of Roddenberry than perhaps even he anticipated, showcasing the "convention years" and his efforts to deal with the *Star Trek* phenomenon, albeit in a slightly altered form. The main gist of the script is that the lead character, writer/producer James MacNorth,

gets involved with beings who possess telekinetic abilities and who reside in a commune of sorts while awaiting the arrival of extraterrestrials known as The Nine. More importantly, from a biographical point of view, is the situation under which we meet MacNorth.

MacNorth is the creator of a television series known as *Time Zone*, the "futuristic adventures of a group of fictional characters who wander through various sci-fi dimensions via some sort of 'time capsule.'" He is at a podium, speaking to a large group of fans who have gathered for this convention. The speech he is concluding probably came directly from one of Roddenberry's lectures: "...to accomplish all that, television must become something more than an electronic billboard designed to sell beer and hemorrhoid ointments. What it *can* become is a way of all humans everywhere having access to the recorded knowledge of all humanity. If we can begin to make that happen, the barriers which have held so much of humanity down, those which have held so many of us apart...those barriers will begin to crumble. We tried to take a small step in that direction during our *Time Zone* television series. But television must be released of its commercial bondage if it is to realize its real potential of bringing the world together....for that great stride of soul which is *vital* if humanity is to have a future."

This, naturally, is greeted by a standing ovation. Following the speech, MacNorth is hustled off stage by security and asked for autographs, queried as to the status of the *Time Zone* movie supposedly in development, forced to listen to songs written by fans of the show, tries to cope with a skeptical reporter who views the whole thing as a money-making ploy, and so on. At one point, the reporter named Calvert gets into an elevator with MacNorth and they're joined by "an almost nude young body [that] just manages to make it inside. About sixteen years, this fan teenager wears only three very small triangles of

Gene Roddenberry on stage at a Star Trek convention (photo copyright ©1994 Karen Witkowski).

metallic cloth glued to her extraordinarily well-proportioned young body. Young flesh and muscles still quivering from her dash into the elevator, she bubbles, all in one breath, to MacNorth." Apparently this young woman wants to wear this particular outfit in the costume contest, but the convention committee is against it. MacNorth doesn't really want to get involved in the issue—it's not his place—and he tries to politely tell her so. Then she laughs, surprised that he doesn't recognize her as one of the night security guards at his room. Calvert raises an eyebrow.

CALVERT : Night security guard?
TEENAGER: Mister MacNorth has round-the-clock protection.
CALVERT: Oh, I'm sure he do.
MACNORTH: I see. You've got your story.
CALVERT: I've got *your* story.

By the time MacNorth gets back to his hotel room, he's exhausted. He asks his convention secretary, Sherry, if the committee has sent up his check yet, because he can't even afford to pay her if they don't. Sherry has to ask how someone can write a hit television series and practically need food stamps. MacNorth ignores the question, choosing, instead, to meet with a pair of people who he promised a friend he would talk to. Harwood and Mara are the couple who will ultimately involve him in the adventure with The Nine. During their conversation, Mara implies something about MacNorth being ill in a sexual manner, to which, Sherry defends him. When they're alone, MacNorth turns on her.

MACNORTH: What in the hell do you know about my love life?
SHERRY: Some of those sweet little things out there, they talk.
MACNORTH: They also fantasize. Sometimes in letters to my wife.
SHERRY: She doesn't understand how a man worries about keeping young?
MACNORTH (means it admiringly): You've been around a bit, Sherry.
SHERRY: Enough to know you ought to prove to yourself that Indian chick is wrong. You ought to get it out of your mind this minute.

MacNorth is obviously tempted, but he doesn't give in to it. Upon arriving home, we quickly learn that the studio doesn't like his *Time Zone* movie script and they're resisting the clause in his contract which says he will produce. Additionally, a deal with Warner Brothers has fallen through and he can't seem to function in bed with his wife, Kathy.

The following morning he arrives at the studio and talks to the studio guard, who he queries as to whether the man's heard anything about the movie.

STUDIO GUARD: You already know their main gripe about you.
MACNORTH: I had to push hard, to make *Time Zone* what it was.
STUDIO GUARD: And since then? You want me to be honest, Jim? You can't keep shoving down people's throats how you were right and how wrong and stupid they were.

In a meeting with his lawyer, Keeble, MacNorth is told that there is no way for the studio to violate the contract. MacNorth argues that all the studio has to do is keep them in court for a year or more and they'll win because he can't afford to fight them. Counters Keeble, "I am *not* letting them get away with this! We're also going to sue for your television profits. I can't see any way they can gross something like twenty million on your show and still be in the red."

MacNorth still believes that he'll go broke fighting them, until Keeble brings forth an offer from Harwood and Mara for him to work on a script for them, for which he will be paid $25,000. At first he's skeptical, not believing in the paranormal or telepathy, and adamant that he will not prostitute himself or his fans.

MACNORTH: I've got how many *Time Zone* fans? Ten million, fifteen million? More than half of them kids who might believe anything I put into a script. They want me to say that this crap actually exists. Telepathy, fortune telling, bending spoons with your mind. "Don't go to a doctor when you're sick. Go to some mystic who'll heal you by touching you. Don't listen to your professors, listen to those voices from outer space..."

He starts to be swayed, however, when he reads the proposed contract further, in which they detail that he only has to write about that which he sees and believes. Ultimately this leads him to the commune and the rest of the adventure unfolds.

While the viability of *The Nine* as a whole remains questionable (although Jon Povill, who would co-write a second draft with Roddenberry, has announced his plans to bring the script to life), it nonetheless provides an interesting look — through fictional eyes — of Roddenberry's life at the height of *Star Trek* hysteria; an hysteria that would completely occupy his life throughout the '70s.

THE TREK BEGINS ANEW

Although the reasons aren't entirely clear, *something* was causing the revival of *Star Trek* innumerable delays. Nonetheless, Roddenberry was given his old office at the studio and told to write a movie script for a low-budget feature film.

"They turned me down a couple of times," Roddenberry said, "then finally they said, 'Write a script and we'll give you an office on the lot and think about it.' They were not that serious about [it] when we first started. I think they had in mind a $2-$3 million picture. We debated a long time whether it would be a two-hour TV film or a movie for theatrical release. I didn't want to do it for television. When the original *Star Trek* ended, Paramount thought it had a real loser on its hands, a stinker. Oh, they'd make a couple of bucks on reruns but they *knew* the show would never amount to much. They destroyed all the sets. Everything. Even Spock's ears. I felt that for TV, the limited budget allowed just would not suffice for the rebuilding of the sets and of the Enterprise. It would be the same quality as on the old show and, after all these years, I felt that they wouldn't be good enough. They said, 'Okay, we'll do a theatrical release. Go write a script.'"

One of his first efforts was a prequel to the original series. "I think," said Roddenberry in 1975, "what we're going to try to do in this particular motion picture is to go back to the beginning, maybe see the Enterprise being built in orbit, maybe get into why this strange half-breed Vulcan/Earthman Spock joined a paramilitary organization, why the captain picked this acid-tongued doctor and answer a lot of questions that the fans have had over the years."

Interestingly, Roddenberry adamantly fought a revision of that idea developed by producer Harve Bennett and screenwriter David Loughery for a proposed *Star Trek VI*.

When Roddenberry's prequel idea was shot down, he immediately set upon developing another story. Although little is known about the resulting script, entitled *The God Thing*, reports have stated that the premise questioned the very nature of God and the universe around us. Paramount was apparently not interested in a script which, essentially, pit Captain Kirk against God.

"I handed them a script and they turned it down," Roddenberry stated matter of factly in 1980. "It was too controversial. It talked about concepts like, 'Who is God?' [In it] the Enterprise meets God in space; God is a life form, and I wanted to suggest that there may have been, at one time in the human beginning, an alien entity that early man believed was God, and kept those legends. But I also wanted to suggest that that might have been as much the Devil as it was God. After all, what kind of god would throw humans out of Paradise for eating the fruit of the Tree of Knowledge? One of the Vulcans on board, in a very logical way, says, 'If this is your God, he's not very impressive. He's got so many psychological problems, he's so insecure. He demands worship every seven days. He goes out and creates faulty humans and then blames them for his own mistakes. He's a pretty poor excuse for a Supreme Being.' Not surprisingly, that didn't send the Paramount executives off crying with glee. But I think good science fiction, historically, has been used that way—to question *everything*.

"[Anyway,] the movie then sagged for quite some time," he continued. "It really got bogged down. I didn't hear anything for over three months. Meanwhile, unknown to me, the executives then in charge were interviewing writers, accepting outlines. I found out about all this quite by accident. None of the outlines were accepted. I think the main reason for all the problems with those scripts rested in the fact that most

Roddenberry with most of the Star Trek *cast at the unveiling of the space shuttle Enterprise (photo courtesy NASA).*

of the people making decisions concerning the film knew little or nothing about *Star Trek*. As it turned out later on, several of the principals had never even seen the show."

By 1976, *Star Trek* was celebrating its ten year anniversary, and the show's fan following was continuously growing larger, with the demand for a new film or television series growing more vehement. It had been seven years since the last new episode, and the only difference between then and now was that the idea of reviving the show, in one format or another, was actually being considered by Paramount.

At the same time, America was preparing for the next phase of its exploration of the final frontier: the space shuttle. This was the year that the orbiter would lift off into space via rocket boosters, and land like a plane. But first, there was the matter of the experimental model, which was designed to test the landing procedures, but not actually fly. The fans of *Star Trek* deluged President Gerald Ford with letters, and it was only

a short matter of time before the President of the United States made the official announcement: this particular shuttle would have the name *Enterprise*, after the starship from the famed television series. And to help celebrate the occasion, Gene Roddenberry and the cast from the show were invited to play a part in the ceremony on September 17, in which the shuttle would be hauled out of its hanger for the first time.

"They rolled out the space shuttle Enterprise," Roddenberry recalled. "The military band marched out and the leader raised his baton. I was waiting for 'Stars and Stripes Forever' or 'America the Beautiful,' or something. Instead, they played the *Star Trek* theme. Twice. I had this funny feeling in my stomach, you know, like that was going just a little too far. People ask me, 'Aren't you proud about the space shuttle?' Well, sure. But this morning we were all feeling uncomfortable. There were senators, generals and politicians all around. And the band was playing the *Star Trek* theme. I thought to myself, 'Geez, these are the people who are running our country!'

"I must admit that when they first announced that the shuttle was going to be named after the Enterprise, I didn't completely approve. I was afraid that my friends at NASA and the space industry would think that it was a shrewd publicity ploy for the movie. You know, everyone has this stereotyped idea about producers who wear Hawaiian shirts, smoke big cigars and do anything to see a few lines in print. And that's all untrue. It was the *Star Trek fans* that started all this. They began a letter-writing campaign to the President. I completely disassociated myself from it. I would have preferred the shuttle not bear a military name like the Constitution or the Enterprise. I would have named it after a famous rocket scientist.

"But a friend of mine told me later that I was just too close to the whole project to see it for what it was. The role of the arts, he said, was changing. The very function of art today is to give people goals, to inspire them. And apparently the Enterprise has inspired a lot of people."

Indeed. So strong had *Star Trek*'s following grown, that the show truly became a part of the national social conscience, and Paramount was not oblivious to this fact. Despite Roddenberry's concerns that the naming of the shuttle after his starship would come across as a cheap, albeit inventive, advertising ploy, it didn't hurt the studio's enthusiasm to bring the Enterprise to the big screen. If any attempt to do so seemed likely to happen, it would probably be the one initiated in July of 1976. Jerry Eisenberg was hired as producer, with Phil (*Invasion of the Body Snatchers, The Right Stuff*) Kaufman directing. Scripting were a pair of English writers named Allan Scott and Chris Bryant, whose credits included *Don't Look Now* and *Joseph Andrews*. Their experience in science fiction was non-existent, but what they lacked in knowledge, they made up for in enthusiasm, and a willingness to learn.

Roddenberry stated, "I'm very excited about some of the ideas they've come up with. The concept that only a science fiction writer can write science fiction motion pictures is ridiculous. Look at me. I came up with STAR TREK and I was a dramatic writer. I wrote for TV.

"I'm very pleased with the way the film is going," he added. "We've just signed Phil Kaufman—who's done many fine films—to direct. Things really began to change around here when the studio shifted its power base and David Picker took charge. He put Jerry Eisenberg in command of the film, and Jerry knows how to deal with the front office quite well. Once these men entered the picture, things began to move quite smoothly.

"It's taking more time than usual to come up with a good script, because we're faced with some unusual problems. This is not just another movie — this is *Star Trek*. A lot of people in the business have said to me, 'Hey, it should be easy to do the film. Just do an extended TV episode. You've done lots already, just do it again.' Well, I didn't want to do it that way. A movie is different from a TV show in a lot of ways. For one thing, the audience has made an investment in the film. They've shelled out money for the ticket, as well as for parking, baby-sitters, maybe dinner. They don't want to see a TV show on the screen. They're a captive audience and they want something special. It's like getting a book and finding out it's lousy. If you've been given it as a present, you figure, gee, since I got it for free, it's no big deal that it's bad. But if you've paid $8.95 for it, you get a little pissed off.

"With the *Star Trek* script, we have defined personalities and really can't do anything contrary to the behavior patterns we've already established in the past. We're finding out that it's easier to work from scratch in terms of a storyline, but because all the details of the film are so well known already, it's getting harder and harder to come up with something new. I don't know what we'll finish with at this point, but I'm sure it

will be a film that has a lot of entertainment value — action, adventure and a little comedy. I want a *2001*."

Unfortunately, he didn't get it, and neither did movie audiences get a new film version of *Star Trek*. Instead, the path would make a twist back to television.

TV TREK—TAKE 2

And the Earth shook.

If it didn't, then it must have been a movement of damn near equal proportion to the fans of a little television series they had refused to let die. They had taken "control" of the show's destiny by generating an unprecedented amount of enthusiasm, resulting in a phenomenon whose closest relative was probably Beatlemania circa 1964. They gathered together at conventions, met their idols, penned original fiction dedicated to the characters and ideals of the show, and never stopped hoping for the day when it would be resurrected on either television or the movie screen. In the middle of 1977, it seemed as though their efforts had finally borne fruit: *Star Trek* was returning to television.

The original cast, with the exception of Leonard Nimoy, who for career and litigation reasons did not wish to play the role of Spock on a weekly basis, had actually been signed to reprise their most famous roles, scripts were being developed and sets constructed for the brand new starship Enterprise. Everything was coming together, allowing *Star Trek* to touch a new generation in the same way as it had the previous one.

For some time, Paramount Pictures had dreamed of starting a fourth network to compete with the three majors, much as the Dumont Network did during television's Golden Age. To this end, they contacted independent stations all over the United States and began offering product to fill one night a week with new programming, corner-stoned by the series entitled *Star Trek II*.

Roddenberry grew more vibrant with each passing day, as a seven year battle to bring *Star Trek* back seemed at an end, and he was essentially being given the opportunity to top himself, although he never really looked at it that way.

"Those [original] episodes will always be there for what people want to make out of them," he told *Starlog* at the time. "We're making a new set of them ten years later under very different circumstances. I think neither takes away from the other. The worst that can happen is someone would say that Roddenberry couldn't do it a second time. That doesn't bother me, as long as I did my damnedest to do it a second time."

What was truly exciting to him was the opportunity to deal with different social issues in a new and fresh style, as television had been altered considerably by such series as *M*A*S*H* and *All in the Family*. Gone were the days when you *had* to hide your ideas within entertainment, for fear that network censors would not allow the show on the air. Things had changed to such a degree, that television was actually *challenged* to express itself in new and different ways.

"Dialogue is more naturalistic on television today," Roddenberry explained. "Direction is more sophisticated. There are better methods of optical effects. There are better methods for special effects. The audience is certainly more sophisticated and able to reach their minds out further. The audience is ready for statements on sex, religion, politics and so on, which we never would have dared to make before."

On July 15, 1977, Gene Roddenberry issued a memo telling the production crew of *Star Trek II* that they needed to come up with a new bible for potential writers. Producers Bob Goodwin and Harold Livingston, Story Editor Jon Povill and several others began making contributions to this item, which had proved a successful tool during the course of the original series. The "bible" which eventually evolved, stated

that the series would chronicle the second five year mission of the Enterprise. While in drydock following its initial mission, the vessel had been completely refurbished.

James T. Kirk, we learn, has refused a promotion to admiral so that he can command the starship on its newest voyage. All of his original crew have been reassigned to him, with the exception of Mr. Spock, who has "returned in high honor to Vulcan to head the Science Academy there." In updating the series and attempting to fill the void created by Spock's absence, three new characters were added and hopes were high that actor Leonard Nimoy would frequently reprise his role of Spock for guest appearances.

In the guide, Roddenberry, who would make similar statements when originally discussing *Star Trek: The Next Generation* nearly a decade later, wrote, "We will use science fiction to make comments on today, but today is now a dozen years later than the first *Star Trek*. Humanity faces many new questions and puzzles which were not obvious back in the 1960s, all of them suggesting new stories and themes."

Defining the basis of a *Star Trek* story, the guide notes that such stories are about people, and not science or gadgetry; that each should always be told from the point of view of Captain Kirk and the crew, that the regular characters are heroes and should always react as such, and that home base is the Enterprise.

From here, the guide details the intricacies of the Enterprise's weapon and defense abilities, followed by a character breakdown, focusing on the new additions.

Lt. Xon, a full Vulcan, has taken the place of Mr. Spock as ship science officer. This twenty year old, who is "a genius even by Vulcan standards," was destined to prove himself as capable as his predecessor. The primary difference between the two is that Xon has virtually no knowledge of the human equation,

and realizes that the only way he will be able to equal Spock is by making an effort to touch his repressed emotions, thus allowing him to more fully relate to the crew. Roddenberry wrote that "we'll get some humor out of Xon trying to simulate laughter, anger, fear and other human feelings." Interesting to note is that the Spock-McCoy feud would have carried over to Xon and the doctor, with the difference being that McCoy believes their "feud is a very private affair...and McCoy has been known to severely chastise (in private) those crewmen who have been unfair to the Vulcan in comparing his efforts to Spock's."

The second new character mentioned is Commander Will Decker, Enterprise first officer who is something of a young Captain Kirk. The son of Commodore Matt Decker, who met his demise tackling "The Doomsday Machine," he comes quite close to worshipping the captain, and would "literally rather die than fail him." This is in direct contrast to the somewhat antagonistic Kirk-Decker relationship demonstrated in *Star Trek: The Motion Picture*. Essentially Decker is a captain in training, and the idea was that the audience would watch his gradual growth during the five year mission. In many instances, he would lead landing parties, thus alleviating the perpetual logistical flaw of the initial *Star Trek* TV series: a ship's captain would never beam into potential danger as often as Kirk did, and it's a format change which would eventually be incorporated into *The Next Generation*.

In a sense, this would make the situation more logical and would have given the Decker character an opportunity to develop. In addition, we could have witnessed Kirk's frustration at not always being directly involved with beam downs.

The final new addition to the crew would have been Lieutenant Ilia, the bald Deltan, whose race is marked by a heightened sexuality that pervades every aspect of their society. Additionally, Ilia, as is common among

David Gautreaux, the actor signed to replace Spock, seen here in screen test for his role as Xon in the proposed Star Trek II *television series of the mid '70s (photo courtesy David Gautreaux).*

her people, is abnormally intelligent, second, perhaps, only to Xon, and gifted with some rather unique esper abilities. As noted, "unlike the mind-meld of Vulcans, it simply is the ability to sense images in other minds. Never words or emotions, only images, shapes, sizes, textures. On her planet, sexual foreplay consists largely of lovers placing images in each other's minds." Like Decker, Ilia made it into the first feature film, and remained essentially as the guide depicted her.

These character profiles were followed by a breakdown of the original crew, an explanation of the standing sets, description of equipment and an explanation of terminology. It concluded with some very basic questions, followed by the appropriate answers. For instance:

Q: What is Earth like in *Star Trek's* century?

A: For one thing, we'll seldom take a story back there and, therefore, don't expect to get into subjects which would create great problems, technical and otherwise. The U.S.S. on our ship stands for 'United Space Ship'—indicat-

ing without troublesome specifics that mankind has found some unity on Earth, perhaps at long last even peace. If you require a statement such as one that Earth cities of the future are splendidly planned with fifty mile parkland strips around them, fine."

The *Star Trek* feature films have provided tantalizing hints of the future, but never delved into it in great detail. Some things, one would assume, are best left to the imagination. As it stood, the show's bible was an efficient guide to the dos and don'ts of *Star Trek II*.

It all became a moot point, however, when—after having a dozen scripts written, sets constructed, the cast signed — Paramount dropped the idea of a television series and decided that a feature film was the way to go.

THE MOTION PICTURE

"It was a combination of things," said Gene Roddenberry in regards to the decision to make a feature film as opposed to a new series. "Five years ago, Paramount began looking at the remarkable rerun of the *Star Trek* series — and they began to say, 'Well, gee, maybe we *do* have something here.' And it resulted in, four years ago, my checking into the studio with the idea of putting together a *Star Trek* feature. At the time, the plan was just to do a modest-budget feature; and they were convinced they had a sufficient audience. But we couldn't come up with a script that Paramount really liked. Paramount wasn't that much into science fiction at the time. I think a lot of studios at the time had a rather simplistic view of science fiction—rocket ships and blasters and high adventure—the kinds of things that, really, you saw in *Star Wars*, though probably with a few more half-nude women. I just wasn't interested in doing a space pirate type of show—a film is just too great an exertion

of time and energy. The concepts I was working in and trying to get by at the same time had some fairly complex and, I thought, daring thematic material. And that just kind of shook them up, because they weren't thinking of science fiction as being a really heavy thematic thing. We finally ended up starting to do it as a spectacular for television to open up a new series. But about that time, *Star Wars* did come along and showed that there was, indeed, not only the audience that they thought might be there, but a rather unusual-sized one at that. They have been moving toward it for a number of years. Not fast enough to suit me, nor with a large-enough budget, but they were moving."

Star Trek: The Motion Picture was officially announced on March 28, 1978. Leonard Nimoy had been signed to reprise his role of Spock (effectively knocking actor David Gautreaux's Xon off the Enterprise) and Academy Award winner Robert Wise was set to direct what began as a $15 million film. It seemed as though Roddenberry's dream was truly becoming a reality. Unfortunately, filming began with an incomplete script and a special effects debacle that hoisted the budget to upwards of $44 million—at the time one of the most expensive films ever made.

Things were certainly not easy for Roddenberry during production. First off, a major struggle took place between he and screenwriter Harold Livingston, who ultimately quit the project three times due to what he termed Roddenberry's interference. Livingston wanted to update *Star Trek*; to make it palatable to a modern audience and not cling to so many aspects of the '60s television series. Roddenberry, on the other hand, had his own feelings as to what made *Star Trek* work, and was not willing to allow anyone to alter that image. Added to this was his limited control on the project, having no choice but to acquiesce to Robert Wise on many aspects of the production. As he quickly discovered, producing a big-budget

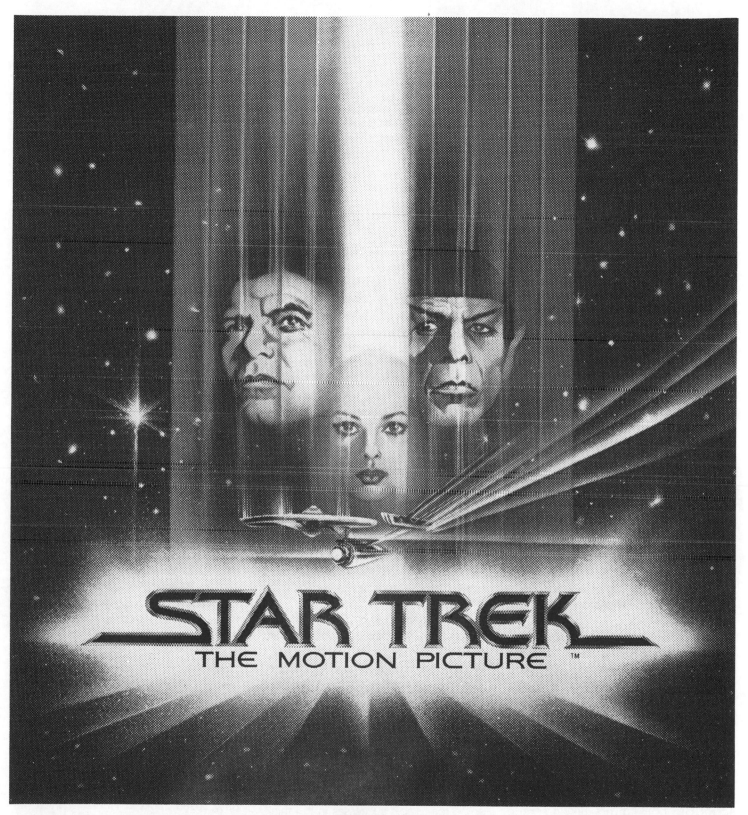

An ad slick from the promotional campaign booklet handed out to movie theatres in conjunction with the release of Star Trek: The Motion Picture (courtesy United Artists Theatres).

motion picture was *not* the same as producing a weekly television series.

In terms of having control, he stated, "I suppose as much as I have the personality to take over. But more is not always more in making a movie. Making movies is quite different than making a television show. In television, I had directors that came and went, different directors every week. Naturally I had to assume a lot of control over the initial show because it was my idea, and I wanted all of the directors to be directing the same Mr. Spock next week as they directed last week. In a movie, however, which is a director's medium, I can hardly get a director of the quality and ability of a Robert Wise and then walk in and say, 'Listen, I want you to do everything exactly as I tell you.' When you bring in Robert Wise, you're bringing in his talent, his ability of wide-screen movies."

The script, based on the "In Thy Image" episode for the proposed *Star Trek II* series, deals with a NASA space probe (Voyager 6), having achieved consciousness and now seeking its creator. If not responded to, the probe, which calls itself V'ger, will destroy all life on Earth.

The original story, based on Roddenberry's *Genesis II* outline "Robot's Return," was written by Alan Dean Foster, then the screenplay was penned by Harold Livingston, rewritten by Roddenberry and then back and forth between he and Livingston throughout production.

"It started off a bit simpler," admitted Roddenberry, "because it had been written as a two-hour television program. It got more and more complex as it got to be a bigger and bigger movie, and we started adding things on to make use of the wide-screen, big-vision, like the wing-walk, where they go out on top of the Enterprise saucer section. I put that in. I put the climax of the show inside V'ger, where the original script did not. I'm not taking screen credit because we had a writer who worked very hard on it. He felt he

deserved credit and my policy is to never get into a credit dispute. That was my policy all through *Star Trek*. If a writer felt he wanted it badly enough to have a Guild action on it, I'd withdraw."

Upon its release, *Star Trek: The Motion Picture* was considered nothing short of a disaster. It was far too long, focused more on special effects than characterization and failed to maintain some of the most basic aspects of the original series that made it such a sensation. Added to that was the similarity of the plotline to several episodes of the show, most notably "The Changeling" and "The Doomsday Machine."

Roddenberry explained to *Starlog* magazine, "After having done 78 episodes covering a fairly wide field, it would have been hard to do anything and not have it bear some resemblances. I think that [the film] appeared to resemble [certain episodes] more at the end because many of the things that made this script different were, bit by bit, sliced out of the movie. They were the 'talky' things. The personal stories were excised from the script or the shooting schedule. Then it became....more and more like things we'd done in the past. We had a two-hour television script, which that story was right for, rather than being given the time to....really get the major motion-picture story. Had we done that, we probably would've had none of those complaints and an even better film.

"My attitude on *Star Trek* is this," he continued. "I think that while the film failed in a number of areas where I would have liked it to have succeeded, it was a successful adaptation of the television story to the screen. We could have done more—and we could have done a lot less, but we did what we could under the time, conditions and circumstances—and the fact that God double-crossed us by making us fallible. The film has some failures....it also has some remarkable successes in it. I think, considering the way it all happened, we came out with a remarkably good film

and I'm very pleased to have been a part of it."

As *Star Trek: The Motion Picture* moved on to an ultimate $175 million gross, word of a Gene Roddenberry-produced sequel began making the rounds. One proposed plotline, according to *Starlog* magazine, had the Enterprise travel backwards in time to save the life of President Kennedy. As a result, all history would have been changed. Reportedly, this tired retread of "City on the Edge of Forever" would have concluded with Spock firing a deadly phaser blast at the president to set things straight. Nothing more was heard of this premise.

Then rumor was that the followup would be the ultimate Klingon story, delving deeply into the nature of the Klingon Empire.

"We know a little bit more about how to use *Trek* in motion pictures," said Roddenberry in 1980. "The second run in anything is easier. If you've ever played golf, the second try you can always sink the putt. It's that first shot at the whole....The sequel story is much more intra-crew, intra-character. It has many more of the difficult decisions that Kirk always had in the TV episodes; decisions about morality and ideals—but I'm not going to say anything more. It's good *Star Trek*. It would have made a good three-parter on the TV show — if I'd had the money to do it."

Many of Roddenberry's views of the *Star Trek II* script would ultimately prove themselves correct. Ironically, he would have little to do with the final film.

EXECUTIVE CONSULTANT

When Paramount Pictures rejected Roddenberry's sequel script, the writer/producer was asked to leave the lot with his long-time secretary, Susan Sackett. Harve Bennett [as detailed later in this volume] was brought in as Roddenberry's replacement, and Gene was given the title "Executive Consultant." Roddenberry's view of the situation, insofar as what he said to the press, was that this was fine with him.

Explained Roddenberry in 1984, "One has to recognize that film and TV are different mediums. TV is a very introspective thing in which you get inside of the heads of the people you see there and you do an awful lot of close shots. TV really gets inside the characters. Motion pictures, on the other hand, are more of a spectacle. This is why in motion pictures Dolby sound works so well. It's also why, in spooky pictures, they blow cold winds on you or rock the seats in earthquake pictures. The spectacle is what is important there. There has to be some difference. Motion pictures today are much affected by the great successes such as *Star Wars*, which are rather spectacular and full of special effects.

"My contract," he elaborated, "gives me the total right to produce and write all motion pictures. But I did *Star Trek* 79 times. I just can't be a creature of *Star Trek* all my life. I wanted to see bright, new people come in and put a good stamp on it and add certain differences. As the consultant, they send me everything from the first story idea to the final draft of the motion picture. I also see the dailies and rough-cuts and all of that. I make my comments to them. I have told them the only time I would say, 'No, stop, I refuse to put my name on it,' is if they should break any of the basic things about *Star Trek*....I'm certainly not going to insist on taking my name off or breaking the contract merely because they don't have the uniform I like or merely because they want to crash the Enterprise. If you're going to have good people, you've got to give good people some latitude to do it their way."

Philosophically this was sound, but Roddenberry made no bones of the fact that the only Harve Bennett-produced film he approved of was *Star Trek IV: The Voyage Home*, finding that *The*

Wrath of Khan, The Search for Spock and *The Final Frontier* were not what he considered truly representative of *Star Trek*.

Throughout the first half of the 1980's, there wasn't much heard from Roddenberry, except for the fact that he had plans to become a full-time novelist, based on the success of his novelization of *Star Trek: The Motion Picture*. Published at the same time as the film's release, the notion of writing novels seemed to touch a chord with him, and pointed out a future direction.

"I guess that if I had my absolute choice, I'd like to end up writing only novels. It's the one type of writing which you have about the greatest freedom," he said. "You can live anywhere. You don't have to live near Hollywood. You can work on your own time and schedule. I have more latitude and freedom that commercial television no longer offers and that cable and satellite television may offer, at which time I'll come back. I may continue to work in today's television for economic reasons depending on how other projects develop."

A novel he spoke often of — which has never seen the light of day — was *Report From Earth*, which featured an extra-terrestrial named Gaan who comes to Earth and starts to observe mankind through his eyes, allowing the author to put his own philosophical stances down on paper. In the pages of *Starlog*, he pointed out, "What I've discovered, is that to practice seeing the world through an invented alien's eyes is not only an exhilarating and fun way to examine yourself and the whole planet, but it creates an unusual kind of logic system. The secret is identifying with the alien so completely that prejudice about myself and Earth begins melting away—and somehow shedding of personal prejudice seems to open up a person's mental processes. You think in new dimensions and at new speeds. The more I polish Gaan and practice putting myself in his place, the more discoveries I make."

At the 1984 Worldview convention, he added, "Gaan was originally a marine lifeform, its home being a far distant methane sea planet, its profession scholar, its specialty the study of life on ocean planets similar to its own, which all members of Gaan's life form had believed to be the only environment capable of evolving intelligence. Their way of studying other intelligences is to stay unobserved while learning the languages and customs of a new world, after which they fabricate a perfect duplicate of that world's intelligent life form, into which a scholar like Gaan then places its own consciousness. It is a study method we ourselves may learn to use in centuries to come. What better way to study another intelligence than from the perspective of living with them as one of them?

"My novel has so far gotten Gaan to our planet, let him recover from his shock of finding an intelligent form on the dry crust of this strange poisonous world, and watched him grow accustomed to these ugly human things stumbling about on stalk-like appendages, burdened with the full weight of gravity. While this is happening, Gaan's technicians in orbit discover a dead, frozen, perfectly preserved human body whole bulky outer covering bears the initials CCCP. Having now a pattern from which a human replica can be fashioned, there is no way a scholar like Gaan can resist this opportunity to study a remarkable new world. In the novel, the time is today and Gaan has begun to live among us, studying us.

"How enjoyable and informative it is to look at this world through the eyes of an extraterrestrial scholar and stranger. Try to imagine how wildly funny each evening's TV news report becomes—and what it is like to go out onto the streets, into shopping malls, and to other places and see the incredible and colorful things that are happening. I have difficulty seeing a better way to gain new perspectives and test old perspectives on the happenings of today.

"The more one becomes a Gaan, the less encumbered one is by earthly racial backgrounds, politics, beliefs, passions, superstitions, preferences, intolerances, hopes and fears. All that one sees through Gaan's eyes is what exists, what is happening at what rate, affected by what other factors. Observe, compute, analyze, and viola!—perhaps not all of tomorrow appears, but some very useful approximations of it will almost certainly come into view. Those capable of using an extraterrestrial's eyes as an excuse, as a challenge, as an exciting game, improve on their ability to estimate where today may be taking us.

"When Gaan looks at the topics we are studying today, he confesses some puzzlement over why we are not paying more attention to the following questions: if automation puts half our work force on the street (and we dare not call that impossible), what of the police? If they are overworked and outnumbered, how do we increase their numbers, their legal powers? What kinds of better tools should we provide? Better weapons, too? What limitations? Shouldn't we be considering possible scenarios, recommending options and limits?

"Prison experiments have demonstrated that implants can trigger alarms if the wrong prisoner enters the wrong area. Or even trigger chemical release incapacitating the person. Is this a valid parole device? Is this a legitimate possibility for the protection of law-abiding citizenry from 'trouble makers'? If disorder threatens our cities, should we consider travel passes that limit which vehicles can travel which areas? What about cordoning off trouble areas or designing special television networks to produce 'patriotic' TV, motivating changes in people's attitudes and desires and values?

"We are perilously close to being able to manufacture non-narcotic drugs offering a broad selection of mood alterations at a cost of pennies. Do we distribute these legally? Do we prefer

that these become criminal substances? Do we continue to maintain the criminal status of all drugs? The truth is that drugs actually represent something that's very wrong in our society. I submit it is frightening that when a person reaches adulthood or adolescence, they need some sort of help to make life happy. What emotional things are we doing to those people who need a substance to get by? We should be examining that, not the criminal aspect of drugs. It may be that unless our world becomes more perfect, some people are always going to need mood changers.

"Can our political system survive television's Hollywood method of casting candidates and presenting issues? Is there a self-ordained messiah in our future? Are there indications of a public hunger for this? Is there a very obvious trend toward more and more simplistic answers to life's problems?"

He summed up by turning Gaan's eyes on our planet and having this alien comment on humanity. "Despite what sometimes seems insurmountable evidence to the contrary," Roddenberry said, "I am now inclined to believe that they will ultimately survive. I look forward to the day when these humans, who are so much more than they yet believe they are, will at last understand that the Cosmos outside and the Cosmos inside themselves are one and the same."

To this date, *Report From Earth* has not seen publication, and one wonders if it ever will. Roddenberry did have a history of promising novels that never appeared, including adaptations of his *God Thing* screenplay and the rejected sequel to *Star Trek: The Motion Picture*.

Besides being given a star on the Hollywood Walk of Fame, not much was heard from Gene Roddenberry in the 1980's, until *Star Trek*'s 20th anniversary in 1986 and the announcement in October of that year that the show would be returning to television.

THE NEXT GENERATION

Shortly after the release of *Star Trek: The Motion Picture* in 1979, there was a steadily diminishing number of independent television stations carrying the original series five nights a week. Paramount, concerned that their golden goose was losing its ability to lay eggs except for one feature film every two years or so, decided that they needed to pump new life into the franchise. Hence their decision to launch a new syndicated television series, ultimately entitled *Star Trek: The Next Generation*, which would feature an all new cast. Naturally there were innumerable fans who claimed that a *Star Trek* without Kirk and Spock would not work, and this undoubtedly filled Roddenberry and those chosen to bring the series to life with some amount of fear. Five years later, however, *The Next Generation* is often deemed *Star Trek*, while the classic cast adventures are looked upon as nice nostalgic visits with old friends.

At a *Star Trek* convention, Roddenberry explained to the captive audience how the series came together.

"There is no prostitution in making something that you like for yourself," he began. "If other people happen to like it, wow, that's wonderful....I'd like to talk to you today about something I've never really discussed: what led up to *Star Trek: The Next Generation*. Many people have wondered about that. How did it happen, what were our thoughts during it? I had a lot of personal resistance to this. The first *Star Trek* took years out of my life, separated me from my family and kept me away from my children and I really didn't want to go through that again when Paramount asked me if I would like to bring *Star Trek* back.

"And there was a career consideration. Why rock the boat? You're ahead, you've got a show that's a success and suppose you go in and everything goes boom, nosedive? No television series had ever succeeded in coming back again. None. It never happened. Then I had an interesting reaction at first from fandom. People were writing me and saying, 'If you get rid of Kirk and Spock, you've gotten rid of me too.' We got literally tens of thousands of letters like that. Some people may say 'Good,' but what *Star Trek* has always been about is variety and diversity as the point of the whole universe. There were physical considerations too. At 67 years old, I am not the same man I was when I was 45 when I started *Star Trek*.

"Put yourself in my place. You think you did it all, that you're really basically responsible for the first *Star Trek*, but so many years have gone by and success has many fathers. For 22 years there have been a collection of people who have said, 'He didn't really do it. It was me, or my brother, or my friend or this or that person.' I found myself thinking, 'They could be right.' The first sign of insanity is that everybody is out of step except you. The net result of all of this made me mad, very angry. *Star Trek*, I said to myself, may be an ego-bent dream, and the rumormongers may be right, but at least I'm going to have the courage to say 'Fuck you' as I go back to it. The more I considered it, the angrier I got. If someone could create *Star Trek* more easily, why didn't more people do something like it in the 22 years since we did the original series? Paramount, meanwhile, when I turned them down had someone else work on a new *Star Trek*. It had a Vulcan captain and a lot of space cadets who seemed to mainly say, 'Gee whiz, Captain.' I really feared doing it until I got angry enough to try.

"Then something else happened. There was a new management at Paramount. Those of you who know me know that I have criticized Paramount many times in the past, and I think with great justification. I even had a secretary who wore a T-shirt that said, 'Paramount is a Klingon Conspiracy.'

"But there was new management there and management seemed

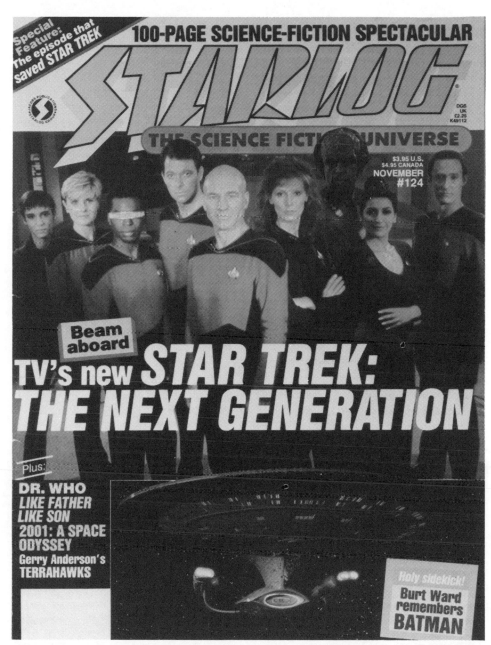

As heralded on this edition of **Starlog** magazine, 1987 saw the creation of **Star Trek: The Next Generation.**

interested in what the creative people did. So they said they had a new way of distributing it, a thing called first-run syndication. And I said, 'Yeah, yeah. But who will my censor be? It'll probably be those same people I had all along who had a deathly fear of open-mouth kissing.' They said, 'No, we'll tell you who your censor will be. The censor will be you.' Which was hard to believe. That's kind of crazy. That's like giving the key to

the asylum to the inmates. But a Paramount executive said, 'Roddenberry, we established that you were a little crazy years ago when you insisted that the starship should have mixed races aboard, and since then we've learned to go along with you.' Believe it or not, that's how it happened. I want to give credit to Paramount, because in all the years and all the months of making this new show, we never got a single telephone call from Paramount saying, 'Don't do that, you can't do that, think twice about doing that.' Paramount has done exactly as they've promised."

Syndication, as he later found out, provided an interesting problem as well. "What we've discovered," he said, "is that this is much more complex than the old system of shooting a pilot and laying out your format and then having time to study what you've done while you wait for the pilot to be sold to the network."

In the start-up period, Roddenberry called together some veterans from the original series, including producers Robert Justman and Eddie Milkis, and writers Dorothy Fontana and David Gerrold. Milkis quit the show before the series premiered, Dorothy Fontana didn't quite make it through the first season, Robert Justman quit for health reasons and David Gerrold departed the fold about six months into the development of the show. Those early days, while filled with creativity, were also rather tumultuous, culminating in David Gerrold's actually going to the Writer's Guild and claiming that he co-created the series and wrote its bible. Things were ultimately settled, though the results of that settlement have never been released. The series credit stands as it had from the beginning: created by Gene Roddenberry.

Of the situation, Roddenberry told a convention audience, "As I understand it, David Gerrold wanted to have co-credit for creating *Star Trek: The Next Generation*, which is absolute bullshit. My way has always been to bring people in and say, 'What do you think? What do you think of that?' That's how I worked and how I work at present. This is the first time somebody has said, 'Oh, because you asked me what I think, suddenly I'm the creator.' It's a very annoying thing for me. He is saying, 'You have lied in taking the credit.' I am not a liar."

Nonetheless, throughout its first two seasons — particularly the first — Paramount Pictures practically had to

install a revolving door to handle the entering and exiting writers and producers who toiled in the 24th century and were, for one reason or another, let go. Numerous cries were heard, ranging from the fact that Roddenberry's lawyer was calling the shots, that Roddenberry himself had become power hungry and took to punishing writers he was displeased with, that Writer Guild rules were being broken constantly and that the production was in chaos.

While the place to explore all of these elements lie elsewhere, Roddenberry had his own response to the so-called revolving door and the people who passed through it. These words, in fact, echo those he spoke during the run of the original series when he rewrote scripts penned by science-fiction veterans. More recently, however, there was a harshness to those words, a determination to let one and all know that he wasn't — if you will — taking any shit.

"I only know one way to make a show like this and to start a new show—my way," he said. "I'm sorry, it is goddamn well going to be my way, with the way I draw the characters and the way I say the story should go. The changes [between shows] is the power structure. I've never been in the position I am now, so naturally it's new to me. To have total acceptance of the *Star Trek* idea by the studio....it is a lovely position of power and opportunity that comes when you're accepted. Very few people have gotten into this position.

"[Paramount leaves] me alone, but it wasn't always so. When we were first talking about the new show and would I consent to do it, it wasn't as it is now. Much of what is now grew out of those days, grew out of decisions that I made. Rick Berman can tell you marvelous stories about the first year of *Star Trek: The Next Generation* when I had some studio junior executives troop into my office and pull out a script and say, 'All right now, on page one there is this comment,' etcetera. Rick remembers very

well that on that day I shut these guys up forever by telling them that they did not have the right under our contract to come in and talk to me about the script, what to change, or what to do."

In the over two decades between the creation of the two series, both the television medium and Gene Roddenberry himself had gone through a period of growth, which he happily discussed.

"Time has passed," Roddenberry related, "and television has become freer and it excites me to be able to explore these things in a more relaxed way. I can talk about sex now in ways that we were never able to in the previous show. I want to talk about, not just homosexuality, but all types of sexuality. What is truth? I want to talk about crises of our time, the problems of our time, and the challenges of our time. I've mentioned before that people were very shocked when I put multi-racial characters in the original show. People can't expect me to put multi-racial characters in the new show and expect it to be exciting because it's been more or less solved or on its way to a solution. The new viewers will be as shocked by what I do as the early audience was. And as a result, I intend to talk about shocking things. That stimulates people and gets them to thinking and we need that on television. The typical television program that has a villain explains that he is a villain simply because he's a bad guy. I don't intend to let us do that. We don't want heavies because they wear black hats. We want heavies who are motivated to be heavies."

Roddenberry maintained that the crew of the starship Enterprise NCC 1701-D would not only be continuing the mission of its predecessor to boldly go, but would seek out a quality of life as well. For this reasons, families are a part of the starship's complement, and the characters all get along famously—a point which has riled many writers who feel that such an approach creates a homogenous atmosphere devoid of conflict.

"It can tie your hands," Roddenberry admitted, "but I saw it was necessary. You can hardly have people from this ideal world with the same smallness people have today. We have no violence. Our people don't allow it, which sounds like death in a series. People have learned to live with hatred. Our people get along beautifully. In their future, they've learned to accept we are all creatures of passion. But they have evolved into people who can live with each other, which we are trying to do today. Perhaps there are things that can't be solved with a shootout in the last act. There's excitement and challenge in life without those things.

"In the early days of television," he continued; "you almost had to have a shootout at the end of every Western. My feeling about violence in films is similar to my feelings about sex in films. If you are going to do a movie about violence, then do a movie about violence; but don't say that 20 pages of script have gone on and there's no violence, therefore we should have some. Do your movie about violence. Do it honestly about violence and thoughtfully about violence; then move on to other subjects. The same with sex. *Star Trek: The Next Generation* is the product of my mature thought and having achieved a majority of years. I used to think that *Star Trek* was very good about being nonviolent, but still there are episodes that I rushed over. Kirk would pick up the challenge of another race a little too fast for my comfort. I made quite a change of attitude and direction of the show when I did *The Next Generation*, because the new captain is not apt to do those things."

While the butt of enormous skepticism when *Star Trek: The Next Generation* was announced, Roddenberry had the last laugh when the show went on to phenomenal success. Critics claimed that a *Star Trek* without Kirk, Spock, McCoy and the rest of the classic crew would never fly, yet audiences took to Picard, Riker, Data, Crusher, Troi, Tasha, Geordi and Worf in a big way. They

claimed the show wouldn't survive beyond the first season, it's now in its fifth with well over 100 episodes to its credit—surpassing the 78 of the original series. A show without internal conflict would never grab the imagination of the audience—it has. Overall, *Next Generation* has put all naysayers in their place, securing itself a comfortable position in the annals of television and pop culture history. Will the show have the endurability of the original? That's a question which will be answered over the next two decades or so.

Before his death, Roddenberry made it clear that while he was responsible for creating *Next Generation* and pushing it forward into production, the series was placed in the hands of executive producers Rick Berman and Michael Piller, who have taken the child and nurtured it to maturity without violating Roddenberry's overall vision.

"I consider it a master stroke getting [Rick Berman]," said Roddenberry. "He is responsible for the cutting of our films and the choosing of directors and so on. We have a good staff now. It is very pleasant to realize we have, in various stages, some 20 scripts in the works and perhaps 15 of them were on my desk the day we began shooting the fourth season. We never had 15 scripts of any kind before. These were fairly finished and arguable. There were people who wanted changes, and in many cases that was the right way to go. But we had 15 rough-draft scripts. I look at every script, but I don't necessarily study every rewrite. I see the original when it came in and so trust Rick Berman and Michael Piller that probably the next version I see is the semi-final or the final. They are very much a part of the structure of the picture. I no longer think, 'Let them turn in anything; I can fix it.'

"It is such a delight to see finished pages come in and be able to think that their creativity is so good. I applaud the people who did it. [Rick and Michael] have accepted my philosophy, and I have few quarrels with them.

There were a couple of times when one or the other has said, 'I saw a scene you rewrote' or 'I saw your note saying rewrite this, and I wish you wouldn't in this case.' In one instance, it was a religious objection which slapped religion unfairly in the face. Another was a political situation that they felt strongly about.

"I had insisted that the film be cut a certain way. They both said, 'We can understand your reasoning, but we think it is wrong.' I argued and argued and finally realized that there was no point pushing it further and asked myself, 'After all, is this small point I'm making really worth taking the whole thing to pieces?' I decided it wasn't. If they had brought up something that was terribly serious about life or religion or politics, yes, I wouldn't go along with that.

"There is so much in the show that I never dreamed of. It's because very bright people have carved something out of it. If there is a facet of my character, it is that I think humans are exciting and interesting child creatures. The problems with the Writer's Guild [first season] weren't serious. The problems were more with writers. Maybe if I were a director it would have been easier, but to have yourself rewritten by a fellow writer! There were a lot of bloody noses and I received some punches, but I'm a stubborn person, and the dust is all settled now. It is possible for us to improve our show, our writers to use their brainpower to create shocking things."

As the 1990's came into being, Gene Roddenberry was stricken with a series of strokes that slurred his speech and left him partially paralyzed, confining him to a wheelchair for the most part. It all came to an end on October 24, 1991 when a massive stroke ended his life.

But for many, it will not be the frail, elderly man in the wheelchair they remember, but the stubborn, obstinate and imaginative captain of the continuing legend of *Star Trek*. It was his boundless energy and imagination that gave birth to a saga which often brought him into conflict with others and resulted in one of the most memorable pop cultural phenomenons of the 20th century. Without conflict, art would wallow in mediocrity. Despite the vehement arguments and disputes he had over the years, his vision lives on and will continue to be carried forth by others. New Great Birds of the Galaxy like Rick Berman, Michael Piller and Jeri Taylor, executive producers on *The Next Generation*, *Deep Space Nine* and *Voyager*, captured the spirit of Roddenberry's creation and continue to explore brave, new worlds and civilizations, as did those who recently closed the log book on the voyages of the original starship Enterprise.

When asked by his official biographer how he would like to be remembered, Roddenberry replied, "That I had great patience with and great affection for the human race. That I did not believe problems needed to be solved immediately, in present-day terms, and, strangely, that I had a philosophy that did not know what 'immediately' was. Perhaps 'tomorrow' is 500 years from now. What we humans are is really a remarkable thing. How can you doubt that we will survive and mature? There may be a lot of wisdom in the old statement about looking on the world lovingly. If we can, perhaps the world will have time to resolve itself."

Since Roddenberry's death, numerous people — friends and colleagues — have paid tribute to his memory and that which he has left behind. But it's actually a writer by the name of Carey Wilbur, whose contribution to the mythos was the original episode "Space Seed," who succinctly captures the appeal of *Star Trek* and Roddenberry's philosophy.

"People want to believe there's going to be that glorious period of space flight," Wilbur says simply. "We want to believe that there's something out there. *Star Trek* offered the human race a future, and God knows we need the promise of the future."

Gene Roddenberry with Majel Barrett during a TrekCruise shortly before his death (photo copyright ©1994 Karen Witkowski).

THE LIEUTENANT
E P I S O D E   G U I D E

The Lieutenant
29 One-Hour Episodes in Black and White
Starring:
Gary Lockwood
(Lieutenant William T. Rice)
and Robert Vaughn
(Captain Raymond Rambridge)
Executive Producer: Norman Felton
Producer: Gene Roddenberry

Episode #1
"The Art of Discipline"
Written by *Archie L. Tegland*
Directed by *Robert Butler*
Guest Starring:
Anne Helm (Laurice Arnold), John Considine (Sgt. Leonard Arnold), Don Penny (Lt. Stan Harris), Biff Elliott (Sgt. Mack Borgman), Mark Cavell (Cpl. Andy Lavoni), Alan Reed, Jr. (Lt. Sigmund Miller), James Henaghan (Pvt. Sam Kegel)

OFFICIAL SYNOPSIS: Lt. Rice is placed in charge of a platoon of demoralized "goof-ups" with orders to shape them up for inspection within 10 days. Realizing the men had hated their previous lieutenant, a harsh fire-breathing officer, Rice decides to befriend the men, much to the despair of Captain Rambridge. Rambridge attempts to convince Rice that, as a leader of men when the chips are down, he cannot request or bargain for obedience — it is something he must command.

Note: *This episode was directed by Robert Butler, who would go on to direct, among other things, the first* Star Trek *pilot, "The Cage."*

Episode #2
"In the Highest Tradition"
Written by *Blanche Hanalis*
Directed by *Marc Daniels*
Guest Starring: *Andrew Duggan (Peter Bonney), Martine Bartlett (Stella Bonney), Russ Conway (Col. Morley), Leonard Nimoy (Gregg Sanders), Majel Barrett (Ruth Donaldson), Don Penny (Lt. Stan Harris), Bob "Alabama" Davis (Sgt. Arons), Michael Macready (Lt. Grady), George Petrie (Photographer)*

OFFICIAL SYNOPSIS: When World War II Marine hero Pete Bonney becomes the subject of a Hollywood war movie, Lt. Rice is assigned as technical advisor in the recreation of the bloody fighting in the Pacific. Rice discovers that Bonney's heroism under fire has gone unrewarded all these years and his shocked reaction is reported in the press. The hornet's nest consequently stirred up in the Pentagon in turn terrifies Bonney, who is afraid the true story of his actions will expose him as a false hero.

Note: Marc Daniels would go on to become one of the primary directors of the original Star Trek, while Leonard Nimoy would portray Vulcan Science Officer Spock in the series, animated spin-off, six feature films and an episode of Star Trek: The Next Generation, Majel Barrett went on to play Nurse Christine Chapel on the series, married Roddenberry and made numerous guest appearances as Mrs. Troi on both The Next Generation and Deep Space Nine.

Episode #3
"O'Rourke"
Written by Jay Simms
Directed by E.W. Swackhamer
Guest Starring: Eddie Albert (R. Cameron O'Rourke), Bobby Diamond (Pvt. Floyd James), Jay Stine (Cpl. Victor Ganz), Wayne Heffley (Sgt. Edgar Brill), Carmen Phillips (Lily), K.L. Smith (G/Sgt. Jack Arpel), Larry Thor (Lt. Col. Bruce Mahlon), Maurine Dawson (Sheila)

OFFICIAL SYNOPSIS: Cocky and caustic R. Cameron O'Rourke, World War II Marine and now a famous writer, clashes immediately with Lt. Rice in a fighting-knife fracas when he is assigned to do an article comparing today's Marines with those of 20 years ago. Capt. Rambridge, fuming when he discovers that O'Rourke intends to "expose" today's Corps as soft and coddling, nevertheless orders Rice to continue to cooperate. O'Rourke, with constant acid criticism, creates a scene in the Grog Shop and later disobeys Rice's orders by taking part in a live ammunition exercise.

When the life of a man is endangered, the situations explodes into a violent judo-karate battle between Rice and O'Rourke.

Episode #4
"Between Music and Laughter"
Written by Sy Salkowitz
Directed by Vince McEveety
Guest Starring: Patricia Crowley (Susan Rambridge), Don Penny (Lt. Stanley Harri), Henry Bechman (Major Al Barker), Michael Stefani (Capt. Mitchell Perry), John Harding (Lt. Com. Charles Harnel), Carmen Phillips (Lily), Chris Noel (Ginny)

OFFICIAL SYNOPSIS: Following their divorce, Susan Rambridge arrives unexpectedly at Camp Pendleton in an effort at reconciliation with Capt. Ray Rambridge. When fun-loving Susan had married the reticent captain, little did either suspect their different attitudes toward life and people could wreck their marriage. Very much in love, they still couldn't live together successfully as husband and wife, and since had been equally unhappy alone. Susan charms Lt. Rice into acting as an unwitting go-between with the reluctant Rambridge, hoping to find that divorce had been a mistake.

Note: Director Vince McEveety went on to direct several episodes of the original Star Trek.

Episode #5
"Captain Thomson"
Written by Sheldon Stark
Directed by Leon Benson
Guest Starring:
Paul Burke (Capt. Kenneth Thomson), Richard Anderson (Lt. Col. Hiland), John Milford (Sgt. Kagey), Lisabeth Hush (Mrs. Thomson), Don Penny (Lt. Stan Harris), Ken Tobey (Sgt. Baker), Carmen Phillips (Lily), Chris Noel (Jean)

OFFICIAL SYNOPSIS: Aggressive, combat-tough Captain Thomson is assigned to a "paper-pushing" desk job after knowing the grueling realism of guerilla warfare, where there are only "the quick and the dead." His dissatisfaction

immediately antagonizes his superiors and subordinates alike. During simulated field exercises, he suddenly assumes command of Lieutenant Rice's platoon as if it were actual war, jeopardizing military property and endangering Rice's career as well as his own pending promotion. He knows that to report the incident "by the book" will endanger his own career, while delaying the facts may cause Rice to take the brunt of the blame. Thomson must decide whether to live with his lie or with a clean conscience.

Note: One of the guest stars is Richard Anderson (Lt. Col. Hiland), who is best known to genre fans for his roles in Forbidden Planet, The Six Million Dollar Man/Bionic Woman (as Oscar Goldman) and The Night Strangler.

Episode #6
"Lament for a Dead Goldbrick"
Written by Sy Salkowitz
Directed by Robert Butler
Guest Starring: Robert Duvall (Richard Whitley), Joseph Campanella (Major Jason Clark), Don Penny (Lt. Stan Harris), Carmen Phillips (Lily), Dallas Mitchell (Public Relations Officer), John Zeremba (Pete Hartley), Holly McIntire (Connie Langford), Larry Thor (President of the Court), Chris Connelly (Pvt. Russell), Michael McDonald (Neal Pierson), K.L. Smith (Sgt. Arpel), James Seay (Chief of Staff), Stephen Mines (Pvt. Richards), Richard Butler (Runner)

OFFICIAL SYNOPSIS: When Pvt. Joseph Morrell is drowned during a night maneuver, Lt. Rice is charged by a famed magazine correspondent, Richard Whitley, of being the direct cause of the man's death when he sent Morrell on the mission in rough terrain. Capt. Rambridge warns Rice that any attack on the dead man would only make Rice look bad, despite the fact that Morrell had been a notorious goldbrick who avoided duties by claiming "illness." Whitley, knowing Rice had given Morrell a bad time in an attempt to make him "shape up," loses his professional objectivity and lashes out at the Marine

Corps, charging "whitewash." Rambridge discovers the psychotic reason behind Whitley's hatred for officers and, in a climactic hearing room scene, springs a surprise witness in Rice's defense.

Episode #7
"A Touching of Hands"
Written by Sy Salkowitz
Directed by Don Medford
Guest Starring: Ina Balin (Jan Everest), Yale Summers (Lt. Barry Everest), David White (Major Amory), Barbara Bain (Cissie Van Osten), Hal Gould (Lt. Col. Wade), June Vincent (Martha Amory), Barbara Babcock (Doris Broxton), Carmen Phillips (Lily), Maurine Dawson (Paula Watsor), Rita Kenaston (Ellie Holtman)

OFFICIAL SYNOPSIS: Jan Everest, wife of Lt. Bill Rice's close friend, is innocently drawn into a romantic situation with Rice when they share a committee assignment in preparation for the Navy Relief Ball. They begin to painfully enjoy one another's company....especially Jan, who has found life with her hardworking husband increasingly boring. The simple act of touching hands in public becomes the object of malicious gossip, ultimately threatening to ruin a happy marriage and two officers' promising careers.

Note: Guest star Barbara Bain (Cissie Van Osten) would, of course, go on to Mission: Impossible and Space: 1999.

Episode #8
"The Two-Star Giant"
Written by Beirne Lay, Jr.
Directed by Richard Donner
Guest Starring:
Neville Brand (Gen. Ira Stone), Richard Anderson (Col. Clinton Hiland), Don Penny (Lt. Stanley Harris), Linda Evans (Nan Hiland), Yale Summers (Lt. Barry Everest), Sheila Rogers (Mrs. Ira Stone), Hal Gould (Lt. Col. Wade), Sherwood Keith (Police Chief McElwaine)

OFFICIAL SYNOPSIS: Nan Hiland, spoiled daughter of a Marine officer, throws a romantic monkey wrench into Lt. Bill Rice's unexpected assignment as aide to General Stone, a crusty, battle-scarred veteran. Rice must struggle not only with Nan's interference but with his own inexperience in the assignment when he accompanies the General to Washington for a grueling session before a congressional fact-finding committee. Yet, as Stone fights for his reputation and career, it is Rice's strength and common sense that provide help at the most criticial point.

Note: The episode was directed by Richard Donner, whose feature film credits now include Superman: The Movie, Ladyhawke, the Lethal Weapon trilogy, The Omen and Maverick.

Episode #9
"Cool of the Evening"
Written by Sheldon Stark
Directed by Robert Gist
Guest Starring: Kathryn Hays (Carol Wayden), Norman Fell (Jerry Belman), Michael Strong (Peter Clay), Jack Albertson (George O'Leery), Don Penny (Lt. Stanley Harris), Henry Beckman (Major Adam Butler)

OFFICIAL SYNOPSIS: Lt. Bill Rice answers the screams of Carol Wayden in an alley behind a nightclub and routes her assailant, comic Jerry Belman, before police arrive. Carol, a school teacher working as cigarette girl in the club, panics when she realizes her reputation is at stake. Accusing Rice as her assailant, she forces him to face a civil court where circumstantial evidence and her own false testimony threaten to destroy his military career.

Episode #10
"To Set it Right"
Written by Lee Erwin
Directed by Vince McEveety
Guest Starring: Dennis Hopper (Cpl. Pete Devlin), Don Marshall (Pvt. Ernest Cameron), Woody Strode (Sgt. Holt), Nichelle Nichols (Norma Bartlett), John Milford (Sgt. Kagey), Preston Pierce (Pvt. Peter Vronsky), Bill Wilson (Pvt. Barlow), Ed McCready (Baylor)

OFFICIAL SYNOPSIS: Old hates are stirred up within Rice's platoon when a young Negro replacement locks horns with a Caucasian classmate from high-school days. The conflict between the two men is perplexing to Lt. Rice, especially since neither can give a valid reason for their mutual dislike. Rather than transferring the new man, Rice attempts to solve the problem by forcing the two to work as a team during maneuvers. When this fails, Rice makes an unusual last ditch effort to reconcile the two. The outcome surprises even him.

Note: Two more Star Trek alumni populate this episode: Don Marshall (Pvt. Erenest Cameron), who would appear in season one's "The Galileo Seven," and Nichelle Nichols (Norma Bartlett) who would go on to co-star as Lt. Uhura.

Episode #11
"A Very Private Affair"
Written by Gene Roddenberry
Directed by Buzz Kulik
Guest Starring:
James Gregory (Sgt. Horace Capp), Laura Devon (Lane Bishop), Steve Franken (Lt. Panosian), Bob Elston (Lt. Ditser), Susan Silo (Marie Eckles), Jan Stine (Pvt. Eckles), Harold Gould (Lt. Col. Wade), Stuart Margolin (Cpl. Purveau)

OFFICIAL SYNOPSIS: Fresh out of Annapolis, Marine Second Lieutenant Bill Rice reports to his first duty station at Camp Pendleton. A frosty reception by Capt. Rambridge, his company commander, jolts Rice's morale. Everything seems to go wrong. He is assigned to investigate a serious grudge battle between two enlisted men over a girl, which the entire company is attempting to hush. Without the cooperation of his men, and without time to prepare for the war exercise, Rice's first experience as platoon leader in a mock battle turns into a fiasco. Yet the lieutenant is determined to get to the bottom of the case he is investigating and redeem himself as a leader in the eyes of his men.

Note: Guest star James Gregory (Sgt. Horace Capp) would guest star in the Trek episode "Dagger of the Mind" and play the gorilla General Ursus in Beneath the Planet of the Apes.

Episode #12
"A Million Miles From Clary"
Written by Ed Waters
Directed by Don Medford
Guest Starring:

Bill Bixby (Stew Sallaway), John Doucette (Sgt. Clintock), Russell Thorson (Mr. Sallaway), John Milford (Cpl. Kagey), Frank Gardner (Pvt. Matthews), Mario Roccuzzo (Pvt. Barducci), Jack McCall (First Lieutenant), Morris Chapnick (Corpsman), Carmen Phillips (Lily)

OFFICIAL SYNOPSIS: Lt. Bill Rice watches his life-long friendship with Stew Sallaway dissolve into steaming jealousy over a beautiful young woman when his former schoolmate is assigned as an enlisted man to Rice's platoon. Sallaway, taking advantage of their friendship, selfishly demands impossible professional and personal favors. Faced with the dissention and resulting ill-feeling among his men and criticism from Capt. Rambridge, his superior, Rice makes a decision that will determine both his and Sallaway's future friendship and military careers.

Episode #13
"Interlude"
Story by Robert E. Thompson
Teleplay by
Margaret and Paul Schneider
Directed by Richard Donner
Guest Starring:

Joanna Moore (Julie Havener)(, Arch Johnson (CDR. Harry Engstrom), Conrad Negel (Admiral Havener), Don Penny (Lt. Stan Harris), Peter Hansen (Dr. Sidney Oliver), John Garwood (1st Patrolman), Richard Adams (2nd Patrolman), Marcia Ganva (Nurse)

OFFICIAL SYNOPSIS: A shattering car crash, paralyzing one side of his body, leaves Lt. Rice embitterd in a backwash of self pity until he is taunted back to reality by the vivacious Julie Havener. Gradually they fall in love without Rice learning that she is also a patient, suffering from an

incurable brain tumor. From the courageous girl, he finds strength to undergo a delicate spinal operation which can cure him — or cause his death.
Note: Co-writer Paul Schneider ultimately wrote several episodes of Star Trek, most notably "Balance of Terror," which introduced the Romulans.

Episode #14
"Instant Wedding"
Written by Ellis Marcus
Directed by David Alexander
Guest Starring: Jeremy Slate (Boxer), Marlyn Mason (Carol Jean), Martin West (Kelso), Don Penny (Lt. Harris), Bobo Lewis (Vera Hockstadter), Madge Blake (Millie Brinkerhoff), David Morick (Sgt. Blake), Barnaby Hale (Chaplain Vaughn), Eve McVeagh (Marge Fowler)

OFFICIAL SYNOPSIS: Lt. Bill Rice faces a string of frustrating dilemmas when it falls his lot to keep a Navy wolf from the door of his fellow Marine officer's beautiful but perplexing sweetheart. First he finds himself forced into proposing in "John Aiden" fashion, then he must arrange a full-scale military wedding. Just when everything seems under control, romance turns cool only moments before the wedding march — and he learns how a lieutenant feels in the role of marrige counsellor. But, his biggest crisis is yet to come, when the Navy begins to storm a position held by the proud Marines.

Episode #15
"Capp's Lady"
Written by Robert J. Shaw
Directed by David Alexander
Guest Starring: James Gregory (Sgt. Capp), Nina Talbot (Marie Newton), John Milford (Sgt. Kagey), J. Lewis Smith (Sgt. Patterson), John Newton (Sgt. Murray), Chuck Haren (Cpl. Sandow), Lenore Roberts (Jane Kagey), Frank Gardner (Pvt. Miller)

OFFICIAL SYNOPSIS: Lt. Rice is about to lose his most valuable non-com, and, worse, he will have to face the wrath of his commander, Capt.

Rambridge, for the martial "foul-up" of one of his men. Grizzled Sgt. Capp finds himself in the unenviable position of having to marry Marie Newton, whose motives and reputation seem highly questionable. He comes to Lt. Rice, 24 years his junior, in romantic desperation. Rice no sooner gets Capp off the marriage-go-round when the love-smitten Sgt. proposes again. In a last ditch effort, Rice intervenes and Marie insists that Capp must choose either her or the Corps.

Episode #16
"To Take Up Serpents"
Written by Jay Simms
Directed by Andrew V. McLaglen
Guest Starring:

Steve Franken (Lt. Sam Panosian), Tom Simcox (Capt. Parker), John Alderman (Lt. Eddie Fiske), Gregory "Pappy" Boyington (Col. Boyington), Michael Ryan (Lt. Comm. Johnson), William O'Connell (Lt. (J.G.) Wade), Anna Lisa (Manager), John Milford (Cpl. Pagey), Pat Priest (Diane), Drlene Sturt (Pat)

OFFICIAL SYNOPSIS: Famed World War II fighter ace Gregory "Pappy" Boyington is featured in a dramatic story filmed on actual locations in a secret area of the El Toro Marine Air Station in California. Lt. Bill Rice faces his first experience in an F4B Phantom jet, the free world's fastest airplane, with a feeling of terror. On an air-infantry exercise, he jeopardizes his own life and that of a pilot friend when air sickness renders him helpless. Filled with self-doubt, Rice forces himself to test his courage air-borne in a second, even more difficult flight.

Episode #17
"The Proud and the Angry"
Written by Jerome B. Thomas
Directed by Andrew V. McLaglen
Guest Starring: Rip Torn (Sgt. Karl Katen), Richard Rust (Pvt. Steven Grace), Miranda Jones (Mrs. Nancy Kasten), Gilbert Green (Col. Timothy MacAdams), Chris Connelly (Pvt. Derek Russell), Bob

Davis (LCDR. Farley Crosse), Barnaby Hale (Capt. Earl Cook)

OFFICIAL SYNOPSIS: Lt. Bill Rice arrives on a secret assignment at Marine "boot camp" in San Diego to investigate charges of training brutality against harsh Drill Instructor Sgt. Karl Kasten. Masquerading as a "boot" recruit in grueling training with Kasten's platoon, Rice is nearing the end of his investigation when he is ambushed and severely beaten by an unknown assailant. Rice sets a trap for his attacker and hopes the result will exonerate Katen, thus saving the reputation of a valuable non-com.

Episode #18
"Alert"
Written by Lee Erwin
Directed by Don Taylor
Guest Starring: Charles McGraw (Sgt. Ernie Trgg), Ted Bessell (Jim Douglas), Sharon Farrell (Pam Canford), Don Penny (Lt. Stanley Harris), Steven Marlo (Sgt. Warren Perry), George O'Hanlon (Jeweler), Eddie Carroll (Pvt. Z. Wesley Martin), Chris Connelly (Pvt. Russell), Theodora Davitt (Laurie Douglas)

OFFICIAL SYNOPSIS: Just about the time Lt. Rice is thinking seriously about marriage, Capt. Rambridge notifies him his platoon is being called to immediate battle alert and will be flown to an international "hot spot" overseas. Realizing that this might be "the real thing," Rice's test as a leader of men comes when he not only must brush aside his own disappointment but also decide whether or not his top sergeant, Perry, should be left behind to remain with his panicked and expectant wife.
Note: Director Don Taylor would go on to helm Escape From the Planet of the Apes.

Episode #19
"Man With an Edge"
Story by Beirne Lay, Jr.
Teleplay by Lee Erwin and Beirne Lay, Jr.
Directed by Vince McEveety
Guest Starring: Chad Everett (Lt. Kingsley R. Kane), Joan O'Brien (Lt. Ruth Riley), John Milford (Sgt. Kagey), Kevin

Hagen (Lt. Col. Harris Farrell), Paul Newlan (Col. High Kingsley), Paul Newlan (Col. Hugh Kingsley), Don Penny (Lt. Stan Harris), Henry Beckman (Major Al Barker), Carmen Phillips (Lily), Jim Drum (Sgt. Victor Tate), John Lindesmith (Corporal), Sandra Grant (Helen), Caray Foster (Jan)

OFFICIAL SYNOPSIS: Lt. Rice's command and respect of his men is threatened when a football-hero-turned-Marine, Lt. Kingsley Kane, is placed in temporary command of the platoon, Rice being raised to Capt. Rambridge's post of Company Commander during Rambridge's absence. Rice cannot overcome jealousy when, under Kane's leadership, the platoon performs better than it had under him. It soon is evident that the hard-driving Kane is using the men to further his own personal stature, fighting a 365 day war to win, rgardless of the means. Realizing his report on Kane will determine whether Kane will retain permanent command of the platoon, Rice is forced to make an "objective" decision whether or not to expose Kane's underhanded methods.

Episode #20
"Fall From a White Horse"
Written by George Eckstein
Directed by John Brahm
Guest Starring: Andrew Prine (Lt. Gerald Allison), Katharine Ross (Elizabeth Sharp), Karl Swenson (Lt. Col. Morley), James Callahan (Lt. Markley), Don Penny (Lt. Harris), Penny Stanton (Mrs. Gorson), Dorothy Neuman (Mrs. Lanyard)

OFFICIAL SYNOPSIS: Lt. Rice receives an unexpected shock when he becomes involved with a girl of questionable reputation, then is appointed by Capt. Rambridge to defend an officer friend accused of a vicious hit-and-run. In his first assignment as a court martial defense counselor, Rice knows Lt. Gerald Allison can prove his innocence, yet Allison foolishly believes his testimony will damage the reputation of girlfriend Elizabeth Sharp. Rice must either remain silent and risk Allison's acquittal or expose the girl's past.

Episode #21
"Mother Enemy"
Written by
Robert J. Shaw and Gene Roddenberry
Directed by Vincent McEveety
Guest Starring: Neva Patterson (Vera Delwyn), Walter Koenig (Sgt. John Delwyn), Jennifer Billingsley (Ginny McBane), Carmen Phillips (Lily), Preston Pierce (Cpl. Peterson), Chris Connelly (Sgt. Ciancola), Paul Comi (Cpl. Kasten), Paul Lambert (Claude Gorman)

OFFICIAL SYNOPSIS: Lt. Rice recommends Sgt. John Delwyn, one of his men, as a candidate for officers training and is shocked to learn from Capt. Rambridge that Delwyn's mother is the top-ranked woman Communist agent in the U.S. Still firmly beleiving in Delwyn's loyalty, Rice must cope with the mother's charge that the Marine Corps is practicing "guilt by association." A furious Delwyn breaks into a Communist rally and publicly defends the Marines against his mother to her face. Rice, impressed, still must decide the question: could Delwyn, in all good conscience, fight his own mother if it came down to armed conflict between the Communists and the free world?
Note: Guest star Walter Koenig (John Delwyn).....did anybody say Chekov?

Episode #22
"The War Called Peace"
Written by Anthony Wilson
Directed by Andrew V. McLaglen
Guest Starring: Donna Anderson (Laura Ann Morrissey), Lloyd Bochner (Dr. Alexander Denning), Denver Pyle (Major Mathew Morrissey), John Marley (George Bardel), Tom Drake (Sgt. Lester Curtis), Clement J. Stadler, Col. USMC (Lt. Col. Watts), Robert LaVarre (Master Sergeant), Ed Long (Frank Hoving), Richard Chambers (Larry Quillin)

OFFICIAL SYNOPSIS: When a dangerous national security leak is discovered on a top secret missile project, Lt. Rice is sent to the base disguised as an engineer to ferret out the cause. He discovers Dr. Denning, a young scientist, has rebelled against the harsh "by-the-book" security rules set down by Major Morrissey. Denning, who has been courting the major's daughter, explodes when he discovers Rice's casual friendship with the girl. He purposely divulges a secret to the press and is fired from the project. Rice suspects the fault does not totally lay with Denning when he discovers a shocking incident in Major Morrissey's past. Col. Clement Stadler, technical advisor for this series, plays the role of Col. Watts, marking his dramatic debut.

Episode #23
"Tour of Duty"
Written by Art Wallace
Directed by Andrew McLaglen
Guest Starring: Ricardo Montalban (John Reading), Louis Nye (Lt. Commander Green), Bobby Pickett (Alvin Hopgood), Marian Collier (Claire Marton), Kelly Thordsen (Chief Burton Reynolds), John Rodgers (Petty Officer Irving Marshall), Ted Knight (Yeoman Hollander), Carey Foster (First Girl), Chris Noel (Second Girl)

OFFICIAL SYNOPSIS: As duty officer at Shore Patrol Headquarters, Lt. Rice meets Sgt. John Reading, veteran Marine who has just returned to the U.S. only to learn his wife had been killed two days earlier in an auto accident while with another man. Later, Reading buys a gun, intending to kill the man. Meanwhile, Rice is involved in other people's problems; assisting a young officer's wife to locate her husband, a young sailor who has misplaced the hotel in which he left his new bride and disclose an officer imposter. In a mad race against time, Rice tries to find Reading in an effort to dissuade him from murder.
Note: Richard Montalban starred in Gene Roddenberry's first science fiction effort, The Secret Defense of 117. Writer Art Wallace penned the Star Trek episodes "Obsession" and "Assignment Earth," and helped to develop the original Dark Shadows as well.

Episode #24
"Operation-Actress"
Written by Robert J. Shaw
Directed by Leonard Horn
Guest Starring: Leslie Parrish (Toni Kaine), Leora Dana (Edith Kaine), Oliver McGowan (Martin Norman), Don Penny (Lt. Stan Harris), Robert Karnes (Lt. Col. A.J. Vilardi), Carmen Phillips (Lily), John Rayner (Arnold Brecher), Richard X. Slattery (Police Sergeant), Dallas Mitchell (Capt. Parker Hanes), Wayne Heffley (U.S.M.C. Director), Molly Dodd (Mrs. Vilardi), Susan Oakes (Karen), Robert Winston (Johnny), Lee Delano (Skeeter), Richard E. Butler (Lt. Wilson), Bob "Alabama" Davis (Sergeant)

OFFICIAL SYNOPSIS: Lt. Rice leaves the rugged Marine camp life for a tour of duty as a technical advisor on a Hollywood film. He's promptly smitten by the charms of Toni Kaine, the beautiful and very spoiled star of the film. When she innocently drops in on a late night party, Toni winds up in jail with her so-called friends, charged with disorderly conduct. The notoriety of the arrest causes the Marine Corps to withdraw support of the film. Toni, in a desperate effort to salvage her public image and stardom, decides to associate herself publicly with a popular cause....the U.S. Marines. She stuns everyone, especially Rice, by announcing she is accepting his proposal of marriage.

Episode #25
"Green Water, Green Flag"
Written by Sy Salkowitz
Directed by Leon Benson
Guest Starring: Richard Anderson (Lt. Col. Hiland), Jan Merlin (Lt. Joe Worth), Don Penny (Lt. Stan Harris), Nancy Rennick (Lt. Leslie Collins), John Milford (Sgt. Kagey), Lew Gallo (Major Atkins), Bill Cort (Lt. Duncan Martin)

OFFICIAL SYNOPSIS: When Capt. Rambridge falls critically ill, Lt. Rice is suddenly faced with the responsibility of commanding an entire company during helicopter maneuvers at sea. A feud erupts between Rice and his "chopper"

pilot which almost ruins the maneuvers and threatens the two officers' careers. The episode was filmed aboard the aircraft carrier U.S.S. Princeton, and features Marine pilots and personnel recently returned from duty in Southeast Asia.

Episode #26
"To Kill a Man"
Written by Gene Roddenberry
Directed by Vincent McEveety
Guest Starring: Greg Morris (Crew Chief), Richard Evans (Co-Pilot), George Shibata (Militia Major), Gus Irikonis (1st NCO), Joseph Hoover (Pilot), Lew Gallo (Lt. Col. Everett Anderson), Paul Mantee (Major Eric Dennis), Linda Ho (Tuyet Le), Frank Leo (Capt. Nicholas Hughes), Jim Henaghan (Corporal), Edwin Cook (Contractor), Barnaby Hale (Marine Captain), George Sims (2nd NCO), Jerry Fujikawa (Chinese Trader), Irene Tsu (Hoa Luu), Beulah Quo (Village Woman 1)

OFFICIAL SYNOPSIS: For the first time in his career, Lt. Rice finds himself the target of a real bullet, in a blistering adventure based on the war in Vietnam. As a courier carrying top secret papers, Rice is sent to South Vietnam where he meets his firebrand, idealistic counterpart, Capt. Myang Dee. The two form a close friendship which meets a crucial test when their helicopter is shot down in a hail of rebel bullets. A shocking, bizarre twist of fate leaves Rice staring death in the face at the end of a blazing machine gun. Filmed with the cooperation of the U.S. Marines, many scenes were actually photographed in war-torn Vietnam.

Episode #27
"The Alien"
Story by George Eckstein
Teleplay by Robert Wesley
Directed by Michael O'Herlihy
Guest Starring: Madlyn Rhue (Jackie Madian), Frank Maxwell (Sgt. Heylek), Danny Nagai (Li), Henry Beckman (Major Barker), Carmen Phillips (Lily), Rita Lynn (Social Worker), Larry Thor (Detective), John Hart (Capt. Quincy), Evelyn Scott

(Mrs. Heylek), Richard Tyler (Lt. April), Sharyn Hillyer (Reservations Clerk)

OFFICIAL SYNOPSIS: Capt. Rambridge finds himself in a sentimental situation that leads him into a romantic dilemma when a 10-year-old Korean orphan arrives as his ward. Prior to his divorce, adoption arrangement had been made that Rambridge knows he cannot fulfill unless he remarries, a step he considers more seriously as his affection for the youngster grows on his flight to America. But, the mutual attraction between Rambridge and Jackie is clouded by the circumstances of the proposal. Their quest for an answer is interrupted when Lt. Rice reports the boy missing and a frantic search is launched, leading to the Marine Base's artillery impact area.

Episode #28
"Gond the Sun"
Written by Robert Dozier
Directed by James Goldstone
Guest Starring:

John Anderson (Joe Hammond), John Beal (Ben Rice), Joan Tompkins (Elsie Hammond), Sherry Jackson (Maggie Shea), Henry Beckman (Major Al Barker), Steve Hollister (Minister), Ray Teal (Coolidge), Strother Martin (Taxi Driver), Kipp King (Ed Colmbs)

OFFICIAL SYNOPSIS: When a young marine is killed on the grenade range, through is own negligence, the task of representing the Corps to the parents falls to Lt. Rice. The assignment takes Rice to a small community near his hometown, where he meets with an unexpected hostility from his own father. More shocking is the accusation made by the victim's father, holding him personally responsible for the tragedy. Rice finds himself faced with a difficult decision — whether to preserve the man's memory of his son or disclose the truth about the accident that caused the boy's death.
Note: Director James Goldstone helmed the second Star Trek pilot, 1965's "Where No Man Has Gone Before."

Episode #29
"A Troubled Image"
Written by Herman Groves
Directed by Don Medford
Guest Starring: Pilar Seurat (Manisahn Jorada), Richard Anderson (Lt. Col. Hiland), Ed Asner (Walter Perry), John Milford (Sgt. Kagey), Chuck Haren (Cpol. Sandow), Jerry Hausner (Murtchison), Steven Bell (Lt. April), Jo Helton (Sister Lucita), Carmen Phillips (Lily)

OFFICIAL SYNOPSIS: Manisahn, dazzling beautiful Vietnamese Army officer, invades Lt. Rice's life when she becomes one of a group of foreign women officers assigned to his class in combat tactics. Believing his tactics are more romantic in nature than military, she gives the startled Rice an icy brush-off and drives herself to the physical breaking point in order to prove herself a good "soldier". When Manisahn learns that she may not pass the rugged field maneuvers due to a mysterious fear, she desperately decides to rely on her womanly wiles.

GENESIS II
EPISODE GUIDE

Episode 1
"Genesis II" (Pilot)
Written by Gene Roddenberry
Directed by John Llewellyn Moxey
Starring: Alex Cord (Dylan Hunt), Percy Rodreiguez (Primus Isaac Kimbridge), Ted Cassidy (Isiah), Lynne Marta (Harper-Smythe), Tito Vandis (Yuloff)

SYNOPSIS: When Dylan Hunt comes out of suspended animation, he is stunned to learn that he has been "asleep" for over a century and that during that time period the world has fallen into ruins due to a nuclear war. As the plot unfolds, Hunt finds himself torn between the scientists making up PAX — whose mission it is to help rebuild the Earth — and the somewhat more barbaric mutants known as the Tyranians.

Episode #2
"Planet Earth" (Pilot)
Written by
Gene Roddenberry and Juanita Bartlett
Directed by Marc Daniels
Starring: John Saxon (Dylan Hunt), Janet Margolin (Harper-Smythe), Rai Tasco (R. Kimbridge), Ted Cassidy (Isiah), Christopher Cary (Baylock)

SYNOPSIS: In this remake of "Genesis II", Dylan Hunt reawakens in the year 2133 and immediately joins up with PAX. In a double-tiered storyline, Hunt goes up against the Kreeg, mutants interested only in weapons and warfare, and a community where females reign supreme and males are little more than slaves.

Episode #3
"Strange New World" (Pilot)
Written by Ronald F. Graham
Directed by Robert Butler
Starring: John Saxon (Captain Anthony Vico), Kathleen Miller (Dr. Allison Crowley), Kenne Curtis (Dr. William Scott)

SYNOPSIS: This time out, PAX is located on an orbiting space station, the crew of which is placed is suspended animation for 180 years when the Earth is devastated by a series of meteors. When they revive, they head back to the planet's surface to see what has survived and to find a place where mankind can reclaim the world. In the midst of this, they come up against a society of clones who want to use their bodies to keep their community going.
Note: "Strange New World" is vastly different from "Genesis II," and didn't involve Roddenberry at all. The following "episodes" are based on Roddenberry's original premise, not this rewritten version.

Episode #4 (Unfilmed)
"Company 'B'"
Written by Gene Roddenberry
SYNOPSIS: Members of PAX accidentally free a trio of super soldiers, who were genetically trained to win any conflict they are involved in. At the moment, the world of the future is their target.

Episode #5 (Unfilmed)
"The Electric Company"
Written by John Tomerlin

SYNOPSIS: A city known as Pharos — which still has the capability of electricity — becomes the battleground as PAX inadvertently becomes involved in a conflict between the Ataluk, a primitive tribe located at the sub-polar regions of North America, and the technology and war-loving Tyranians.

Episode #6 (Unfilmed)
"The Secret Weapon"
Written by Gene Roddenberry

SYNOPSIS: A totalitarian community must be stopped when their leader comes into the possession of a series of nuclear weapons that survived "The Great Conflict."

Episode #7 (Unfilmed)
"London Express"
Written by Gene Roddenberry

SYNOPSIS: When the PAX team surfaces in the remains of what used to be London, they find themselves the pursued in a vicious fox hunt initiated by the ruling class. Their only chance is to get to the sub-shuttle and head back home — if they can.

Episode #8 (Unfilmed)
"Messiah?"
Written by Gene Roddenberry

SYNOPSIS: When they are temporarily trapped in a desert community while enroute to North Africa, Hunt and the rest of his team are stunned to witness what appears to be a retelling of the Christ legend as a man named Carst comes out of the desert and appears to be a messiah.

Episode #9 (Unfilmed)
"Geronimo IV!"
Written by Gene Roddenberry

SYNOPSIS: An idyllic farming community seems to be ripped apart when a man named Geronimo, claiming to be the descendent of the original, takes over and rules with an iron fist. PAX decides that he must be stopped but upon recognizing that the people in that community are spineless and without the desire to develop further, they wonder whether stopping Geronimo is the right thing to do after all.

Episode #10 (Unfilmed)
"The Radiant One"
Written by Gene Roddenberry

SYNOPSIS: A community consisting of radioactive descendents of people who survived the Great Conflict live in a virtual Garden of Eden. When they are discovered, however, it becomes apparent that the isotopes which have become part of their genetic make-up are deadly to outsiders.

Episode #11 (Unfilmed)
"Robot's Return"
Written by Gene Roddenberry

SYNOPSIS: A team of astronauts arrive on Earth from a Jupiter mission which was reported missing some 200 years earlier. It turns out, however, that these astronauts are really intelligent robots which have come to Earth seeking those who sent the original team out all those years ago. However, seeing the shape the planet is in and recognizing the fact that these "barbarians" may one day reach for the stars again, the consider the possibility of destroying all life on Earth.
Note: This storyline ultimately served as the basis of Star Trek: The Motion Picture.

THE QUESTOR TAPES
E P I S O D E   G U I D E

Episode #1
"The Questor Tapes" (Pilot)
Written by
Gene Roddenberry and Gene L. Coon
Directed by Richard A. Colla
Starring: Robert Foxworth (Questor), Mike Farrell (Jerry Robinson), Dana Wynter (Lady Helena Trimble), Lew Ayres (Dr. Vaslovik), John Vernon (Jeffrey B. Darrow), Majel Barrett (Dr. Bradley)

SYNOPSIS: Dr. Vaslovik's android creation, Questor, is brought to life but some of his memory tapes are damaged in the process. As a result, Questor is determined to find his creator, who is missing, and to discover the purpose of his existence. To help him accomplish these goals is Jerry Robinson, Vaslovik's assistant and the head of Project: Questor.

Episode #2 (Unfilmed)
"Think Love"
Written by Larry Alexander

SYNOPSIS: Questor and Jerry Robinson must use their resources to help a man named Crighton, who it has been determined will play an integral role in the development of the human species, resulting in the natural development of extrasensory perception in individuals. Complicating the situation is a teacher named Shelley, who Jerry falls in love with. The results nearly cost he and Questor their lives, while almost denying Crighton to humanity.

Episode #3 (Unfilmed)
"The Surgeon Without a Heart"
Story by Gene Roddenberry
Teleplay by Juanita Bartlett

SYNOPSIS: The subject: Harvard Educator Michael Hughes, who has come up with an innovative way to teach culturally deprived children. The problem is that Hughes, whose teaching will impact on humanity, has suffered a heart attack and the only person who can save him, Dr. Parker, is going through a variety of emotional problems which will undoubtedly result in Hughes' death. Questor has to take Parker's place in the operating room, but a malfunction causes the android to start to believe that he actually is Parker.

Episode #4 (Unfilmed)
"Rosemary"
Written by Irving Elman

SYNOPSIS: Jerry Robinson and Questor must rescue kidnap victim Garth Arliss, who is in the midst of developing a revolutionary means of disposing of radioactive material. This process, which would be worth millions, is something he wants to bestow upon the world for free. His kidnapers, however, have other plans.

The late Gene L. Coon takes a break from writing to pose for the camera (photo courtesy Jackie Coon-Fernandez).

GENE L. COON
"The Forgotten Gene"

Novelist. Marine. Screenwriter. Producer. Humanitarian. Scrabble player.

These were a few of the dichotomies of Gene L. Coon, and the legacy he left all that *Star Trek*'s become has never been fully explored before.

While *Star Trek* has suffered its share of fatalities beyond Gene Roddenberry in 1991, including the passing of Jeffrey Hunter and John Hoyt (respectively Captain Christopher Pike and Dr. Boyce of the original pilot, "The Cage"), art designer Michael Minor and Merritt Buttrick (David Marcus in *The Wrath of Khan* and *The Search for Spock*), the passing of Gene Coon went largely unheralded. In fact, it is this forgotten Gene who may very well have defined *Star Trek* for future generations.

Indeed, Coon's contributions to the series were important enough for William Shatner to mention him at the commemoration of the Gene Roddenberry Building on the Paramount lot several months before Roddenberry's passing. Shatner continues to herald Coon's contributions to the series as its producer for much of the first and second season. Coon's uncredited rewrites and frequent use of a psuedonym (Lee Cronin) gave him an anoymity that few people who have worked on *Star Trek* ever had.

"In my opinion," offers Shatner, "Gene Coon had more to do with the infusion of life into *Star Trek* than any other single person. Gene Roddenberry's instincts for creating the original package is unparalleled. You can't even discuss it. He put it together, hired the people and the concept was his and set in motion by him. But after 13 shows, other people took over. Gene Coon spent a year and set the tenor of the show. Gene [Roddenberry] was more in the background as other people actively took over."

For producer Harve Bennett, who steered the *Star Trek* feature film series for nearly 10 years, Coon was an inspiration. "Gene Roddenberry was the Douglas McArthur of this particular campaign, the George Patton," says Bennett. "And guys like Gene Coon were the Omar Bradleys."

Coon, a chain smoker who died after a swift bout with lung cancer in 1972, joined the original *Star Trek* during the first season and remained with the show until midway through its second. His illness happened so suddenly, many of his closest friends didn't realize he had died until days after the funeral. His contributions to his profession in general and *Star Trek* specifically, are monumental. In terms of the latter, it was Coon who created the Klingons in "Errand of Mercy" and devised the Organian Peace Treaty; the "Prime Directive" was a result

of his pen as were the dynamics of the Spock/McCoy relationship and the frequent humorous interludes that punctuated the series in its first two seasons.

Jimmy Doohan, who plays Scotty, credits Roddenberry with having given Coon the opportunity on *Star Trek*.

"The gorgeous thing about Gene Roddenberry is that he recognized Gene Coon," says Doohan. "I've worked with Jackie Gleason before he became famous and what's amazing to me is how he recognized the genius in Art Carney. If Jackie hadn't liked Art, he wouldn't have been there. But Jackie did like him and he knows real talent when he sees it because he's a real talent himself. That's also Gene's talent in picking people like that."

Veteran writer/producer Glen A. Larson, whose years of experience in the industry include producing such respected television fare as *Quincy*, *Knightrider* and *Battlestar Galactica*, had worked with Coon while the two of them were on the staff of *It Takes a Thief*. During their tenure together, Larson came to look upon Coon as a mentor.

"I used to listen to him talk about the business a great deal," reflects Larson. "That was really my whole introduction to television, through Gene. I think Gene Coon was the spirit and soul of [*Star Trek*]. I don't think the show would have gone in the direction that it did nor had its enormous credibility if not for Coon. From what I could tell, Gene *was Star Trek*. When he was no longer there, I think the show quickly denegrated to monster of the week, which was always the danger of science fiction in television, because you generally don't have the people around with the intellectual capacity to really explore important themes without making them so obscure that there's no hope of holding an audience. Gene had a good sense of drama in addition to strong concepts."

Jackie Fernandez, Coon's second wife, points out that "Science-fiction per se was not a particular choice for him. It was a genre he did, but he didn't

think of himself as a science fiction writer at all. If you hadn't had that name on it, it was just another drama which Gene was interested in. Another thought, another quest, another way to look at a situation from a different angle. It just happened to fall into a category that was too much; it was overwhelming."

Coon's arrival in the middle of *Star Trek*'s first season was, according to associate producer Robert Justman, just enough to "save" Roddenberry's life.

"Gene was fatigued and so was I," says Justman. "We both nearly didn't make it through the first season because of overwork. We were at our wit's end. I was so tired that first season that I came unglued one night at home. My wife called Gene and said, 'That's it, I'm taking him away.' You try working for about six months, seven days a week and averaging three or four hours of sleep a night with enormous pressure. Eventually something's got to give. It happened to be me that night and Gene was next. We were both basket cases. As a result of that, I think that's how Gene Coon came to be on the show. Gene Roddenberry just couldn't do it by himself. He was excellent, Gene Roddenberry wrote wonderful scenes, but it took its toll."

When Gene L. Coon joined the *Star Trek* staff as line producer, Roddenberry became executive producer.

"I had no choice," said Roddenberry. "The only way I could get people like Gene Coon to come in and produce — and I needed a producer, more helping hands — was to become executive producer, actually a supervising producer. Today, it would be different. No one would object to a very complex show having two, three or even four line producers with a supervising producer over them. In those days, it was unheard of, but I just had to get some extra people in any way I could. I had found myself working 12 or 14 hours a day and I could no longer do it. Everyone on our staff was in the hospital at least once during those three years just from total exhaustion. We were doing a

The pen of Gene L. Coon transformed McHale's Navy *from a one-hour dramatic series to a half hour sitcom (photo copyright ©1962 CBS).*

half a science-fiction movie every week. Imagine what a burden that is. Science-fiction movies usually take 20 weeks to do. We were doing one every week!"

"Honestly speaking," says Robert Justman, "Gene Roddenberry would have died if he didn't have Gene Coon or someone to do this. Gene Coon was a brilliant find; you couldn't find anyone better. The problem is that we wore him out, which is why he ultimately left in the middle of the second season."

Gene Coon was born in Beatrice, Nebraska and educated within the public school system in both Nebraska and California. Following high school, he attended Glendale College.

In 1942, he enlisted in the United States Marine Corp, where he spent four years. During that time, he was stationed in the Pacific and the Far East. Taking part in the initial occupation of Japan, he was ultimately sent to China, ostensibly to help repatriate the Japanese, but he ended up editing and publishing a small newspaper. For eight months he remained in Northern China, and then went stateside where he

became a radio newsman, member of the National Association of Radio News Directors, and a freelance writer. He started writing for the television series *Medic*, and this led him on his path to full-time teleplay writing. Over the next few years, he turned out numerous scripts for such series as *Wagon Train, Bonanza, Have Gun Will Travel, Rawhide, Alcoa Premier, The Eleventh Hour, Hotel de Paris, McHale's Navy, Riverboat, Suspense, General Electric Theatre, Mr. Lucky, Peter Gunn, Ichabod and Me, The Virginian, Destry, Kraft Summer Theatre, Dan Raven, Project 120, The Restless Gun, Rescue 8, The Eve Arden Show, Follow the Sun, The Islanders, Adventures in Paradise, Dragnet, The Rebel* and *Maverick.*

In the early '60s, Coon went to work at Universal Pictures. At the time he was being represented by Lester Colodny, who solicited business at the studio and met up with company vice president Jennings Lang.

"They had a series on the board called *McHale's Navy*," Colodny, who also represented the likes of Neil Simon,

Woody Allen and Mel Brooks, explains, "and Jennings Lang loved the idea, but the script didn't work. The original version was a one hour drama and it was terrible. Jennings said, 'How do we make this work?' I said, 'I represent a writer by the name of Gene Coon. He has great credits, he's very talented.' I brought him in and made a deal for him to write two pilots. Gene took a dramatic series and made it into a half-hour comedy, and they started making the pilot."

McHale's Navy, of course, went on to become a hit series and inspired a couple of theatrical spinoffs. Meanwhile, Colodny had a falling out with his agency and was hired by Lang to serve as an executive in charge of new programming development, and Coon was made head writer.

One of their first projects came together when Lang went to Colodny and said, "Lester, we own all these Frankenstein movies. How do we make a series out of this?"

"Gene and I started watching the Frankenstein movies, and the more we watched them, the more we were falling on the floor screaming," smiles Colodny. "We were laughing and I turned to him and I said, 'Wouldn't this make the funniest series in the whole world?' We put our heads together, and between the two of us we came up with the concept of *The Munsters*. We took the idea back to Jennings Lang and he said, 'You're out of your mind.'"

However, the head of MCA and one of the most powerful men in Hollywood, met with rapid success in placing the proposed comedy. "[Later], Lew Wasserman, the head of the studio, told us, 'We sold your crazy, god-damned series. We don't understand it, but we sold it.' Then they gave it to other people and they made it into a kid's show. Our version was very funny and very hip. We were doing a satire of *The Donna Reed Show* with monsters, because we wanted to do something very adult. The first two scripts were a very sly, tongue-in-cheek and arch take-

As originally conceived by Gene L. Coon and Lester Colodny, The Munsters (right) was intended to be a hip take-off of The Donna Reed Show (left).

off on *The Donna Reed Show*, but *The Munsters* never became that.

"During this time," he adds, "they would get Gene to fix everything. Whenever there was something going wrong, they would call Gene Coon. He would fix scripts, he would fix pilots. He was a jack of all trades."

Also working in the New Projects department was Mort Zarkoff, a writer who ultimately became great friends with Coon.

"The charge we had," says Zarkoff, "was to come up with new projects. We would develop new concepts, new ideas, bring them on to script form and hopefully we would create little units that would then produce the shows. Some of us would work in little teams, sort of pair off, then we would all come together and pair off in different ways. It was highly productive and highly energetic. The spark to it all in terms of sheer energy and ability to turn out work was Gene. He was an incredible source of creative energy. We would all work and write scripts, but it was a question of degree. Most of us could turn out so many pages a day, and Gene would lock himself in the office and the pages would just pour out. And the material was good. We reworked a little bit of it, but he would get into that 14-cylinder

typewriter of his and zip the pages off. They were, without a doubt, some of the cleverest, craftsman-like work that I'd seen in a long time."

Jackie Fernandez warmly reflects on her late husband's method of writing. "He really thoroughly enjoyed writing," she says. "I've heard so many writers complain about how agonizing it is for them. He wasn't one of those people. He *loved* to write. He bounced out of bed in the morning at 5 or 6 o'clock, went straight to the writing room with his old beat up typewriter, and the cigarettes and pipes, and he just wrote his brains out until about 1:00, when he stopped and then our life took off. We just had fun for the rest of the day. I never once heard him complain about writing. It would have been unthinkable for him to be anything else but a writer.

"He loved the excitement and the thrill," she elaborates. "His way of writing was going to bed with the thought in his head of what he had to come up with, and then it was there when he got up. It was just there. He went from sleeping soundly to getting up feeling fresh, and it just came out of his fingers onto the typewriter and he just never had to think about it."

One of the things that impressed Lester Colodny most about Coon, was the man's ability to effortlessly segue from one genre to the other—often at the same time.

"Gene could work on so many projects at the same time because he taught himself something called automatic writing," Colodny details. "He had this crazy concept in which he hypnotized himself, and he was convinced that he could put himself in a state of almost disembodiment In which once he was ready to write, after having thought out the story and worked out what he was about to write, he would go into a room, put on some Jazz music and sit down at his typewriter. His fingers flew like you never saw in your life. He would be in a state of self-hypnosis, which he called automatic writing. His mind was only focused on one single thing: that script. The most astonishing thing you've ever seen in your life."

Writer/producer John Furia, Jr., former President of the Writer's Guild and friend of Coon who worked with him on *Kung Fu*, notes, "Gene was an extremely prolific writer. He wrote novels and lots of television in lots of genres. A lot of prolific writers tend to be sloppy, facile and not very good. Gene was not that. He just happened to be a writer who wrote fast. He cared a great deal about writing. I think there were a lot of things he cared about. He loved to talk, he loved writing. A lot of writers kind of write defensively and hate the process. I sometimes say I have a love/hate relationship with writing. I hate to be doing it, but I love it when I'm finished. But Gene really relished the process of writing itself.

"He lived well," Furia continues. "He liked good food and good wine. Unfortunately he loved to smoke, a pipe and cigarettes. He was a man of some contrasts. He talked tough — he was not a sentimental man—but he was a very tender and caring man. I don't mean he had a foul mouth, but he was a Marine and I guess once a Marine, always a Marine. And he was tough-minded. He had strong ideas, strong convictions and held to them tenaciously. He was great company. Writers like to get together and talk with other writers because they're sometimes interesting conversationalists. Gene was certainly one of those. He loved to talk. He came out of that era of writers like Hemingway, Chandler, etc., who wrote some pretty strong, tough stuff, but he was just the opposite. He was not self-promoting, a very shy man. He was a terrific writer."

David Gerrold, who was given his first opportunity to write for television when Coon purchased his "Trouble With Tribbles" script for *Star Trek*, recalls, "He was a remarkably straight-forward human being. There was no performance about him. I have to contrast him with Gene Roddenberry on this. Gene Roddenberry was always doing the performance of a great man, and people were awed because they would go into his office wanting to see the great man, and of course he would do the performance. Gene L. Coon didn't do the performance, he just did Gene L. Coon. He was very accessible, very straight-forward and very un-pretentious. He was *real* candid. If there was a subject that he

for one reason or another didn't want to discuss, he wouldn't lie or anything, he would say, 'Well, that's not really to be discussed.' You understood at all times exactly what you were dealing with. There were no code phrases.

"A lot of what happens in television today," he adds, "is that people speak in codes, and you have to try and decipher what they really want, what they really mean, what's really going on. With Gene L. Coon, everything was 'no bullshit.' So it was real refreshing to work with him, because he'd say, 'We can't do this because of that'....or he would say, 'We don't have pockets on the uniforms.' There was no philosophical discussion of why we don't have pockets in the 23rd century. It was just, 'The uniforms were designed without pockets.' I suggested a couple of things one time where I said, 'We could do this down on the planet as a redress of the transporter room.' And he said, 'I'll tell you why we won't do that. We want to keep the look of the Enterprise unique.' There was no, 'We wouldn't have this kind of thing down on the planet because....' It was always, in nuts and bolts, we're making a television show here. That was very refreshing, because what we've got now is that *Star Trek* has become this whole religion, people argue about this, that and the other thing; there's a significance about it. With Gene Coon, there was an understanding first, that what we're doing is television, good television. We're not on a mission from God. We're here to entertain the audience. I think he had the clearest sense of the show, of what it really was, and approached it with the nuts and bolts attitude that, 'Yes, we know we're doing noble humanity out there, but we've got to tell a story, pull a rating and please the network."

Jackie Fernandez concurs with Gerrold's assessment, adding, "David's right on the mark professionally and in his personal life as well. He was exactly the same at all times, so you never wondered what he was going to be like today, or in this situation or that situation. He was

kind of like a grown up Huckleberry Finn. It was a great quality, because everybody knew where they stood and didn't have to do any tap-dancing.

"Gene Roddenberry's personality," continues Fernandez, "even though he was a very soft-spoken man, was a very expansive, huge personality, bigger than life, so to speak. That ran true to form when it came to the show. Gene Coon's personality was quite the opposite. He was introspective, he was quiet, content to let others shine— Roddenberry, me or anyone else who wanted to shine. He would let them and just be there. His enjoyment was participating when it came to conversations, and we had a house filled with things to do such as chess, pool, scrabble, swimming or whatever. People were over all the time and Gene Coon loved participating, but he didn't need to be the star. Never needed to be the star."

Dorothy Fontana, who had once upon a time worked as Gene Roddenberry's secretary and eventually became a writer, story-editing *Star Trek* (among numerous other shows), has her own fond memories of Coon.

"Gene Coon as a person was a very interesting man," she warmly recalls. "He had been a combat Marine in World War II. He had his share of narrow scrapes. Even though he looked like a heavyset, jolly man, I'm sure he had his harrowing times when he was in combat. He had a delicacy of writing that was really remarkable. A subtlety of relationships that shows in the writing. He had a great sense of humor. He was never one of those people who would say, 'I absolutely don't agree with you. This is my opinion and I'm not going to change it.' He would listen to what someone else had to say, their opinion, mull it over, give it some thought, he'd go and find out more about it before he ever came back and said, 'No, I'm sorry, I don't agree with you.' Or, 'Yeah, you're right, I'll look into this more.' His secretary was a young black woman who had very much gotten into Malcolm X's philosophy and she was telling Gene about it. Gene said, 'Well, I don't know. Is he going to be speaking? I'll go down and listen to him talk.' And they had these discussions on the black movement and all that involves, the philosophy of life that involves, the determination of the black people to be more equal. Gene was always an open-minded and fair man. I always liked that about him, because I think it showed up in his writing and I think it made him a good writer."

"He was a liberal man," notes Mort Zarkoff, "to the extent—I don't know if you want to get into politics—he had a love for man and a love for the fairness and unfairness, as it were, to different groups of people in the world. I think that was reflected in his work as well. He seemed to build into characters the dynamics of the human condition and the unfairness that exists in the world. Therein lies a great deal of the edge of his dramas."

Says Lester Colodny, "Gene was always a commentator in everything he wrote. Everything had a message. He was very tuned in to things. You know how many years ago you're talking about? Gene was so aware of the ozone layer, of forests being decimated. If you go over the episodes he did, so many of them have an underlying message that they were very apropos to our culture. Whatever he wrote—he could write the funniest comedy—there was always a sociological point of view that had to do with the betterment of mankind. He was very dedicated in that way. Of all the people that I've met in my life, I would say he was one of the most guileless people I've known. There were no hidden agendas. No bullshit."

David Gerrold agrees with this. "I think he was extraordinarily compassionate in the way he dealt with people. I mean compassionate in the sense that he was considerate of other people's feelings. I never saw him hurt anyone. He was always watching out for the very best. If you had a suggestion, he would listen

and actually consider whatever you suggested. There were suggestions I made where he said, 'Well, yeah, but here's why we can't do that.' And there was one time I made a suggestion where he said, 'Yeah, I like that. We'll do it.' So you knew that he was listening. This made him a good producer. He didn't have to be the guy who did it all, who knew it all. He didn't have to micro-manage. He didn't care where the good ideas or the good stories came from. All he had to do was make sure that the good stories got made and the bad ones didn't. A very down to earth attitude. Gene L. Coon was the guy who had a good sense of recognizing what was a doable story. He could recognize a doable story and had a good sense of how to translate it to television. "He asked me to do a rewrite of 'I, Mudd.' He said, 'We want to get to the planet faster at the end of act one, and [Steve] Kandel gets us there at the end of act two.' I read the first draft Stephen Kandel script, and it was good. I thought it was shootable. But I understood it when Gene Coon said, 'Structurally, we want to do this instead.' I understood exactly what he wanted. First of all, he was testing me to see if I could rewrite, I'm sure of that, but secondly, more important, he was teaching me something about story structure. When you're going to a planet with an interesting problem, you want to get there quickly. He said, 'How can you cut two acts down to one, and how can you fill the extra act?' He gave me some suggestions and instructions and let me go home. I brought it back over the weekend and he said, 'That's it, you've got it.' My feeling is that Coon's strength was that he was receptive, he listened, he understood what would make a good television story, he had a great sense of structure and great sense of dialogue. I think he was just an all around good producer."

From 1964 until 1967, Coon wrote the screenplays for a variety of films (*The Killers, The Raiders, Man in the Shadow, No Name on the Bullet, First to Fight, Journey to Shiloh*), and penned the novels *Meanwhile, Back at the Front*

and *The Short End of the Stick*, but he seemed to find his true niche in *Star Trek*.

Examining the chronology of *Star Trek*, it becomes obvious that many of the show's more memorable aspects went into effect during Coon's reign.

"If you look at the episodes that Roddenberry was responsible for in the beginning," notes Gerrold, "which was pretty much like the first 10 episodes, there's not a lot of that noble purpose there. There's a bumbling around trying to find out what the show is about, yet at the same time they did some great episodes. Because no one knew what *Star Trek* was, they were continually inventing it. You see stuff like 'Charlie X,' 'The Enemy Within,' and they also did a lot of rip-offs — 'The Galileo Seven' was *Flight of the Phoenix*, 'Balance of Terror' is *The Enemy Below* — and so they didn't really know what they could do with the show yet. When Gene L. Coon first came on board in the second half of the first season, you start getting things like the Prime Directive and a lot of the stuff that was later identified as the noble parts of *Star Trek*. Gene L. Coon created that noble image that everyone gives Roddenberry the most credit for.

"When Gene L. Coon came in," Gerrold elaborates, "one of the things that happened is that by then they knew what they could do, and he would concentrate on those areas. The episodes he did were more sure of themselves, but they weren't as adventurous in the same way. The characters by then were more established, so Coon let the characters have the relationships with each other. The advantages were that when Gene L. Coon took over, the characters locked into place very tightly and crisply. And it became Kirk, Spock and McCoy. Before that time, there was a vagueness because Roddenberry didn't know who or what the show was about. After Gene Coon took over, he decided it was about Kirk, Spock and McCoy, and the other characters were ancillary. That became kind of the formula, which was successful."

As noted earlier, the majority of

Gene Coon is generally given credit for locking down on the idea that Star Trek *was really about Kirk, Bones and Spock (photo copyright ©1966 NBC).*

Coon's scripts contained thinly-veiled social commentary, which became a staple of the series and something that is generally credited to Roddenberry.

"We never sat around talking about that kind of thing," says Dorothy Fontana. "I think that's just the kind of writing that Gene Coon did. It influenced the writers who came in, who were structuring their story. You could see this kind of flow happening. Another thing that happened is that the humor between the characters began to become more and more developed, particularly the Spock and McCoy relationship became a lot more fun. It evolved into what it ultimately became, which was a basic friendship. It was a friendship conducted with little insults and jabs, but it was always fun. The verbal fencing matches. It was fun to create those conversations once we started getting into them. I think Gene Coon led the way on that."

Says David Gerrold, "Roddenberry always took the show too seriously and everybody preached. I think Roddenberry wanted to be a preacher and couldn't make it or something. Everybody preached and Gene said,

'No, in the future our people work together,' but what he would write would be sermons. In Gene L. Coon's scripts, people interacted with each other in a whole different way and didn't preach, although it was mandatory to do a little preaching at the end of the script where the captain explains—the captain being the father figure. Gene L. Coon's characters joked with each other. At the end of 'The Apple,' they're on the ship and McCoy is musing over the influence they may have had over these people, the introduction of concepts like heaven and hell, and Spock makes this remark about who the Devil would be. Kirk and McCoy say, 'Who would have pointed ears and arched eyebrows?' and they're both walking around him. That's definitely a Gene L. Coon thing, the characters playing with each other. I think that's why the fans loved the show so much. While our people were having an adventure, they were never too busy to snipe at each other, which was the way they showed their affection. I think there was never a question of how much Spock and McCoy loved each other, and that was shown by how vicious they would get when they would start sniping at each other. I think a lot of that was Gene L. Coon."

In order to fully realize Gene Coon's profound contribution to the *Star Trek* mythos, one must have a thorough understanding of the episodes he was involved in and the ideals they represent.

In "Arena," when a Federation starbase is destroyed, the Enterprise sets off in pursuit of the attackers. Enroute they enter an uncharted sector of space where Kirk and the commander of the other vessel, the lizard-like Gorn, are transported to a planet's surface. There they are forced to carry out their barbarism against each other in a battle to the death, with the loser's ship and all those aboard being destroyed. What follows is a savage struggle, with Kirk's ultimate humanity sparing both he and the Enterprise.

According to the on-air credits,

the script for "Arena" was based on the Fredric Brown short story of the same name. "What happened," says Dorothy Fontana, "is that Gene wrote the script as an original. When it was read by research, they said, 'Oh, this is very much like the Fredric Brown story.' Gene said, 'Yes, you're right. I must have read it and just didn't realize it.' So he instantly gave story credit to Fredric Brown and Mr. Brown was properly paid. The way the development came about, the relationship between the antagonists—Kirk and the Gorn—had a lot of nice stuff to it. It could have been just a brute contest, but it wasn't. It turned out not to be that way."

At the outset of "A Taste of Armageddon," Ambassador Robert Fox is on board the Enterprise to negotiate a peace treaty with the planet Eminiar VII, despite that world's obvious lack of interest in such a treaty. Kirk himself points out, "It *is* their planet, Mr. Ambassador," but Fox arrogantly forces the starship forward. It is a short matter of time before they find themselves immersed in an interplanetary war between Eminiar and Vendikar, which is being fought by computers. Said computers pinpoint the location of theoretical bombings, and people living in those areas voluntarily march into disintegration chambers so that their respective societies will live on. Naturally Kirk takes it upon himself to destroy the computers and force these planets to realize the true impact of war. "Death, destruction, disease, horror," says Kirk. "That's what war is all about. That's what makes it a thing to be avoided."

"A Taste of Armageddon" is generally considered to be one of the most powerful allegories ever presented on the Vietnam war.

"The original story and script was by Robert Hamner," recalls Dorothy Fontana. "Gene did a rewrite on that. I think some of the things he added really had a lot to do with the character of Kirk. To the best of my recollection, it was Gene Coon who wrote the speech at the end that man has a reputation as a killer, but you get up every morning and say, 'I'm not going to kill today.' It seems to me that Gene Coon added that speech in particular. It was one of those things that began to identify Kirk far more solidly than we had before."

Adds director Joseph Pevney, "The final speech from Bill, the demand for peace and not giving up human lives to a computer, was rewritten several times until we got it the way we wanted. Gene Coon rewrote the script and it was quite powerful."

"Space Seed" became an important moment in *Star Trek* history in that it paved the way for the motion picture *Star Trek II: The Wrath of Khan*. In that episode, Enterprise comes across a derelict "sleeper ship" named the Botany Bay, which contains a crew of approximately 70 men and women in suspended animation. Led by Khan Noonian Singh, these people turn out to be the result of genetic experimentation on Earth in the 1990's. Basically a race of supermen, with strength and intelligence nearly 10 times that of an average person, they had attempted to take over the Earth and triggered World War III, the Eugenics War. They managed to flee in the Botany Bay, and are now revived in the 23rd century.

"Space Seed" gave us a little bit of Earth history and a taste of what the world would go through before reaching *Star Trek's* era.

Surprisingly, Khan Noonian Singh may never have come into existence at all if it hadn't been for Captain Video. "Hell," laughs writer Carey Wilbur, who wrote the first draft, "the plot for 'Space Seed' comes from an old *Captain Video* I did some 30-odd years ago. It was a crazy story where we did the legend of men being turned into beasts, and our villainess had been transported from the days of Greek mythology to the future. So in doing 'Space Seed,' we took away the mythological powers and replaced them with a genetically altered human being."

As a writer for hire, Wilbur

submitted the script which was rewritten by Gene Coon. "I had no qualms about Gene rewriting me," he points out. "He was an excellent writer and certainly knew the show better than just about anyone."

Next up for Coon was one of *Star Trek's* most popular episodes, "The Devil in the Dark." When miners are being murdered by a creature that can move through solid rock, chief engineer Vanderberg contacts the Enterprise and asks for assistance in hunting it down and putting an end to the threat. The starship arrives with Kirk and Spock leading a landing party to investigate the situation. What they discover is that this so-called creature is actually an intelligent being known as the Horta, and that it has only killed to protect its young, which are encased in silicone shells that the miners mistook for worthless rocks.

David Gerrold opines, "I would have to point to 'Devil in the Dark' as being the best episode Gene L. Coon wrote, because it really gets to the heart of what *Star Trek* is. Here you had this menace, but once you understand what the creature is and why it's doing what it's doing, it's not really a menace at all. We end up learning more about appropriate behavior for ourselves out of learning to be compassionate, tolerant, understanding. To me, in many ways Gene L. Coon was the heart and soul of *Star Trek*. He was the guy who had to roll up his sleeves and make it work. He was the guy who would do a rewrite if a script needed a rewrite and try to stay true to the original concept. He actually, of all the people who worked there at the time, had the clearest story sense, both in terms of story structure and dialogue. I think that shows in the scripts that he did. 'Devil in the Dark' he wrote over a weekend."

Laughs Lester Colodny, "Not only did he write it in a weekend, but he probably read two books, made dinner for 14, redid the entire front lawn, helped me with 30 pages of my book, rewrote four other pieces for the studio,

went to visit two friends....he was incredible."

In terms of the development of the script idea, Dorothy Fontana recalls, "The costume guy, who did a lot of the creatures for us, came to the studio and said, 'I have to show you this new creature,' and it was this kind of lumpy thing that was orange and misshapen and it was real low to the ground. He put a rubber chicken out in front of the thing. He climbed inside this suit and on his hands and knees he brought this creature over the chicken and the chicken disappeared. After he passed over it, some bones appeared out the back. Gene said, 'I've got to find a way to use that,' and he came up with the Horta. Of course it's a wonderful story, because it's really all about mother love. It was a great story."

"Errand of Mercy" dealt with increased tensions between the Federation and one of their enemies, the Klingon Empire. Kirk is told to secure an alliance with the people of the strategically located Organia. No sooner have Kirk and Spock beamed down than the Klingons arrive, with their military commander, Kor, claiming the world as the latest possession of the Empire. Kirk is frustrated by the absolute complacency of the Organians, and his frustration turns to anger when he learns that things have grown worse between the Federation and the Klingons. It appears that an intergalactic war is about to begin, when the Organians reveal themselves to be something far removed from human, with the power to stop both sides from warring....permanently. There is an amazing scene where Kirk protests the interference of the Organians. "You have no right to interfere," snaps Kirk. "We have the right—" "To wage war, Captain?" asks an Organian. As David Gerrold notes in his book *The World of Star Trek*, "And then [Kirk] realizes that the whole purpose of his mission was to *prevent* a war."

"Gene came up with the Klingons, though we never liked the name," explains Dorothy Fontana. "We said, 'Gene, can't you come up with a different name than Klingon? We hate it.' But we never could come up with anything better, so we left it. Then the Klingons kind of became a stock villain, because they were easier to do in make-up than the Romulans. We wound up doing the Klingons quite a bit and they became a very good adversary, because once you established them, you had to find out ways to explore them."

"The City on the Edge of Forever," generally considered the best episode of *Star Trek* ever produced, opens with the Enterprise in the midst of studying time disturbances in the area of a particular world, when McCoy accidentally injects himself with an overdose of cordrazine. As a result, he becomes a paranoid madman and beams down to the planet's surface to avoid everyone's attempts to sedate him. Kirk and Spock lead a landing party in pursuit, and there they find an ancient stone structure which identifies itself as the Guardian of Forever, a time portal. When the moment presents itself, McCoy leaps through its center and does something in the past that causes history to be changed: the Enterprise is no longer in orbit. To try and counter this, Kirk and Spock pursue him to Earth in the year 1930 in an attempt to remedy the timeline.

Longtime fans of the series know that this episode has been the source of much controversy between author Harlan Ellison and Gene Roddenberry, with the former believing that his original teleplay had been butchered in the rewriting. At the same time, Roddenberry went on to take considerable credit for what is considered *Star Trek*'s shining moment. The episode is seen as a brilliant example of the program and widely perceived as its best episode. According to Roddenberry, Ellison's original teleplay failed to service the series' main characters.

For over two decades, fans have accepted the fact that Roddenberry was responsible for rewriting the show and making it the moving, passionate,

The crew of the Enterprise, happy to be beamin' down to a planet (photo copyright ©1966 NBC).

brilliant work of science-fiction that most viewers believe the show to be. However, Glen Larson disputes the notion that it was Roddenberry who did the rewriting, stating that it was actually Gene L. Coon who was the one responsible. This startling revelation came to Larson's attention during a Writer's Guild Award ceremony in which the script was a nominated entry.

"That night," Larson reflects, "I knew that something was troubling Gene and I asked him what was wrong. And he said, 'There are two scripts up tonight for the Writer's Guild Award, and I wrote them both.' One of them was by Harlan Ellison ["City...."], and he said, 'If Harlan wins, I'm going to die.' Harlan was just an amazingly stubborn person. That night he also told me a story about Harlan. Harlan would write a script that said, 'Five thousand people accosted him on the city streets.' Gene said, 'Harlan, why do you bother writing this into a script that you know is for television? You know we can't have 5,000 extras.' So Harlan would go home, do the rewrite and say, 'Four thousand extras.' And that was his

rewrite. Gene would have to sit down and make a television show out of it. Obviously he kept all of the theoretical things, but he would have to write a script that was a script that could be shot on the stage with a rock.

"But Gene made his contribution in an unheralded way," continues Larson. "His name wasn't on the Ellison script. It is unique in the business these days, it wasn't so much then, for someone to do the kind of work he did and not submit for an arbitration or a credit. It's that simple. An awful lot of guys today will put their name on it and let the Guild fight it out. Coon had a great respect for writers. Therefore, even if he had to do a massive amount of work, he would not take away the guy's credit, which, by the way, is linked to residuals. It was a very generous act on his part. Nevertheless, if you knew a guy was going to stand up and accept an award for what you did, that was more painful than the money. The mere fact that somebody was going to get credit for his thoughts and actual words, because they were so important to him, was almost too much to bear. He shared that with me. He didn't make that a public announcement, but he was feeling great pain. Harlan would stand up and bow from the floor."

As far as Roddenberry's taking credit for the rewrite, Larson offers, "Gene [Coon] was there. Gene made the show work. Gene was the guy and later on, when *Star Trek* gained prominence, I was always surprised at what I heard Roddenberry say, because there are people who create something who don't know how to make it work on a week to week basis, a show to show basis. I suspect that's kind of the way Roddenberry was. I'm not an expert on that. I'm giving you this directly from the horse's mouth, because [Gene Coon and I] used to sit there and talk about things every day."

The Enterprise is literally snared by the hand of the Greek god Apollo at the outset of "Who Mourns for Adonais?" Apollo has decided that the time has come for mankind to worship him again. Kirk must use the force of the starship as well as crew woman Carolyn Palamas, who is in love with Apollo, to combat his powers and gain their freedom. Finally realizing that the species cannot be forced to worship, that it must chart its own destiny, Apollo moves to a spiritual plane, joining the other gods who had long ago realized that their time had come and gone.

There is a moment on film in which Carolyn is assaulted by a storm that is representative of Apollo's fury. As originally written, the script ended with McCoy announcing that Carolyn was pregnant with Apollo's child. There had been talk on staff of doing a follow-up story in which she deals with giving birth to a Demi-god, but no one could whip the story into shape.

Of this script, Fontana notes, "I think Gene basically enhanced the relationships, the fact that the god wanted this woman to not only be his consort, but foremost among his worshippers. And then the antagonistic relationship

between Kirk and Adonais. Kirk wasn't going to fall on his knees and worship a god. No way. Again, it was a matter of character development."

Episode writer Gilbert Ralston explains, "I'm an expert in Grecian history, and I got interested in some of the characters tucked away in my various textbooks. Using Apollo just seemed like a good idea, and Gene Coon liked it very much. I liked *Star Trek* because of Gene and some of the people who originally worked on it. Their conception was highly intellectual and very sophisticated, and it was fun to write because they were apparently very demanding in so far as literary quality was concerned. Shows like that were always a pleasure. It was a *people* show, without an emphasis on stunts and special effects. It was about people, and the fact that one had funny ears didn't make any difference. They were not afraid to emotionalize what they did and, in its own peculiar way, it had a kind of reality which I think was very important. I think *Star Trek* will continue as a kind of quasi-classic for a long time to come."

Captain Kirk does the computer shuffle again in "The Apple" as the Enterprise goes to a world run by Vaal, an ancient computer that controls the laws of nature as well as the inhabitants. While this is an idyllic world, the people are exactly like children. No cares. No concerns, thus allowing Vaal to take care of them and their, in turn, making offerings to "Him" in appeasement. Kirk decides that they must see this is wrong; that they have a right to govern themselves.

Actor William Campbell, who became friends with Coon after playing Trelene in "The Squire of Gothos" ("Gene made friends with him when he was the only actor on the set who Gene saw read a book," smiles Jackie Fernandez), points out, "Gene recognized some of the shortcomings of *Star Trek*. He saw the cult atmosphere and felt that no American would go along with that concept — being policeman of the universe. It was a little L. Ron Hubbardish.

Here you've got a leader who's omnipotent, this rocketship is a city traveling around spanking people who are getting out of line. You don't tell Captain Kirk what to do, because he's boss. There's no sitting down and saying, 'We're having a meeting of the council to find out if we're going to let you do this.' He knew the impossible parts of it, but he said, 'We can take young people—because they're going to be the leaders of the future—and show them that right should be right, because today we don't know who the good guy is.'"

In "Metamorphosis," Kirk, Spock and McCoy are transporting the extremely ill Federation Commissioner Nancy Hedford to the Enterprise via the Galileo, when they are captured by an energy cloud that brings them to Gamma Canaris N. There, they meet Zephram Cochrane, a famous scientist who disappeared over a century earlier and hasn't aged a day. Cochrane, it's revealed, told the energy cloud—an intelligent creature he refers to as "The Companion" — that he was lonely; that he needed companionship. Instead of freeing him, the Companion brought the Galileo there. Ultimately, this turns into a cosmic love story between Cochrane, the Companion and the dying Hedford.

"This was a very delicate and touching love story," enthuses Fontana. "The idea that a man could accept a relationship with this alien, and the young woman, to save her life, accepted the alien into her body. It was really a lovely story and a very touching one. I think Gene did it with great deftness and delicacy."

Although not credited, Coon added quite a bit to "A Piece of the Action." A century after the USS Horizon visited Iotia, the Enterprise arrives to examine the level of "contamination." What they find is a society based entirely on a book detailing the mob wars of Chicago in the 1920's. After initially approaching the inhabitants — mob bosses and all — on an intellectual level, Kirk realize that he's got to do as the

In a scene from the infamous Star Trek *blooper reel, the cast enjoys one of their seemingly frequent laughfests.*

Romans do and it's only a short matter of time before he and Spock come on like mobsters, slang and all.

Points out Fontana, "I think one of the main things Gene added was Kirk and Spock really getting into the gangster stuff, and the whole business with Kirk trying to drive the car. That was certainly Gene Coon, which added so much to their characters. Again, you get another look at the relationship between these two men, and also the fact that they had a sense of humor."

"Gene Roddenberry and Gene Coon didn't want a '20s or '30s type pulp," explains writer David P. Harmon. "They wanted an inch of truth and from there you could expand. They knew exactly what they were looking for, and although it was hard work, you didn't mind rewriting until it was exactly right. [In those days] we all pretty much wanted to be playwrights, and television was considered a stepping stone. The two Genes had the same regard for the writer and his script as the writer himself did. They gave you great freedom to experiment and any success for that show

stems from them. The rest of us had to take a few steps back and bow to their sensitivity, their knowledge, their respect for their fellow writers and, most of all, to the fact that they both loved what they were doing. To them, *Star Trek* wasn't just another job."

"Bread and Circus" has the Enterprise proceed to planet 892 IV, where they discover a society that resembles Earth in the 20th Century, though there is an ancient Rome slant to it in that gladiator battles are televised as sport for the public. Captain Merik, Kirk and company learn, had previously gotten sucked into the politics surrounding "the game," eventually having his crew beamed down one by one so that they, too, could participate. Mixed in with this is the struggle of what everyone assumes are "sun" worshippers, but who turn out to be servants of the "son" of God, Jesus Christ.

"Certainly there was a nice philosophy going on there with the worshipping of the son," says Fontana, "and then the indication that it was the son of God; that Jesus or the concept had appeared on other planets. I thought that

was a nice touch. There have been other stories written with the same theme as the main point, but just adding it at the end really seems quite nice."

Opines director Ralph Senensky, "There were things about that script which weren't working. Both Gene Roddenberry and Gene Coon were writing on that show as we were shooting. I do remember that my concern was that the whole thing about the 'sun,' which they talked about from early on, might not be a mystery when we got to the end. We didn't want to tip that we were doing a Christ story from the word go. That took some doing because it wasn't really in the script, but they did it. They were sealing up the loose ends, because originally when they were talking about the sun you knew right away that they were talking about the son of God."

Following "Bread and Circuses," Gene L. Coon left *Star Trek* for reasons which aren't entirely clear. According to Dorothy Fontana, "He was actually having some physical problems. Sitting at his desk and typewriter a lot was bothering his back. He left because he was having a medical problem. He had it taken care of and went on to *The Name of the Game*."

One *Star Trek* production source offers a different possible reason. "Apparently Coon and Roddenberry had something of a falling out towards the end of the second season. Nobody's really talked about it, because the details weren't very well known. Apparently they had a disagreement about the direction of the show or what Coon was doing with the show. I suspect part of it is that Coon was letting the show get too funny. Although the audience responded very well to the humor in *Star Trek*, Roddenberry had gone off on an extended vacation and Coon, during that vacation, bought a lot of scripts and pushed a lot of things through production, and the show worked very efficiently without Roddenberry there. Roddenberry came back and found that a lot of changes had been made. Now I don't know what the cause was, but I think Roddenberry always panicked when he thought he was losing control of something. So they had a falling out and Coon left the show."

Another possible reason might have been tension between Coon and the show's lead actors, William Shatner and Leonard Nimoy, as John Meredyth Lucas, who replaced Coon as producer, attests.

"When I joined the show," says Lucas, "there was a great deal of tension with the actors. Not civil war, but a great deal of tension among the cast and the company. As a matter of fact, Gene Coon took me out to location to introduce me as producer. We came up to the company. When they'd gotten a particular shot, we walked over and Shatner walked away from us. He would not speak to Gene or to me. They were feuding over something, though I've no idea what the problem was. There was tension among Shatner and Nimoy and Gene. Just a great deal that had built up.

"It happens on every show, but it was particularly noticeable on *Star Trek* when I first came in. I won't say I solved it, but I simply ignored it, went on and was on the set a great deal. I tend to be hands-on with everything. It was just a different kind of approach. Whatever had caused the tension, I'm not quite sure. Actors tend to feel that if you're not there all the time and petting them a little bit, or at least there to hear their screams of anguish, that they're abandoned."

Actor William Campbell offers this view: "I don't know anything about the relationship with the two guys, but I can tell you this. What happens to actors when they've acquired a position on a television show, after a short period of time—they can't help it—they become precious, and also recognize that in some ways they can tell producers off, can make their presence felt. They all have ideas.

"I don't remember a situation where Gene Coon would tell either of those actors how to act, nor did he suggest that he was a director, but he did have an inner sense and he might have

held the line on certain things that they would have changed. Or areas where they would have liked another direction be taken, and Gene Coon perhaps debated them on occasion and they didn't like it. But I never heard him say word one bad against anybody."

Notes Jackie Fernandez, "Basically Gene wasn't crazy about actors. They were just too needful and too egocentric. He wasn't. He didn't get along with Robert Wagner either when he went over to *It Takes a Thief*. I would take his feelings about these actors he didn't get along that great with with a grain of salt, because he didn't care for actors in general."

Dorris Halsey, who along with her late husband Reece Halsey, managed Coon, says, "He was happy on *Star Trek* for quite a while. Then both personal and professional things started weighing on him. He was having personality problems with Shatner and Nimoy. He had a very low respect for actors, except his friends. Gene also had a low threshold of boredom."

While Jackie Fernandez—who did not marry Coon until after his time on *Trek* — believes that there may indeed have been a conflict between *Star Trek's* pair of Genes, it was nothing too serious.

"Roddenberry liked the glory more than Gene wanted in the show," she says. "He wanted more guts and less glory. Less raz-ma-taz. Less show business and more thought. Roddenberry wanted more flash into the quirky trappings of science-fiction. Gene was a philosopher in his feelings about thought. There probably was a certain difference there, but certainly not enough to disturb a friendship because they remained friends for as long as he lived."

Glen Larson, based on conversations he had with Coon, believes that the producer had simply had enough of *Star Trek*, and could not work on the series any longer.

"Gene had two scripts on his desk in front of him which he had to rewrite," Larson relates. "He suddenly

put his pencil down and finally said, 'This is it,' and he got up and walked out. It had been an around the clock, very draining experience."

Part of the problem, according to William Campbell, was that high-quality writers were no longer attempting to write for the show. Opines the actor, "I think it was starting to become a tremendous chore to come up with anything new. Don't forget, they were using writers from the outside and it was becoming more difficult to get them. You've got to remember that we're talking about a period when the great writers no longer were doing anything. When television was making its first inroads, you had some of these great people doing television shows."

Coon departed and went to work for Universal Pictures and *It Takes a Thief*, though he nonetheless continued to write for *Star Trek* under the pen name Lee Cronin. This, according to Glen Larson, was *not* by choice.

"At first, Gene Roddenberry wouldn't let him leave because he had a contract," Larson offers. "The only way they'd let Gene out is if he continued to write for the show, and he continued under a psuedonym. He would be in there typing away while we were supposed to be doing *It Takes a Thief*, but that was great because more and more of it fell on me and I became an instant producer. Roddenberry knew they needed Gene, and didn't feel they could function without him, so he had to promise to make script commitments."

Gene Coon's efforts for the third season (under the aegis of Fred Freiberger) — which were apparently written under some form of duress — never matched the power of his earlier works.

His first script — surprisingly from the typewriter that produced "Devil in the Dark" — was "Spock's Brain," generally considered one of the worst episodes of *Star Trek* ever filmed. In it, an alien race actually steals Spock's brain and it's up to Kirk and a zombie-like

Spock to retrieve it.

"I suspect," muses David Gerrold, "that 'Spock's Brain' was Gene L. Coon's way of thumbing his nose at Roddenberry or something. If not Roddenberry, he was thumbing his nose at how seriously the show was taking itself. I suspect what had happened is that they were a little panic-stricken because there weren't a lot of scripts to shoot. The history of *Star Trek* is management by crisis. I think somebody called up Gene L. Coon and said, 'We need a script in a hurry, can you do it?' And he did it under a pen name, and I don't think he deliberately set out to write that show seriously. I don't think there's any way you can take that episode seriously. You've got to take it as an in-joke. What's the stupidest science fiction idea to do? What if somebody stole Spock's brain? I think Gene L. Coon had that kind of sense of humor to do that kind of impish stuff. He had an irreverent sense of humor, and I think he wanted to poke *Star Trek* because someone was taking it too seriously. Maybe it was his way of not buying into it."

"Spectre of the Gun" was a surrealistic remake of *Shootout at the OK Corral* that worked quite well, while "Wink of an Eye" — to which he supplied the story — was an embarrassment. "Let That Be Your Last Battlefield" was a take on racial intolerance, a theme more in the Coon mode though not nearly as subtle as it should have been handled.

Of "Let That Be....", producer Fred Freiberger recalls, "Gene originally had a devil with a tail chasing an angel. We used actor Frank Gorshin and thought, 'What an idea it would be to do black on one side and white on the other, and the other guy has it the opposite way.' *That's* the stupidity of prejudice. There's a wonderful moment when Kirk says, 'What's different about him?' And he says, 'He's white on the other side.' That was a big morality show and I liked the idea of it."

In terms of Coon's overall involvement with the third season,

Freiberger adds, "Gene Coon was a lovely, talented guy who came up with certain stories and said do what you want with them because he couldn't get involved. He worked as much as he could with us and he was a complete gentleman and completely professional about the whole thing."

Dorothy Fontana believes that the seeming drop in writing quality was due to the fact that Coon was under enormous time pressure and forced to write the scripts between his other assignments. "It wasn't like being on a series where you could devote all your time to that series," she suggests. "I think the writing suffers because of that."

"If you're not producing," says Glen Larson, "somebody else takes it and does the rewriting. Knowing his attention to detail and his work ethic, I would imagine that somebody rewrote him. It would be interesting to be able to see his first draft scripts."

Although completely burned out from his experience on *Star Trek*, Gene Coon found work solace on *The Name of the Game* and *It Takes a Thief*, as well as on a vision he had which has subsequently quite literally become a reality.

"Gene wasn't someone who reflected a lot," points out Jackie Fernandez. "He was more interested in what was coming up. He always had ideas and things he wanted to do. I guess it was probably the first in-house video cassette he wanted to develop for hotels —original script programming. We went to Las Vegas, but we couldn't get it going because it was a tied-up town and we couldn't get into it. He was very progressive in his thoughts and didn't think about yesterday."

Adds William Campbell, "Gene put together a company called Unitel. There had already been companies diddling with the idea of video cassettes for hotels and airlines, but Gene was the first guy who actually sat down and thought of this as something that people could play in the home. One of the problems is that that was a very expensive thing to

Departing Star Trek, *Gene Coon next joined the staff of* It Takes a Thief. *Shown here, star Robert Wagner, who portrayed Alexander Mundy (photo copyright ©1968 ABC).*

keep going. He took offices and I think he felt if he would just continue on in television, he was never going to get on in this. He was way ahead of his time in regard to that. I remember that Universal was dealing with Columbia Records, and the idea was to sell shows on records. Well, they're doing it today as discs, aren't they? Universal was fooling around with that in the '50s. Gene Coon actually put Unitel together and he was moving towards something. Of course, unless you're a guy with a big power structure, you're getting into problems with NBC, ABC, CBS....people trying to absorb you. Chances are that if he had lived, he would have continued on and pursued it, and somebody eventually would have bought him out for a bundle."

While developing Unitel, Coon stopped working for Universal. Says Dorris Halsey, "He couldn't stand the atmosphere of being in the Black Tower of Universal. After that it became less glorious. He wrote a lot of *Kung Fu* and various other things."

During the time of *It Takes a Thief*, Unitel, *Kung Fu* and all the others, Coon found true happiness when he married his first love, the current Jackie Fernandez, then Jackie Mitchell. Gene Coon had originally been married to painter Joy Hankins, but from what can be gathered it was not a completely happy union.

"One day we had sat around talking, and he was talking about the one love in his life who had gotten away," recalls Glen Larson, "because her parents had broken it up. He went off to the war and came back and had lost track of her. Once he was driving along Sunset Boulevard and he saw her picture on a billboard."

Explains Dorris Halsey, "Gene's first wife, Joy, was very fond of about 30 cats. As a matter of fact, Gene's parting words to her were, 'This is the last god-damned can of cat food I'm going to open.' It sounds funny in retrospect, but it was a difficult time to go through. Gene had opened a casting book and seen Jackie's picture (she was one of the top models in town), and she had a huge poster on Sunset. Gene and my husband, Reece, were looking all over for Jackie, and when they saw her name in the casting book, Gene reached her and that's all she wrote. Gene moved out from Joy, but it wasn't an easy thing for him to do. Reece went with him to the hotel and I think Gene threw up through the night from leaving his wife. But this was stronger than everything. He had loved Jackie long ago from far away, and he left his wife for her."

Reflects Glen Larson, "I remember having a real heated debate with a director, Don Weis, who did a number of our It Takes a Thief episodes, over Gene. It wasn't a carnal relationship. It was just his first love, he was just in love with her. It was in those days of innocence where people didn't live together. They parted without ever having made love. And Don Weis, who at this point is one step away from W.C. Fields in terms of cynicism, said, 'Come on, you don't hold the torch for someone all those years.' I said, 'I understand.' It's the way it was. He couldn't wait to marry her and I guess it turned out rather well."

Unfortunately, it was a marriage that only lasted about five years, though they were a joyous five years.

"When Gene married a second

time, it was a great love affair," says John Furia, Jr. "He was a mature man when he died, but it was wonderful to see two people together with that much affection for each other."

Jackie Fernandez believes that, "When I came along, he was tired. He was married at the time and that was an extremely difficult situation for him. I think it was a combination of everything and he was just ready to quit. I know, looking back — and I can't prove this — that he had cancer by the end of Star Trek, and that was depleting him. Nobody really knew it, and it may not be true, but I can look back and see that his bronchitis attacks were actually minor attacks of the same thing that happened when he died of cancer. I really think he lived on for five or six years, when he was smoking heavily as always, with the cancer. He was feeling very burned out when I came along. We had so much fun that it gave him a new lease on things. We had a great time and it was a wonderful five years.

"I don't know why, but I think his destiny was that he was not going to live long no matter what."

At the end of June 1973, Mort Zarkoff was having dinner with Gene Coon. "Gene complained of this cough," he recalls. "I believe it was on a Tuesday. The next day we heard that he was in the hospital with pneumonia. A couple of days later he died. It was that rapid. Fortunately, it was that fast. Of course it wasn't pneumonia at all, it was cancer. But....he was here that very week."

"He died very suddenly," concurs Dorris Halsey. "He didn't find out he had lung cancer until they were at the hospital, and he died three days after checking in. While the doctor was telling Jackie that her husband was dying, someone took her purse and all her credits cards. It was a nightmare. Reece would not believe that Gene had lung cancer and had died in three days. He felt somebody did something wrong at that hospital, and never got over it. They had the same birthdate, June 7th, and

we used to have double birthday parties. Reece also died of cancer. It hasn't been a happy conclusion to any of this. Life does go on and not always with a happy ending.

"This is the true American success story with a tragic ending," she continues. "It is truly incomprehensible that somebody who could commit so much to so many different areas, would be felled. It makes you doubt when you don't want to doubt."

William Campbell emphasizes, "Losing Gene was disturbing to anyone who knew him. He was a grand guy and he did have a feel for Trek. No doubt about it, Roddenberry was the one fighting to get the bucks to do the show, but he was thankful, I assure you, that he had a Gene Coon down there actually artistically putting the show together."

As he reminisces over his friendship with Gene Coon, Mort Zarkoff is struck by a particular thought. "Maybe there was a premonition that his life was going to be short, and he just poured his writing out. Whatever was bottled up. Some of us who are lucky enough to live on, dribble it out a little bit every year. But his output was so concentrated and so hot, that it just poured out at once. And we're the beneficiaries of it."

As are the fans of Star Trek, who have embraced many of Gene Coon's contributions since the series went off the air.

During that same time, a great many people have been credited for all that the show was and has become. Yet it is Gene L. Coon who is most noticeably absent; who has not gotten the credit that he so obviously deserves. The reason? Perhaps ego, perhaps the passage of time. Maybe a combination of both.

"Gene died in 1973," offers David Gerrold, "so there's nobody out there tooting the horn for him."

Dorothy Fontana agrees. "He hasn't been around to be a guest at the conventions and the subject of interviews. I think he has suffered for it. But one of the things Gene brought to the series was certainly part of his own personality, and I think that lives on."

In public, Gene Roddenberry made only passing references to Coon's contributions to *Star Trek*, but William Campbell states that, privately, the situation was just the opposite.

"What's interesting," he says, "is that if you had talked to Roddenberry as recently as I did — the last TrekCruise to the other side of Mexico — he [Gene Coon] was the one guy who we talked affectionately about, the one we credited as the maker of *Star Trek*. At the same time, if ever there were going to be plaudits from various organizations, whether it be NASA or this, that or the other, he would revert back to this being *his* show. In private, he took a completely different attitude. In a sense, I guess I don't blame him for that. After his stroke, after he started mellowing and after he saw that this was his shining hour, his legacy, he started to spread this kind of message out to people in regard to Coon. When I talked to him about Coon on the trip, there was almost a tear in his eye, because his death absolutely knocked Gene Roddenberry on his back. He was shocked, and so was I."

"It's a strange system of giving credit where credit is aptly due," opines Mort Zarkoff. "I knew both Gene Roddenberry and Gene Coon, and I can tell you right now, Roddenberry had the greatest respect for Gene Coon, and he told me that years after Gene had died. Gene Coon wasn't Christ walking on water, but I haven't heard anyone — *anyone* — say anything but the greatest stuff about him. I guess it would be interesting to do a little Louis B. Mayer and do the dark side of Gene Coon, but he didn't have one. He really didn't."

At the time of Coon's death, writer William Douglas Lansford wrote a letter to the *WGAw News* which read, "Like many others who knew Gene Coon, I was shocked and grieved by notice of his passing. Shocked, for he had never shown a sign of illness. Grieved that such a sterling man could be so suddenly and

tragically taken from among us. Those whose work and lives Gene touched will, I believe, long cherish the memory of his worth. Those whom he helped and fought for will recall that he was modest, wise, sincere, courageous and selfless. That he gave much of himself to the betterment of his Guild and of his fellow craftsmen. Some like myself owed him more than a lifetime of gratitude could express. There must be many who felt as I, for at the reading of his eulogy by Johhn Furia the house was S.R.O., the sorrow profound. But there was beauty, too, in our communion.

"Gene was a writer, a Marine, a friend, a gentle man. He lived fully. He served faithfully. He died graciously. In his quiet way he met each test of Man's validity."

Interestingly, one of Gene L. Coon's final projects was Roddenberry's television pilot, *The Questor Tapes*, which dealt with an android seeking its creator and its own destiny. To a very large degree, this represented the writer's own view on life.

"That was very important to Gene," says John Furia, Jr., "and something he was always searching for. He talked about it and we had many conversations in that respect. When he was dying, and he died very quickly, he said something that I'll always remember. His wife called me to tell me that he was dead and that he had asked that I give his eulogy. I was not his closest friend, although I felt I was a friend, and she said that he had particularly asked that I do the eulogy because I was the most Christian man he knew. He meant not so much in terms of the Christian religion, but of a spiritual manner. That was important to me.

"He was not an ill man," closes Furia. "I had seen him a couple of weeks before he died. He complained of a cold and told me he was going to the doctor for some tests. Within a very short time, he was dead; he was gone. As I say, he was always a Marine. He was a husky man, a kind of solidly built guy. A

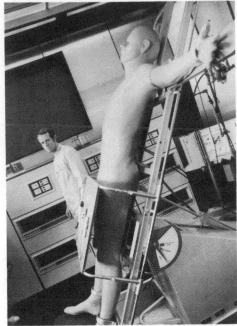
Collaborating once again with Gene Roddenberry, Coon co-wrote the script for The Questor Tapes *(photo copyright ©1974 Universal Pictures).*

very manly man. Yet he turned out such sensitive material. That's what was so fascinating about him. He was a Marine, tough and physical, strong-minded, nobody's patsy, yet a surprisingly gentle and tender man with a great sensitivity, and very gentle and kind to everyone. I don't think you could find anyone who would say other than he was a wonderful guy.

"But that questing was an important part of him. He was a very curious man. Like a lot of writers, he had a great sense of curiosity about everything."

GENE L. COON

June 7, 1924 - July 8, 1973

Memorial services for Gene L. Coon were held in North Hollywood on July 11, 1973. Then Guild president John Furia, Jr. delivered the eulogy. What follows is an edited version.

This is a celebration for Gene Coon. Words and their proper use were very precious to Gene, so I'll remind you that to celebrate means to commemorate or proclaim an event, to praise or extol with appropriate ceremonies. Gene celebrated life. With honesty, candor, love, generosity, humor — yet he delighted in insisting he was a hard-nosed s.o.b.

I loved the man. It was difficult not to. One night at a Writer's Guild meeting — which he attended loyally, but with a certain joy in puncturing our pomposities — Gene broke into a discussion with a mighty, angry shout. He railed briefly about....I don't recall exactly what....and seeing him, I smiled. He was such a gentle man, it was incongruous to watch such an outburst. Afterwards, I spoke to him, and he said, in that delicate, side-stepping way he had, "What the hell were you smiling for?" I told him. Gene asked if I disagreed with him, and I answered: "I disagree 100%." Then he looked at me and grinned contentedly and said in that Nebraska-fed, Will Rogers drawl: "At least, it was damn honest anger!"

You could count on Gene's honesty like the sun rising each morning, and it was just as welcome.

I didn't know a lot about Gene before I met him a few years ago. He was an authentic war hero. He was with the Marines on the Yalu River and on the Long March back. He did then what he always did — what he felt was right. Yet he was very much against war and killing. So he built an armor around his gentle heart, of toughness and of humor.

He wrote about it in his first novel, *Meanwhile Back at the Front*. This is an excerpt from his first chapter:

Right in the middle of the rice-paddy-cum-bass-pond sat the dingy, tattered, disreputable tent of the Public Information Officer....

[It] was long and shabby and full of holes and covered with the mud of a thousand rains and a hundred wild evenings, but it was a little drier than a foxhole and seldom came under direct fire. Through these portals, as the saying went, passed the great of the world of journalism. Pulitzer Prize-winning newsmen, novelists, columnists, military analysts and other liars, think-piece writers and men concerned only with the little picture, world-famous men drawn to the Marine division as by a magnet. As a member of the working press, Ben enjoyed knowing them, talking to them, learning that even the gods of the written word have feet of clay. He liked being in on the top secret that Homer Sespe, that tower among pundits, wore a girdle....It was all very exciting and stimulating, and lost only a little of its glamor when one of the great men drank too deeply and threw up all over his sleeping bag.

But then there were the Andovers....Andover, in spite of his 76 daily newspapers and his 72 million weekly readers was, as the fourth estate rose as a man to testify, a son of a bitch, even a revolting son of a bitch — which, according to H. Allen Smith, is a son of a bitch any way you look at him.

Anyway you looked at Gene, you saw a loving man. He loved his family. He loved Kathleen. He had a love affair going with Jackie that was beautiful to behold, and he was neither shy nor apologetic about showing it. One night at my house, talking good talk, I watched them sitting on my couch, holding hands, and I damned near cried just enjoying them. He loved people. He loved reading. He loved writing with a joy I've never seen in another writer.

Most of us writers have a kind of love-hate relationship with a blank sheet of paper. But Gene exulted in it.

Reading was like eating to him. And he was a gourmand, gulping great portions of history, philosophy, fiction, everything, and savoring the best of it to share with friends. One of the last things he said to Jackie last Saturday was to bring him a book to read.

He wrote with great skill and zest — and also with amazing speed. He concentrated so well, he could pound his typewriter and talk simultaneously. And what talk!

Gene helped a lot of novice writers. He loved people, but he also loved the act of writing and anyone who had the stomach and the head to try it. It was part of his optimism and affection for the human spirit.

Star Trek was very dear to him. One of the most renowned of its scripts was Gene's "Devil in the Dark." In it, he showed us a monster who was a *good* creature, *not* ugly, not evil, though dangerous and terrifying. Gene could see through the facade of people and things, and his vision was bright and warm.

He had an insatiable curiosity. Everything interested him: Eastern philosophy, bagpipe music, his ancestor the Picts, gem cutting, the sounds of good words strung together like a necklace of well-matched pearls, yesterday, tomorrow, the history of the future....A pleasure.....An idea....A texture....Discovery.

With a knife I always believed was deliberately dull, Gene would whittle away at a block of wood and find, hiding inside it, a shape, a form, an idea. He played pool with relish and could spot you a stripe or a solid and still cheerfully whip the pants off you. And not apologize for the insult either.

He was a lousy poker player. I took his seat in a game a few weeks ago in the interminable waiting we endured between caucuses and sidebars in the negotiations to which he generously gave himself. I think that deep down Gene believed the *gavotte* of negotiations was an invention of the devil with a hangover. He did it because it was good for writers. But, as I said, he was a rotten poker player. He didn't have the con for it. Or the description. Or the killer instinct. He just liked to play....Badly.

The thing he played with best was ideas. Like little boys, bartering the mysterious and eclectic and priceless contents of their pockets, Gene would trade ideas with you....I never lost in those trades.

In with my pocket lint of ideas, I've always had some about immortality. If that means being remembered — and treasured — in the hearts of people you knew and loved, then Gene is truly immortal.

Will there be, sometime, another world? I have my dreams. The idea of immortality was not born of any creed or book or religion. It was born of human affection. It will continue to wax and wane, like a moon of time, through mists and clouds of doubt and darkness — as long as love can fill a heart and make it bright and beautiful.

I don't accept nothingness. There must be something. Heaven, Universal energy. God. Hope. Something. Gene is there. And if I know my friend, he is discovering....And finding it fascinating. We, none of us, can ignore our own mortality. But I want to share with you my own hope, my own feelings in confronting it....

Gene mentioned that he was struck by a line of dialogue I had used for *Kung Fu*. It's this: *Before we wake, we cannot know that what we dream is not the truth. Before we die, we cannot know that death is not the greatest joy.*

Gene had a literary streak, and so I've adapted an old Latin verse by the poet Catullus, just for him, for now:

By ways unknown and many mem'ries sped
Brother, to this moment am I come.
That I may celebrate the dead
And I speak of peace with your ashes dumb.
Accept my thoughts. Such heirlooms of past years.
Are joyous things to grace you where you dwell.
Take them, all drenched with a brother's tears,
And, Gene, my brother, now hail....and farewell.

I'd like to suggest we each take a separate, silent, private moment to commune with our memories of Gene....

Fred Freiberger (right) with producer Gerry Anderson, while the two were collaborating on Space: 1999 (photo copyright ©1976 ITC).

FRED FREIBERGER
"The Final Curtain"

When Gene Coon announced his departure from *Star Trek*, more than a few eyebrows were raised in terms of how the show could continue without him. When Gene Roddenberry made it clear that he would not be returning for the show's third season as well, everyone knew that *Star Trek* was in trouble.

On the one hand, Roddenberry was admired for sticking to his guns and refusing to produce the series when NBC changed the show's promised timeslot. On the other, his departure — to some —seemed a veritable slap in the face to the people who labored via a massive letter-writing campaign to keep *Star Trek* on the air. In a sense, it was as though their efforts meant nothing.

Actor George Takei notes, "Gene was aware that even if he had stayed with *Star Trek*, NBC intended to cancel the show after its third year. From another vantage point, maybe it should have been a matter of personal integrity on Roddenberry's part. *Star Trek* was

Gene's creation and the third season would be identified with him whether he liked it or not. If the quality of the show was in some way to erode, it couldn't help but reflect on Roddenberry. Inevitably, it would be Gene's reputation that was at stake. Now, Gene Roddenberry's a human being, so I can certainly understand his position. At the same time, giving myself distance and perspective, I can't help but wish that Gene had looked at the entire picture and realized how *Star Trek*'s third season might finally affect his professionalism and artistic integrity."

"I think the show was hurt twice," offers writer David Gerrold. "Once when Gene L. Coon left and once when Roddenberry left. Roddenberry was at his prime during the days of the old show. He could sit down and a write a script in a weekend. The joke was that he would sit down with a bottle of scotch and when the scotch was finished, the script was finished. He understood television. I've said nasty things about Roddenberry, but there were a lot of things he understood.

"There was a writer who brought in a script and it took two pages of maneuvering to turn the ship around," recalls Gerrold. "Roddenberry crossed off these two pages and Shatner's line was a simple, 'Reverse course.' Roddenberry understood that you have to show it in such a way that the audience understands what's going on. Gene L. Coon understood that too. You have to give Roddenberry credit for getting the show started and getting the show made. I think what really hurt the third season was Roddenberry's not being there either. If he was, there would have been some of that stuff that was there in the beginning. When the show first started, there was a lot of really nice stuff there that you always wanted to see developed. I wish Roddenberry had been there in the third season to take care of his baby."

To make matters worse, the budget for the series was lowered yet again, as it had been at the outset of season two, while cast salaries increased.

"The third season we were reduced to what I call a radio show," reflects Co-Producer Robert Justman. "We couldn't go on location any longer because we couldn't afford it. We had to do shows that we could afford to do. It was quite difficult and that did affect what the concept was. Certain concepts just couldn't be handled. We didn't have the money. The studio had deficit financing situations and every time you shot a show, you lost more money. In those days, they didn't think they had a chance

of syndication, especially since everybody knew that third season was it. They just cut it down to the bone to cut their losses. It was very simple. When you get moved in a timeslot to a night when your audience isn't home, you know that the handwriting is on the wall. Remember, they tried to cancel us at the end of the second season. By the time the third season rolled along, it was no longer Thursdays at 8:00. It wasn't Fridays at 8:00. It was Friday at 10:00. If your audience is high school kids and college-age people and young married people, they're not home Friday nights. They're out, and the old folks weren't watching. So our audience was gone.

This was the less than auspicious situation that greeted Fred Freiberger as he assumed the reigns as *Star Trek's* producer.

Fred Freiberger, raised in the Bronx, New York, had been an Air Force navigator during World War II, and was shot down over enemy territory. As a result, he became a prisoner of war, spending two years in a Nazi prison camp. "I was very nervous," he understates. "I was a Jew in a German prison camp." But he managed to survive. "I was with a lot of my friends and there was a certain   amount of security that way. As officers, we didn't have to work, so we did a lot of reading. We had the theater. I wrote a book while I was there on my experiences."

Once freed, Freiberger proceeded to Hollywood with two of his friends, utilizing back-pay from the Air Force to finance the trip — a trip he would not have otherwise been able to afford. Once there, he'd hoped to get involved in publicity for the studios via a personal contact, but was kept waiting due to an industry strike at the time. During the interim, he decided to write a story, which was sold to Mary Pickford's company, Comet Productions. "Just out of the blue," he smiles, "I was a screenwriter. You know, a kid from the Bronx who came out here."

From there, Freiberger began

writing for radio dramas, penning his first science-fiction effort for a show called *The Clock*. "It was the only science-fiction they ever did on that show," he smiles. He then wrote the story for the Gary Cooper starrer, *The Garden of Eden*, and eventually wrote the screenplays for *The Beast From 20,000 Fathoms* and *The Beginning of the End*. His memories of the former have more to do with the early presentation of the "beast" than anything else.

"I felt we should hold back the beast," Freiberger relates, "and not show it so soon. But [producer] Hal Chester said, 'You don't understand. I've spent a fortune on this thing and if you think I'm going to hold it back and only show it for two minutes, you're out of your mind.' Well, it *was* Hal's film, and so that's why the creature shows up about a half hour earlier in the film than I would have liked. Holding it back and playing up the suspense is the way I would have gone with it."

Freiberger segued to television where he worked on such series as *Ben Casey* and *Slattery's People*. His first genre effort for the medium was *The Wild Wild West*, where he was the fifth pro-

It was Fred Freiberger who set the tone of the phenomenally successful Wild Wild West. *Seen here are Michael Dunn and series star Robert Conrad (photo copyright ©1965 CBS).*

ducer brought on to the show prior to it ever hitting the airwaves. The series was essentially a western flavored take on the then enormously popular James Bond films. It starred Robert Conrad as undercover agent James West (working for President Grant) and Ross Martin as make-up and dialect genius Artemus Gordon.

"They were having problems with it," Freiberger explains. "I was told it was a western but with fun and gadgets and asked if I wanted to come on board as producer. I said, 'Sure, but why do you want me?' And they said, 'We hear you go to Vegas a lot. We want a guy who will take chances.' So I went over there and started working. To give you an idea of what we started to develop, one of the writers I was interviewing came up with the idea of a dwarf named Dr. Miguelito Loveless [portrayed by Michael Dunn], who wants half of Southern California. We did these kinds of wild things. I'd bring in a prince from Russia or have a circus come through town. One of our commandments was that at the end of the second act West has to be in a situation that none of us could figure a way out of, and then of course we would have to devise one. I just didn't want any easy solutions.

"The wonderful thing about science fiction-like elements in *Wild Wild West* is that we could do anything we wanted to get him out of an impossible situation, like putting dynamite in his boot."

As these elements were developed, Freiberger found himself battling the network more and more. The series was expensive to produce and apparently no one at CBS really understood what they had, so there were numerous creative arguments. Ultimately Freiberger, who was involved in the development of the first 10 episodes, was let go. "Then the show premiered," he smiles, "and it wiped out all the competition. The network kept saying they didn't understand the show. *I* understood the show."

His next entry into the world of science fiction came in the form of *Star Trek*.

"I was familiar with *Star Trek* only in that I had seen the first pilot they had done," says Freiberger. "I had seen Gene Roddenberry at the beginning to talk to him about producing the show at the start. I consider myself basically a writer, but I've done a lot of producing. In terms of that he interviewed me as to whether I would produce the show. I was shown the first pilot, and Jeff Hunter was the actor. They had done one with Shatner but hadn't put it together yet. He asked me if I would be interested in producing the show. I said, 'I'd love it.' I like science fiction. I'm not a buff, but as a kid I read *Astounding Stories* and *Amazing Stories*, as well as all the pulp magazines. I was always a big fan of Edgar Rice Burroughs. But I was going to Europe on a vacation that I had planned. I mentioned to Gene — not that it was offered to me, but I was up there as one of the candidates — that the pilot was terrific, and if the job was still available when I got back, I was interested.

"I thought the pilot was pure science fiction," he adds, "and very intriguing. That's what the show should have been. 'The Cage' was what the series was all about. At that time, people didn't accept it. By the time I came back, he had gotten Gene Coon and I was off doing other shows. Then, when third season came along, my agent brought me into Gene's office and he said he would like me to produce the show. Gene said, 'Would you write a script so that we could see how you do?' And I said, 'Gene, I've got a lot of credits as a writer and I don't audition scripts. I'm not up here to audition as a writer. I'm here as a producer. If the requirement of getting the job is for me to write a script, I'll have to pass.' I think Gene appreciated that point of view and he hired me to do the show. Gene Coon had done the first season, John Meredyth Lucas did the second and I assumed he wanted to change producers every year."

Freiberger admits to being a bit uncomfortable at his first meeting with Roddenberry and NBC executives. "Something like 30 people from the network came in," he remembers, "and I was amazed at the contempt with which Roddenberry treated them and I could see they didn't like him at all. I'd thought to myself, 'Holy shit, what have I gotten myself into?'"

Obviously *Star Trek* had changed quite a bit between "The Cage" and the third season, and one must question whether a new producer coming in felt the series to be a daunting challenge.

"It wasn't a question of daunting," Freiberger responds, "it was a question of going in on a show that was being successfully produced with a lot of people involved who were very loyal to the show. You can walk into *Family Affair* and it can be daunting for you. You get into a situation where everybody knows each other and they've been together for some time. I was more concerned with improving the ratings, because the show had about a 20 or 24 share. Today that would be a hit. In those days, even if you had a 30 share, you were very iffy. It was the loyalty of the fans that kept it on when NBC threatened to cancel it. They did keep it on, and it was impressive that NBC succumbed to the campaign. But in all three years, the ratings remained the same no matter what went on. It kept the same fans. Our hope was to improve the ratings, and we tried different kinds of stories. But the ratings always stayed the same....always.

"The show didn't have a big reputation at the time," he points out. "It had a very strong cult following. I remember being concerned about why we weren't increasing our ratings, and, as I understand it, a survey was done and they discovered that although we did have many female fans, women generally seemed to be terrified of outer space. The survey seemed to indicate that women were more comfortable with boundaries rather than the endless expanse of space. At least, that was what was reported to me in terms of the survey. I was doing anything to try to increase those ratings, because we were always on the edge."

Star Trek's survival into a third season was tentative at best, a point driven home by the fact that the show's budget — as previously mentioned — was lowered.

Notes Freiberger, "The cutting of the budget hurt us badly. We had to do at least four of the shows completely on the Enterprise. There were a lot of restrictions, but that's no excuse if the stories aren't very good or aren't executed properly. It's a question of judgment and you have to go with what you think. That's the way television works. I think, on balance, we did some pretty nice stories and some that didn't come out so good. Some shows you're happy with, some you're disappointed with and others you're ashamed of. That's the way it goes, but if you're a pro, you accept those things, you understand them and all you can do is make sure that everybody does their best."

Another mitigating factor, according to some, was the purchase of Desilu by Paramount Pictures; a sale which definitely had a detrimental effect on Star Trek.

"Desilu was like a family," says frequent Trek director Ralph Senensky. "Herb Solow, who was the head of the studio, used to come down and talk with you on the sound stage. He didn't seem like the other studio heads who never seemed to talk to you. Herb went out of his way to help you. Can you imagine a studio working like that? I think when Paramount bought the company, it had a lot to do with the demise of the series. When Paramount bought it, a kind of corporate mentality took over. In a way, I think that's why I resent Paramount having such a hit in Star Trek, because if they had their way, they would have killed it off. It survived in spite of them and now they have this bonanza making all of this money."

Freiberger's problems didn't stop there. Unfortunately, a great many of the creative people involved with the third season were disappointed with the direction the show took. Marc Daniels — who had played so integral a role in the course of the series — directed "Spock's Brain," and decided that one episode under the new regime was enough.

"Fred Freiberger and I didn't agree on what the director's role was," the late Daniels explained. "There are many writer/producers who don't consider the director a partner. They consider him, shall we say, an employee. This is particularly true in episodic TV. They just want you to do the work, get the shots and forget the rest. I didn't particularly care for that kind of thinking."

Margaret Armen, who had written for Roddenberry and Freiberger, explains, "I suppose they were looking for two different types of stories. Fred was looking for all action pieces. That's why he wasn't crazy about 'The Paradise Syndrome.' He didn't think that there was enough violent and terrifying action in it. He didn't realize that the suspense would come from the characters, their relationships and so forth. There was some action in it, but there was no monsters and that sort of thing. So Fred was looking primarily for action pieces, whereas Gene was looking for the subtlety that is Star Trek. Action, but with people carrying the story."

David Gerrold, who has had "sparring" matches with Freiberger in the press before, admits, "I understand Freddy Freiberger's problems a lot better today than I did 24 years ago. Oddly enough, I have a respect for the man that I don't think he realizes. He's able to do something that not a lot of people can do: he can bring in a show on time, under budget. He can do the job. There are people who crumble under that kind of pressure. As a producer, I'm sure his opinions are correct for what he's doing. As a writer, I think his biggest weakness is that he doesn't have a sense of humor. He doesn't allow the show he's working on to have fun."

A major blow came when Robert Justman, who had been involved with Star Trek since "The Cage," announced that he was leaving about two-thirds of the way through the season. "I felt like I was in prison and I had to get out," he exclaims. "I just didn't want to take it anymore, because I was so unhappy with what was happening with the show. We couldn't make the kind of shows we wanted to make because we couldn't afford them, and I felt that the content of the shows was going downhill. It was my feeling that the show wasn't what it ought to be.

"I got on fine with Freddy Freiberger," he adds. "He was a nice man. I think he did what he did as best he could do it. I never had any harsh words. It just wasn't the same without Gene in a hands-on position that third season."

For his part, Freiberger had his own problems to deal with. As he explains it, every television series has its share of difficulties, but Star Trek's were multiplied because "there were so many jealousies going on."

"When you have a second banana, like Spock, who's probably getting more fan mail than the lead, it gets twice as murderous," says Freiberger. "They want the last line, they want this, they want that. They're measuring each other's dressing room. Even this kid, Walter Koenig, was always asking for more. I told the writers to put him in more. So I read Shatner's book [Star Trek Memories], and Koenig is complaining that he's supposed to be representing progressive youth of the decade and the producer finally gave him more to do, and it was establishment shit. So I wrote to Bill and said everytime I start to feel good about Star Trek, something like this shows up. I wish somebody would whisper into that little schmuck's ear that the producer was trying to meet what he asked for. If I disappointed him, the least he could do is understand that an attempt was made to satisfy him and not take a cheap shot. It's that kind of stupid little stuff that drives me crazy."

One primary supporter of

Freiberger is actor William Shatner. "I thought he did a yeoman's job," he says. "There was a feeling that a number of his shows weren't as good as the first and second seasons', and maybe that's true, but he did have some wonderfully brilliant shows and his contribution has never been acknowledged."

Despite any criticisms, Freiberger points out that *Star Trek* had to change by his being involved, simply because the dynamics of the show's producer had changed.

"This is the nature of this business," he explains. "If people come in to produce a show — Gene Roddenberry, Gene Coon — that show has to be shaped in terms of what they think. Each writer comes in. There are so many active writers in the Writer's Guild. Writers have fragile egos. They come in and submit something. You generally know your show better. You change that show. You rewrite that show. You make suggestions. The professional writer who has been in the business and knows what it is, changes it. Some of them will accept the fact that some good suggestions are made. They have to if they want to stay with the show.

"That is the nature of television. That's the nature of Broadway in spite of the Dramatist's Guild contract which says they can't change any words. They just say to you, 'We can't change a line, but I think our backers will pull out of this,' and so they get their way. Who's kidding who? With a novel, if you won't do what the editor says, unless you have a fantastic, powerful name, you just will not get that thing published. That is the essence of the procedure between staff on a show and writers. The writer comes up, tells him an idea. They get an assignment — all of them cutoff assignments, cutoff after story. They then come in with the story; discuss the story with them. They adjust. At no time does a writer have to, if he's got such integrity, say that he cannot accept the change. All he has to do is leave and say, 'Just pay me my money for that extent and I'm finished.' They

The shift of Star Trek's time period to Friday nights at 10 resulted in Roddenberry leaving the series, and Fred Freiberger joining (photo copyright ©1968 NBC).

don't have to go on after that. As I say, they're not crazy about it, do not delight in it, but the nature of the business is to have you conform to what the people in charge of that show set down. All you can do is operate from your viewpoint."

And what was Freiberger's viewpoint? To — hopefully —broaden the viewer base for *Star Trek*. "To do a science fiction show," he says, "but get enough additional viewers to keep the series on the air. I decided to do what I would hope was a broad canvas of shows, but I tried to make them more dramatic and to do stories that had a more conventional storyline within the science fiction frame."

While it's true that the third season lagged seriously behind the first two in terms of production and script value, it nonetheless produced a number of effective episodes.

"Spectre of the Gun" had Kirk and other members of the Enterprise bridge crew the intended targets of the Earps in an Old West setting.

"When Gene Coon wrote the original script," says Freiberger, "it was set in an actual western town. Bobby

Justman and I thought about how we could help it some and therefore we did this surrealistic kind of town to try and give it an other-worldly approach. Vincent McEveety was a hell of a creative director. I thought he did some wonderful things with it. I thought the show came out well, and that was satisfying considering that was my first episode of *Star Trek*, though it aired later in the season."

"Day of the Dove" featured an alien being which feeds on negative energy, and is manipulating a conflict between the Enterprise and a Klingon vessel commanded by Kang. This was a shipboard show that managed to overcome its budget limitations with a thoughtful theme.

"The Tholian Web" had Captain Kirk disappear into another dimension, while those aboard the Enterprise believe that he's dead. Some of the effects may have been hokey, but this was a tremendous character episode — particularly regarding the McCoy-Spock relationship.

"Plato's Stepchildren" had the crew encounter a race of cruel, telekenetic beings. While showcasing the decadence that absolute power can potentially bring to the one wielding it, it was intended to feature a profound television moment in that Kirk and Uhura were supposed to kiss passionately, representing the medium's first inter-racial kiss. Forced to shoot a "softer" version by NBC executives, the creative team presented something of a cop-out, but the episode comes *this* close to delivering the goods.

"The big thing," notes Freiberger, "was who was going to kiss Uhura, a black girl. We had quite a few conversations on that one, because someone said, 'Let's have Spock do it,' and I said, 'No, if we have Spock do it, we're going to have all these people screaming that we didn't have the guts to have a white man kiss her.' We went through a whole thing, but it all worked out and Shatner said to her, 'It's not that I don't want to, but I don't want to humiliate you.' That's a show I'm very proud of."

Of that kiss, William Shatner recalled, "They said, 'Would you mind?' and I said, 'Mind? No, I don't mind.' And then they kind of backed off on it, in that I was being *forced* to do it. It wasn't Kirk actually kissing Uhura. It was Kirk being forced by some power beyond there — to kiss her. So the edge was taken off the first interracial kiss on television by the fact that this guy was going, '...uh, argh, not me—no—kiss.' But it was part of the whole story. The story involved Kirk's having to do things against his will. And, of course, Spock, as well. Spock was being forced to kiss Christine Chapel, who was in love with him, and they were protesting too.

"There's a very basic thing going on there, if you think of the reality of what is happening — not only the plain knowledge of what the next step can be — but the bottom line is probably that you can't protect that woman. That's basic. It's biological. If you can't do that, what good are you? And yet, we all know that we can get into situations where we are powerless even to protect a person we

love. That is the essence of terror. And then what do you do? Well, Kirk was saying things like, 'Don't let it bother you, it's going to be okay, just go with it, it'll be all right.' And Uhura, knowing what is was doing to him was trying to protect him, too — saying that it *was* going to be all right, no matter what, and she was not afraid. Well, they both were afraid, and had every right to be. But they did what they could — for each other.

"I'm well aware that there could have been different ways to write the scene or play it," added Shatner. "We did try some variations. There could have been a whole different story, if anybody had wanted to emphasize an interracial love story. But in fact, that wouldn't have made the point as effectively. Kirk and Uhura wouldn't even think of a kiss or a love story as interracial. That would be the last thing they would think about. If we did any good with that kiss or anything on *Star Trek*, it was to push in the direction of not having to think about that."

In "Let That Be Your Last Battlefield," the Enterprise finds itself in the midst of a chase between an alien law enforcement officer name Bele and his prey, Lokai. Half the face of each man is white while the other half is black. The only difference is the side on which the particular color is.

"That was originally a Gene Coon story brought to me," relates writer Oliver Crawford, who wrote the teleplay. "It dealt with racial intolerance, and I thought it was a marvelous visual and cinematic effect. The whole point of the story was that color is only skin deep. How could any writer not respond to that? That fit right into today's scene, and I was very pleased with the episode."

"All Our Yesterdays" had Kirk, Spock and McCoy projected back in time, with Spock falling in love and reverting to more barbaric modes of behavior. Again, an extremely strong character episode, which actually inspired a pair of novel spin-offs by Ann C. Crispin.

"I love that episode," smiles

Freiberger. "The woman who wrote it was a librarian at UCLA. I remember when Leonard Nimoy read that script he came to me and said, 'I'm a Vulcan, how can I be passionately in love with a woman with emotion involved?' So I said, 'This is way back in time, before the Vulcans had evolved into a non-emotional society.' He accepted that, for which I was very grateful. One of my favorites."

"Turnabout Intruder" is noteworthy primarily because of the opportunity offered to actor William Shatner. In the story, the bitter Dr. Janice Lester manages to have her mind inserted into Kirk's body, and vice versa. Shatner has to convey the notion that there's a woman trapped within him.

"I have to tell you," says Freiberger, "Shatner is a very creative guy. When I say creative, I mean he's willing to try *anything*. He loved 'Turnabout Intruder.' I was, frankly, a little concerned when Gene Roddenberry came up with a story where Kirk changes places with a woman. When I originally read it, I had said to Gene, 'I wonder what Shatner is going to say about this,' and Gene said he wouldn't have any problem with it. He was right. When I mentioned it to Shatner, he just loved the idea."

As the season progressed, it became obvious that *Star Trek's* five year mission was winding down a couple of years earlier than planned. Despite this, Freiberger believes that the morale on the set was fine until the last few shows, when the end was approaching.

"When they cut the budget down, you know that's not a good sign," he says. "The last couple of shows the morale went down a little, but prior to that I hadn't noticed. Despite that, if you're a pro, you do the best that you can right up until the last minute. Listen, three years for a show — any show — isn't bad, especially when the ratings are so low."

Freiberger's next genre effort took him to England, where he served as second season producer of Gerry

The morphing alien Maya (Catherine Schell) was a creation of Freiberger's for the second season of Space: 1999 *(photo copyright ©1976 ITC).*

Anderson's *Space: 1999*, the series that — believe it or not — had the moon blown out of orbit and sent hurtling to different galaxies where inhabitants of a lunar colony met alien lifeforms. Given full creative control over year two, the first thing Freiberger did was present an analysis of what he felt was wrong with the series.

"In the analysis," he explains, "I said that if you're appealing to an American audience — which they desperately wanted to do — you can't have the show take place in what looks like a big living room. They had a big living room rather than a spaceship, which is how it seemed to me. I said, 'You've got to streamline that.' Also, if you're going to have a professor, have a young guy with a beard, rather than someone like Barry Morse, who's a wonderful actor. But you want some youth in there and you want a love interest."

To this end, Freiberger created the characters Tony Verdeschi (Tony Anholt) and Maya (Catherine Schell), an alien who could transform herself into various creatures and objects by rearranging her molecules. Even the lives of stars Martin Landau (Commander John Koenig) and Barbara Bain (Dr. Helena Russell) were spiced up in an attempt to draw viewers.

"You have to have some tension," adds Freiberger in terms of what he tried to bring to the show, "and someone that you care about. You have to care about the people when you see them in trouble. Also — and I guess this was my *Star Trek* influence — I felt that you can't automatically regard those you meet in space as the enemy. Whatever they're doing, they're doing out of their own needs and motivations. You're not going to be evil for the sake of being evil."

Most of Freiberger's suggestions were implemented, but *Space: 1999* didn't survive past its second season. The producer nonetheless remembers the experience positively.

"As a matter of fact," he notes, "I

Lee Majors as Steve Austin, The Six Million Dollar Man *(photo copyright ©1976 Universal Pictures).*

liked it better than *Star Trek*, although it wasn't nearly as authentic. If you set up that you're traveling at warp eight in *Star Trek*, you've established what that is. But here, to think that the moon has been yanked out of orbit and sent hurtling with the necessary speed to get to another galaxy, was a bit hard to believe. But everyone accepted it. I thought it was great fun."

Next up for Freiberger was *The Six Million Dollar Man*. Based on Martin Caidin's *Cyborg*, the series starred Lee Majors as former astronaut Steve Austin who, following a crippling accident, is transformed into the world's first bionic man.

"A very pleasant experience," says the producer of the enormously popular series. "I thought Lee Majors wasn't the greatest actor in the world, but I found him to be one of the most professional. He was always on time, even if he was out boozing the night before. I found him to be a lovely guy, and I thought the show's premise was great."

The syndicated *Adventures of Superboy* followed, a series for which Freiberger served as story editor. Set at Florida's Shuster College, the series in its first year chronicled the adventures of Clark Kent/Superboy, Lana Lang and their friend T.J. White.

"The format was tough," Freiberger admits, "because they wanted him to be a school boy, and you had to contrive like mad for situations for him to get in to. I enjoyed it, though. We only had 20 minutes of air time, but I thought we managed to put in an awful lot of stuff. When I first went in there, I said I would like to, in a sense, do a *Star Trek* type of show in terms of a small morality play. Why couldn't we do scripts that say something? They got very nervous about that and I said, 'Look, I'm not trying to solve the world's problems with it, but I think if we say

Freiberger served as story editor on the first season of The Adventures of Superboy, *which starred John Haymes Newton as the Boy of Steel (photo copyright ©1987 Viacom).*

something meaningful in terms of the relationships, it would be important.'

"[Executive producer] Ilya Salkind had some dream that he was doing a little feature in every episode," Freiberger laughs. "That's the expression he used. He hired all these young directors who would take out humor, take out motivations. I was story editor, so I didn't have any control over that kind of thing. All I could say was, 'For Christ's sake, they're taking all the fun out of the scripts.'"

According to Freiberger, things got worse when the producers replaced John Haymes Newton with Gerard Christopher in the lead role, while simultaneously trying to entice more adult viewers.

"I thought they were nuts to let John go," he says. "He was a very good kid and his acting was improving. More importantly, he symbolized what the all-American boy was. But he wanted more money and instead of paying him, they fired him.

"We had that lovely gal, Stacy Haiduk, who was so charming and lovely and played a high school girl so well. Then they put her in these tight-fitting dresses with her knockers hanging out, and I said, 'What the hell are they doing?' They had some dream that they were going to get adults to watch the show. We were already in the top 10 or 15 all the time. What more could they want?"

While Freiberger currently lives in semi-retirement, it would seem that the accomplishment he will always be remembered for is producing *Star Trek*. Sometimes, though, that particular credit isn't always what it's cracked up to be.

"I've been the target of vicious and unfair attacks even to this day," Freiberger points out. "The fact that at the end of the second season, *Star Trek*'s ratings had slipped, it was losing adult fans and was in disarray, carries no weight with the attackers. The dumping was all done on me and the third season. It seemed it was now *Star Trek* law to lay everything on Freiberger. Every disgruntled actor, writer and director also found an easy dumping ground on which to blame their own shortcomings. Whenever one of my episodes was mentioned favorably, Gene Roddenberry's name was attached to it. When one of my episodes was attacked, Roddenberry's name mysteriously disappeared, and only then did the name Freiberger surface. As an example, I read an article, which I think was in the L.A. *Times*, praising 'Plato's Stepchildren' as the first television show to allow an interracial kiss. A breakthrough. Roddenberry was lauded for this, when in fact Roddenberry wasn't within a hundred miles of that episode.

"I have no quarrel to make with the right of critics," he continues, "self-styled or otherwise, to dislike my episodes and to state that dislike. What angers me is when they choose to attack my character, sometimes labeling me as indifferent or uncaring. None of that could be further from the truth, and I'm thankful that on occasion people like Bob Justman have gone out of their way to publicly and vociferously stand up for me.

"I have read that the fans didn't like any of my episodes. If true that hurts me, but there is another truth. In my travels throughout the United States, Canada and Europe, I have run into many *Star Trek* fans, and not one of them has ever treated me with anything less than courtesy and respect. For that I thank them."

Interestingly, speaking of his tenure on *Star Trek* reminds Freiberger of his World War II experiences.

"I thought the worst experience of my life was when I was shot down over Nazi Germany," he reflects. "A Jewish boy from the Bronx parachuted in to the middle of 80 million Nazis. Then I joined *Star Trek*. I was only in a prison camp for two years, but my travail with *Star Trek* has lasted 25 years and still counting."

Like others who toiled in the television incarnation of the final frontier, Fred Freiberger applied his particular skills to *Star Trek*, and attempted to guide the voyages of the Enterprise as best he could and with everything he had. No one could ask more of a Great Bird.

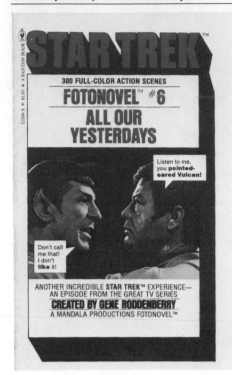

The cover of this Star Trek *photo novel highlights a moment from one of Freiberger's favorite episodes, "All Our Yesterdays".*

From left to right: Leonard Nimoy, General Scott, William Shatner, Gene Roddenberry and Great Bird of the Movie Galaxy, Harve Bennett (photo courtesy Anderson Archives).

HARVE BENNETT
"The Gene L. Coon of the Movies"

Harve Bennett seemed an unlikely choice to assume the mantle of leadership of the *Star Trek* universe; a reign that had lasted nearly a decade. After all, Bennett was best known as a television producer who, despite an array of impressive credits including *The Mod Squad*, the Emmy Award winning miniseries *A Woman Called Golda* and *The Jesse Owens Story*, had little experience producing features. In fact, his only previous trek in the science-fiction genre was as an Executive Producer of *The Six Million Dollar Man* in the mid-70's.

In addition, Bennett, who had worked for the *Sun Times* in Chicago, CBS-TV, ABC-TV and as an executive pro- ducer/writer for Universal, was also executive producer of *Rich Man, Poor Man* and *From Here to Eternity*, both of which helped launch the miniseries as a viable programming entity in the mid-70's. And it was the same Harve Bennett who Paramount Pictures turned to after the debacle of *Star Trek: The Motion Picture* and after having rejected overtures from Gene Roddenberry to produce a follow-up *Trek* picture in which the crew of

the Enterprise goes back in time and inadvertently prevents the assassination of John F. Kennedy (all of which results in Spock's being forced to kill the President. Oliver Stone still swears it was Leonard Nimoy who killed Kennedy).

After failing to elicit interest by the networks in other science-fiction projects such as *Genesis II* and *The Questor Tapes*, Roddenberry returned to *Star Trek* in the mid-70's hoping to revive it first as a low-budget movie, then an aborted television series and, finally, as the sprawling big budget feature, *Star Trek: The Motion Picture.*

"They did *Star Trek I* and it was not successful," says William Shatner. "It was only because of Paramount's belief that there must be some box-office somewhere around that they hired Harve Bennett, who again set the tone of the way the subsequent movies were going to go, and Gene was again in the background position of offering advice, but not involved in the creative process."

Said Bennett shortly before Roddenberry's death, "I had very little to do with Roddenberry on the movies. I was fortunate enough to have a mandate from Paramount to not pay any attention to him, which is easier said than done because he is the master manipulator of a large and loyal following. It's

like the Bolshevik party, it isn't that there were so many of them, it's just that they were so smart and vociferous. He is a remarkable visionary, but a very bad supervisor of other writers. I don't want to rake muck, because it is not my nature to do that. There is a tremendous misconception about Roddenberry. I am his replacement. His vengeance, some say, is *Star Trek: The Next Generation.* He alienated some really creative people who were doing the very best to make his show a hit. That's the summation of what my perspective is.

"Credit for the success of the show of course goes to Gene Roddenberry," added Bennett of the original *Star Trek* television series of the '60s. "There's no disputing his genius. But it also goes to Gene Coon, the hardheaded re-writer who made a lot of things work. I think of myself as the Gene Coon of the feature movies. Fandom never understood the contribution that Coon made to that which they loved in the movies, notwithstanding Roddenberry's genius. It's my gut feeling, knowing all the players and the material, that whenever the name Gene Coon is on the episode as producer, they are generally the best shows."

The name Harve Bennett attached to the *Star Trek* feature films have held a similar meaning. Harve Bennett was chosen to serve as the executive producer of *Star Trek II* because of his intelligence, his ability to articulate and his fund of general knowledge, which has been apparent since the days when, as Harvey Fischman, he was one of the original radio show "Quiz Kids" in the '40s.

"I came to Paramount with no anticipation of doing feature pictures at all," Bennett explains. "I was here to do television. But the second week I was here, I got a call from [studio president] Barry Diller. Now you have to remember that running the studio at the time was Barry Diller, who used to be my assistant at ABC, Michael Eisner, who used to be a counterpart of mine at ABC New York,

and running the entire operation was the great immigrant, Charlie Bludhorn, who built Gulf and Western and bought Paramount. Barry calls me in and says, 'Will you come to a meeting in my office?'"

At that meeting were the aforementioned executives, including Charles Bludhorn, who asked Bennett what he thought of *Star Trek: The Motion Picture.* "I decided that the truth was the only thing I could say," he reflects. "So I said, 'I thought it was boring.' He suddenly turned on Michael Eisner and said, 'See, by you, bald is sexy.'" Bennett was asked if he could produce a *Star Trek* film for less than $45 million, to which he responded in the affirmative, and was given the job. In fact he would produce the next three films for a total cost of about $45 million. It was a task he felt suited for, particularly because his background had been in television, which was the approach Paramount wanted him to take.

"The real reason for this originally was that, at the time of the industry's shakes over *Heaven's Gate* and massive spending on giant pictures, someone conceived the idea of giving this kind of film to the people whose background and training was essentially in the more cost-conscious area of television — which may be a first, as far as we know. I think they chose wisely, because they picked good storytellers and not just people who make pictures for controlled budgets. However, it was never seriously a television project. The minute the script began shaping up, it was clear to all that we had something terrific.

"The main thing that rang false about the first film was that the characters had gone 20 years and hadn't aged, which, to my way of thinking, was totally unbelievable. I felt a major element in future films would be to have the characters age and to focus on what they were going through as people as they did so. At one point, I even sat down with Shatner and told him point blank that there was a real danger in having a middle-aged Kirk running around like a

30-year-old."

Bennett began the process of selecting the storyline for the film by screening numerous episodes of the original television series. While many of them were appealing, the one that absolutely captured his imagination was "Space Seed," which introduced Khan Noonian Singh. At the time, he had asked himself, "Who is the heavy? Who is the black hat? We won't make this picture unless there is a black-hat heavy.' You know, the solution the writers and producers came up with: Khan. I had been watching the *Star Trek* episodes and I said, 'Okay, where's my heavy?' Montalban, especially now that he's become 'Mr. White Suit,' is the best heavy there ever was. Great reverse casting, and it works."

Initially, Bennett wrote a one-page outline entitled *Star Trek: The War of the Generations*, in which a new generation plans to overthrow the United Federation of Planets. Their leader turns out to be Khan, who sees this as a chance for revenge against Kirk and all that the Federation stands for. Next, he had to find someone to collaborate with to expand the premise into a screenplay. "After considering other writers," he says, "I found out that Jack Sowards, a great 'movie-of-the-week' writer, was a great *Star Trek* fan. We talked and he clearly knew more about *Star Trek* than I did, so I hired him. Jack and I went to work, and I say we went to work because the process is like this: you talk, and you rap and the responsibility is that the writer records, in whatever fashion he chooses, the fruits of the give and take of this process. His task is then to go and make it become a script. Jack made an enormous contribution to this picture."

Most notable among them was the idea of killing the Spock character as a means of enticing Leonard Nimoy to star in the film, as the star had stated he had no interest in *Star Trek II*.

"I think Spock is the most important character," admits Bennett. "I've always thought that. I think the fans

validated that in Leonard's first two years on the old series. Remember *The Man From U.N.C.L.E.*, in which the real star was David McCallum, but Robert Vaughn was the star and matinee idol? I think Bill is the centerpiece, but the thing that makes it work is this extraordinary oddball who makes the show unpredictable. I said, 'Leonard, remember *Psycho* and did you see *Dressed to Kill*?' He said yeah, and his smile got bigger and bigger. I said, 'Well, that's what we're going to do with Mr. Spock.' And he said, 'That's fantastic!' And right then and there we shook hands and that was it. Now, that was the beginning of an evolution that got so convoluted that its resemblance to the final film is, of course, a process."

Bennett was speaking of the moment in *Psycho* when the Janet Leigh character is killed — in the *middle* of the film, an unprecedented move at that. The hope was to capture the *Star Trek* audience in the same manner by killing off Spock in an unexpected way in the midst of telling the story. Unfortunately, word of this leaked out (according to Bennett, by Roddenberry) and members of fandom took to a letter-writing campaign that unleashed all their fury. As a result, the death continued to be pushed off until it occurred near the end of the film. After Sowards handed in his draft, Bennett let Samuel Peeples (who had written *Star Trek*'s second pilot, "Where No Man Has Gone Before") take a swing at the story, and then did a rewrite of his own.

"Enter Nick Meyer," he smiles. "When I saw *The Seven Percent Solution*, I was so impressed with the screenplay that I went out and read the book, and I was even more impressed with the book. Nick read my rewrite of Sowards and Peeples and said, 'This has promise. What if...' He signed on and said, 'You write it, and I'll rewrite you....'"

The mix was a great success, resulting in a critically acclaimed film that restored some much-needed luster to the starship Enterprise. Needless to

say, Paramount Pictures was pleased to bankroll *Star Trek III: The Search for Spock*, and Bennett was just as eager to produce. Leonard Nimoy signed on as director, and he began fleshing out the story with Bennett.

"When the draft of the piece was finished and Leonard and I were both very happy with it, we sent it to Bill," recalls Bennett. "He called and said, 'I'd like to have a meeting.' So we came over on a Sunday morning to Bill's house and there was Bill's lawyer, his agent, and one guy who kept his hands over his chest. I thought maybe he was from *T.J. Hooker*, the stunt guy or something. Very intimidating. And he said, 'Are you happy with this script?' I said, 'Yeah, we like it a lot.' Leonard said, 'Promising, very promising.' Bill said, 'Well, I just can't do that.' The complaint was that there wasn't enough of him in the material. That he was standing by, that he wasn't leading. We said, 'Let's talk about it.' There was merit in much of what he said. He said, 'Oh, good. You other guys can leave now.' And the lawyer and the agent left and the gunsel left. And we had five hours of intense conversation.

"You have to understand," he continues, "that is not quite as selfish as it seems. This is their career. It's like a quarterback saying, 'Who's going to be kicking for me?' The actor says, 'How am I going to come off? Are they going to like me? Are they going to love me so that I can make the next picture?' Being a star over a long period of time is a nerve-wracking affair. So that's where his thrust was and we had neglected to protect our star. The compromises that came out of that — some of them were funny. Bill said, 'I think I should be in the scene where Bones talks to Spock.' We said no. 'You see, that's a very lovely scene and I should be there. Why am I not there?' We said, 'Well, Bill, it feels like one of those moments when two guys are joined together and Bones has not really had his moment.' On that one he said, 'Why don't we shoot it both ways?' Then

The cover of Vonda N. McIntyre's novelization of Star Trek III: The Search For Spock, which was based on Bennett's screenplay (cover courtesy Science Fiction Book Club).

dor, a great talent and a great ego. Did you notice the last scene as the cast is surrounding Spock? Who remembers where Kirk is? By himself. He knew where his light is. This is not a fault. It's the way he is. He's a matinee idol in the traditional, historical sense of that word."

In writing the script, Bennett did 12 outlines in all, which took six months. He says the last scene in the movie is the first one he wrote. "Somewhere along the line I read a fan poem in one of the hundreds of fan magazines about *Star Trek*. It was first person Kirk. It said, 'I left you there. Why did I do that? I must come back to you, my friend.' I thought, 'That's it!' I suddenly had a thrust. It got a lot easier from that point. A great motion picture has a very similar last scene. It was almost, beat for beat, the last scene in *The Miracle Worker* by William Gibson. It is the moment in which, after the entire play, little Helen Keller is at the well with her teacher and she begins to get some understanding, and finally with her hand on her face she says, 'Water.' And the teacher says, 'Yes.'"

Contrary to popular belief, the third movie was not in mind when *The Wrath of Khan* was filmed. Bennett explains, "It would have been very easy to say that at the conclusion of *Star Trek II* that all the things we have done to modify the film's ending to be ambiguous about the death of Spock were carefully designed and that the plot for *Star Trek III* was already in my mind. Not true. All of that, like most decisions I have ever made, are done in a flurry of intuitions and sometimes pressure of time. The last weeks of *Star Trek II* were frenetic because of an organized campaign: Don't Kill Spock! And the studio panicked that this would affect the box office. Nick Meyer was steadfastly going to walk on the picture. He said that we said we would kill him, so we're going to kill him. Leonard was getting threatening letters. This was a serious thing and I felt that the compromise we had to make, with Nick's blessing, reluctant though that was, was that we made an

he said, 'Now Bones gets to go up there with the priestess, don't you think I should be up there and do something that makes it all happen?' We said no. He said, 'Well, maybe that's too much.' I said, 'Bill, I'll tell you what you are. You are a quarterback who wants to call the play, run back, throw the pass, catch the pass, score the touchdown and lead the cheers.' He hugged me and said, 'You're right. I can't help it.' Bill is a Shakespearean actor. It shows in everything, even on *Hooker*. He has to wind up to draw a gun. And Bill has, in can-

ambiguity out of the ending by saying, 'There are always possibilities.' We said, 'Who knows with Vulcans?'

"I have said once or twice at a few *Star Trek* gatherings I have gone to that I have always tried to be fair. I have a great affection for these people, even when they're so proprietary that they come over and tell you that you can't do it your way, you have to do it my way. But these people keep that franchise. It is a business. They keep it healthy and strong. They are its lifeblood. So you do not disregard that. To be fair, you've got to give clues and those were the clues we dropped. On *Star Trek III*, I said, 'Look, it's got to be faster and more efficient.' So I was the sole writer, which was the easiest writing job I ever had. The reason for that is, since it was so direct a continuation of *Star Trek II*, the outline was already in place. I knew exactly what I had to do and I did it in six weeks.

"I had to make a story out of the following 'givens': One, there is a casket on a planet that has been created by the reformation of life forces and life has been created from death. Two, 'There are always possibilities.' Three, before he died, Spock said, 'Remember.' Remember what? The puzzle was solved so easily that I think 17 other people could have written the script. If you end a film with a Genesis device that can, in one 'poof,' create life where there was lifelessness, you have created an enormous story device that cannot be ignored. Now the fans would be justified in saying, 'Well, why not just create a planet as a plot solution?' Or, 'What would happen if the Klingons got hold of this? They wouldn't use it to make a planet, they would destroy a planet.' Therefore, the final puzzle-solving was the denial of the validity of the Genesis device. That was — as 'The Lord Giveth, the Lord taketh away' — necessary, or we would have expanded the borders of *Star Trek*, even subliminally, that it would have had the same impact the A-Bomb had on the 20th Century, so as to

make conventional things no longer viable. That's fine, but who needs to restructure *Star Trek* on that basis?"

Writing the script, he ran into other problems set up in the last film. First, there was Saavik. The actress who portrayed her, Kirstie Alley, was unable to work out negotiations with Paramount. "We didn't want to cut [her] scenes," Bennett says, "so we decided to recast the character and keep the part. How did we fare putting Robin Curtis in where Kirstie Alley had gone before? About even." Another character not written into *The Search for Spock*, and quite obviously missing, was Carol Marcus.

Bennett details, "She was the fifth member of a four-man relay team. She was the extraneous character. She was in the story outline. I thought it might be fun to have her relating to David and have something going with Saavik. But then protomatter came up. Then something happened: Did Carol know? If Carol knows about protomatter, everything about David making a mistake — cheating, being responsible — doesn't wash. Then it's not David's ambition, it's mother and son in some kind of Oedipal whim to cheat the world together. And they don't tell Kirk, which is very out of character. Also, then I would have had to kill them both.

"Writer's problem. Answer: Don't get Carol involved. Get her out of this issue. David doing it without his mother's knowledge enriches it for me. And his father certainly doesn't know. If you think it's tough answering that, think of how it was when I tried to explain it to Bibi Besch. She was deeply upset. She cried. She thought it was a rejection of her talent. Bibi's a very adult actress, so you can understand that may sound strange to you, but it's not. She thought she must have done something wrong. But I got a lovely letter from Bibi after the picture opened. It said, 'I've seen the picture. Now I understand. You were right. I hope you can find a place for me in one of the other films.'"

Two other major script deci-

sions, killing David and destroying the Enterprise, were rather easy for Bennett. He believes in a balance. If you get something, you have to pay for it. Kirk gets Spock back, but at what cost? He loses two very major things along the way. Is it worth it? That makes for a good script, and lots of emotion and tension.

"I confess to being old fashioned," Bennett continues. "There is in my vision such a thing as ultimate retribution. The reason David dies, structurally, is because he's messed with mother nature. He allowed himself to bend the rules at the wrong time, in the wrong place. He's there on that planet for only that reason. The whole story dates back to David putting protomatter in the matrix. The death of Spock — everything — rests on his shoulders if you want to blame him for it. Also, we did not feel that the character of David was a viable character upon which to build further stories. We didn't set out to kill him. We didn't even set out to use him, but when I got to the crisis and came up with the idea, 'I'm going to kill one of them,' then, with an eye to plot it, [it] became obvious which one I would have to kill, because it was the one I didn't need. I had no idea what the future of Saavik might be. Clearly, I couldn't kill Spock a second time or the picture would be over, and David was extraneous then. It wasn't the actor's fault so much as the character just didn't make it. It was like the [Decker] character in the first movie: it was a good try, and it is very interesting to see the number of tries to bring 'new blood' into 'the family.' It's hard, and I don't know the answer to that. I've given up trying. I have no desire to bring in new commanders and all that stuff. I don't think the fans want it, particularly."

One of the secondary themes of the film, as Bennett has noted, is not to mess with mother nature. The concept of the Genesis device was too massive to deal with in the *Trek* universe for future stories. It had to be destroyed.

"Gene Roddenberry said, 'Let's try protomatter.' It became a tool for me to solve the problem," he explains, "which is the interjection of a human value system in an otherwise antiseptic, impossible box — the perfect scientist. The value system is ambition. That interested me. It all snapped together. Kirk changed the computer on the Kobayashi Maru scenario before *Star Trek II*. His son says to him, 'You've cheated.' His father says, 'I changed the rules.' Well, it turns out that the kettle was calling the pot black. David says it at a time when he knows he's changed the rules."

The loss of the Enterprise was the big risk in the script — the big surprise — though word of it leaked to the fans and campaigns, not unlike the ones to save Spock, were begun to save the Enterprise from its demise. Admits Bennett, "The death of the Enterprise caused serious ripples. The death of David did not. That's backwards for me. How could you destroy the Enterprise is a burden I take full responsibility for. I will justify it to the end and once again I think I have been playing fair. My choice was a humanistic choice. It began as a writer's problem. Usually it happens when you reach a sticky point. I have a whole justification for it. Oliver Hazard Perry of the U.S. Navy scuttled the Niagra at the battle of Lake Erie and won the battle as a result and took command. Perry happens to be one of James T. Kirk's great heroes. Actually, there is a model of the Niagra in Kirk's quarters for those who love *Star Trek* trivia. So, the scuttling of the ship to achieve the greater good is a tactic. Also, with the death of his son and the hopelessness of the situation, it seemed like the right solution, and also because in the series there had been one notable false countdown.

"There are two elements in the making of a story whether it's on film or not. Suspense and surprise. You're either hoping a character will do something or he does something that you didn't expect. The sure knowledge of the audience saying, 'Oh, no, they're not going to do that,' and the sheer surprise of saying, 'Oh, yes we are.' There are many

other moments in the film which were intended to be one or the other. The death of David is one clear example of surprise, because you're playing off the clichés of the expected. One of the joys of motion picture writing as opposed to television is that you have full use of those two ranges. In television the surprise is limited, and suspense is limited to the fact that the episode must end with the hero surviving."

Star Trek III completed production on schedule and under budget, and went on to a success that rivaled that of *The Wrath of Khan*. "For me," Bennett reflects, "this movie is about honor and friendship and decency and values higher than the complex value system we have inherited since the atomic age. It's a return to innocence."

Considering the success of the film, it's came as no surprise to anyone that Paramount was interested in once again dipping back into the well with a fourth film that would round out an unofficial "*Star Trek* Trilogy."

"In moving through the trilogy," Bennett states, "I confess that every one of the major tricks I learned in television, I used. I'm out of tricks now....[I knew I had to] find another one, because we [had] now completed a trilogy and we have to go where no man has gone before [in *Star Trek V*]. When you go where no man has gone before, you have to build things and then it starts getting expensive. Here are the three tricks of the trilogy: *Star Trek II*, in television we call that the 'bottle show.' The 'bottle show' in television takes place in an elevator that's hopefully trapped between two floors. Or it takes place in a mine shaft where people are desperately trying to save you and you have to stay down there and talk a lot. Sixty-five percent of the film was on the Enterprise bridge in one incarnation or another. It was also the Reliant bridge. And it was also part of the science station. We used the set for 65 percent of the movie and that is an incomparable savings in terms of time, dollars and moves. We'd shoot a

scene, move the people out, repaint it, and it would now be the Reliant.

"*Star Trek III* was the classic television 'the leading man loses his memory' show. I did that on *Mod Squad, Six Million Dollar Man, Bionic Woman*, and you usually do it when your leading actor is exhausted or needs a rest. He's in a coma-like state. In *Star Trek III*, we had a man who was directing the movie, and who had never directed a feature before, and we felt that to act and so forth would kill him. We had our choice of how to utilize that asset, and what we did was we spent most of our money building one great set, the Genesis planet, and the story became let's find him while he directs. [On *Star Trek IV* we decided to use] local location. We've gotta add some size to this picture, so what do we do? We go out. How do you go out in the 23rd Century? You back to the 20th Century."

Together Bennett and returning director Nimoy concocted a tale in which Kirk leads his team back through time to bring a pair of humpback whales into the future so that they can communicate with an alien probe and stop the potential destruction of Earth. While searching for a writer, the film — ultimately to be subtitled *The Voyage Home* — was struck with an interesting dilemma. Eddie Murphy, a golden boy at Paramount at the time, had been pretty vocal in the fact that he loved *Star Trek* and would be very interested in co-starring in the new film.

"Now the meeting with Eddie Murphy was a little bizarre," says Bennett. "He had a separate meeting with Leonard. Leonard said, 'He's a little strange in a room.' So he came in with two thugs, good looking thugs, and they were all in black leather. [We] told Eddie this story and he thought about it for a while and he said, 'It's good. Let me see a script,' and he walked out. We sat there and thought, 'Wouldn't it be terrific to have Eddie in this movie?' Later, the studio started getting very anxious for a very good reason. Here you have a franchise

STARLOG PRESS 0-931064-88-0 K48271 $5.95 U.S.

OFFICIAL MOVIE SPECIAL
The making of this amazing voyage!
Includes eight spectacular STAR TREK posters!

DELUXE EDITION

This magazine, published by Starlog Press, heralded the release of the fourth film in the series, **The Voyage Home.**

called *Star Trek* and it performs in a certain wonderful way. Here you have a franchise called Eddie Murphy and it performs in an even bigger way. Why not take them together and form one franchise? Bad economics because you are probably diminishing by compositing. So the studio was resistant to it, but Eddie has a certain amount of clout and he said that he hadn't decided whether

he wanted to do it or not and so much of the development of the story was with the very distinct possibility that Eddie Murphy was in it."

The search for a scenarist continued until Bennett found what felt like the perfect writing duo. "We went through every writer we could think of," he recalls. "We finally found Steve Meerson and Peter Krikes, whose work

was highly regarded. Nothing came of it. Some of that, in fairness to them, was because we had saddled them with what appeared to be a male character that we thought was going to be Eddie Murphy at one time. Then when Eddie fell out, we had to readjust the script. But, by then, it had turned to paste, it just didn't work."

When Murphy did pull out to do *The Golden Child*, one of Bennett's first creative decisions was to alter the Murphy character into a female marine biologist, who could also serve as Kirk's love interest. "I remember saying, 'Well, I know it's corny, but it would be better if it was a woman. Kirk hasn't had a woman to play to, which he does so wonderfully. The whole series is the woman of the week. Remember that whale special we saw where the girl was bidding adieu to the whales who had to leave Marineland because the female was pregnant and they could not keep them and they had to send them back to the sea and she was bereft? Remember that character? That's the lady,' and Leonard thought that was great. So, now we're getting down to where we've got a movie to make and a whole new script to write. That's when we were fortunate enough to find that Nicholas Meyer was available.

"Nick and I had written the final script of *Star Trek II* in 10 days. This one we wrote in about 20, and it was very simple to do it that way because I took act one and act three and Nick took act two. Now if you think about that in structural terms, I got us into the dilemma and time travel, he carried us through San Francisco, and I got us back. That was like breathing for me because it's pure *Star Trek*, and it was like breathing for him because his irreverence is what really makes the fun. Then we swapped pages and I rewrote him a little bit and he rewrote me a little bit and we put it all together and had a script. Nick always said, 'You know the problem with this script is you've got five endings.' And he was right, we did have five endings. He said, 'Why don't you have the whales save the Earth? That's the end of the picture.' No, I said, that's the end of the picture for the hoped for extended audience who's never seen *Star Trek* before. But for people who have seen *Star Trek* before, we have a trilogy to complete. So we've gotta get them back, get them off the hook and give them the Enterprise back. We've got to do that, so that when we finish this picture, we have brought the franchise back to square one and it can go anywhere it wants to go. That's only fair. Besides, that's what the fans want.' So that's what we did. We kept every ending."

For his part, Bennett wanted *Star Trek IV* to be his final voyage aboard the starship Enterprise. But William Shatner, whose contract guaranteed he would serve as the next film's director and creator of its story, had an extremely long and intense meeting with Bennett, and they ultimately decided to work together. Upon coming aboard, Bennett's major problem was that he didn't like the basic thrust of the story, which basically had the Enterprise encountering God.

"I had not wanted to do *Star Trek V*," he reiterates, noting that when he had been told of Shatner's story approval on the film, he said, "'That's a terrible situation,' especially when I heard the story he wanted to do. The struggle with *Star Trek V* was to take a talented and wonderful man and try to dissuade him from doing the story he wanted to do, at which we did not succeed. If the logline in *TV Guide* does not interest you, then it's a pretty good indication that the premise of the story is not interesting. The log line of *Star Trek V* is, 'Tonight on *Star Trek*, the crew goes to find God.' If you saw that in an episode of anything, you'd say that's a hoot, isn't it? No one is going to find God because that's like finding the fountain of youth, which was, incidentally, Shatner's back-up story. It's like [screenwriter David] Loughery said in *Starlog*, it's a passive premise. It's a premise that the chore became to make the trip as interesting as possible and to that extent we succeed-

ed. To the extent that it was real good until the moment when the inevitable truth poked its head out and said, 'Hey, this isn't really God,' and everyone said we knew that all the time, but we were having a good time up until then. I don't think it failed, [yet] $65 million in gross can be considered a failure. It did 25% less business than the other movies, excluding *Star Trek IV*, which was a phenomenon because it reached beyond the cult.

"Basically, I was called in to control Bill's appetites. They were extravagant because he didn't know anything. He had spent all those years in front of the camera, and believed because he had directed *T.J. Hooker* and Leonard had done it, he could too. Bill would come in and present a concept and he thought he was discovering the wheel. It's funny how first-time directors try to be pioneers in the craft." P i o n e e r Shatner was taken to task by the critics, and the pre-release opinion of what to expect was not enhanced by reports of his going in for reshooting after the film had wrapped, and word that the special effects, which had previously been handled by George Lucas' ILM, were being botched by Bran Ferran.

"I would say we did some optical reshooting," Bennett relates. "We did do a day and a half. Bill directed to tie certain things together compared to hundreds of other movies that go out and shoot five weeks and millions of dollars. You're speaking about a day and a half of pick-up shots. There was an absence of understanding with the Klingons. There was no understanding about why the guy [Klaa] apologizes to Kirk. That was necessary because of the evolution of the Klingon relationship in *The Next Generation*. It was meant to be the beginning of détente, which is an important element in *VI*.

"The show that required patching was *Star Trek II*, [which] required three or four days of reshoot because the original was so hardlined about the death of Spock that it was perceived as

a downer by our first previews, and Nick was rather adamant that it stay that way. The studio and I felt that we ought to leave the picture with all the possibilities of science-fiction bubbling in people's minds. The key phrase that governed that reshoot, and Nick directed it, he did not resist, was that there are always possibilities, and the insertion of 'remember,' which rather blatantly said 'I might be back.' These are tools of the trade. I'm the guy who brought the Bionic Woman back to life after she was dead, dead, dead, so I'm an old hand at how you can change course if everybody wants you to. In fact, it would be fair to say that no matter how big the stories of *Star Trek*, the fact remains it is still a series on the big screen or the small screen. It is a continuing adventure with the same characters and has the matrix and nature of a television series, which is that the characters have to keep coming back and you have to keep making them fresh by exploring new avenues of their lives. That's the tough part of making series-oriented material."

As for the effects, "You should have seen ILM's tests for God. They were silly. We went with the creative judgment that Bran had a more vigorous attack to help us sell the illusions and it was a picture as discussed that needed fancy footwork. In addition to that, it is only correct to note that by the time we were ready to start, ILM was overcrowded. We would have been the fourth or fifth major picture and we would have received at their hands, not withstanding our relationships, the 'D' team instead of the 'A' team. That was an important consideration. All the people we had worked with were booked."

Following the release of *Star Trek V*, Bennett decided to head back in time himself, returning to the 20th century and electing not to participate with the sixth film in the series, *The Undiscovered Country*. "I'm sure glad that it's not my movie," he smiles. "I would not want a movie of mine to be sold as, 'Gee, guys, come to the funeral.'

I think that's a cheat. Come say goodbye to these folks. I'm the guy who killed Spock and brought him back, so I can't be cynical. I also think there has been an erosion and a conversion. of the *Star Trek* cult that first tended to be resistive to *The Next Generation* and then, as the show improved and the habit accrued, they were after getting fresh material as opposed to reruns and the inevitable wait for movies. I think they became very interested in [*Next Generation*] and it became a better show. You can see in all the publications where the letter ratio [stating] 'It's not as good as the old show' began to shift; where the minority opinion is that the original characters were more interesting, and the majority opinion was, 'Hey, let's get on with it.'

"In my opinion," he elaborates, "and marketing never agreed with me, I said, 'Guys, you don't understand. There are so many hours in a *Star Trek* fan's life. Where the cult was used to having turkey dinner every two years and old turkey sandwiches in between, now you've given them fresh turkey sandwiches every Saturday and Sunday, big movie nights.' I know from a lot of mail I've received that people felt about *Star Trek V* that they could maybe see it next week because they didn't want to miss this week's *Next Generation*. After all, turkey is turkey. I think the appetite for the *Star Trek* movies was seriously impacted by the success of the series. Not destroyed, just kind of subdivided and the feeding frenzy that we experienced on *II*, *III* and *IV* did not exist on *V*, even if it had been a better movie."

What could have been one of Bennett's most important contribution to the *Trek* mythos was *Starfleet Academy*, an aborted theatrical prequel to the original series. In a sense, it would have introduced Kirk, Spock and McCoy to each other and the audience.

Starfleet Academy chronicled the story of a young James T. Kirk, a Spock who is estranged from his parents and becomes the first Vulcan to attend Starfleet Academy, and Leonard McCoy,

a 30 year old doctor who attends the Academy after having pulled the plug on his terminally ill father and is searching for meaning in his life. Michael Curtiz' 1940 film, *The Santa Fe Trail*, served as an inspiration for what Bennett envisioned as the classic triumvirate's first trek. The film which could have been made, according to Bennett, for $27 million, would also have avoided the hefty baggage of Shatner and Nimoy's multi-million dollar salaries along with Kelley's take-home of nearly a half a million dollars, and the $125,000 paychecks the supporting players pocketed.

For Bennett, who had spent a decade living with *Star Trek, Starfleet Academy* was not to be. The rejection of the project was a big disappointment for the veteran producer, who envisioned the film as his freshman directorial effort.

"It meant a lot to me because I came out of UCLA film school wanting to be a director and other winds blew me to other ports," admits Bennett. "It was a desire of mine to direct and it was accepted by the studio and, the fact is, part of the deal was for us to do a *Star Trek VII* with the original cast after *Starfleet Academy*."

But once word leaked out about the project, support was marshaled against the film and it was vociferously denounced on the convention circuit by members of the supporting cast as well as *Star Trek* creator Gene Roddenberry. Letters began to pour into Paramount decrying the planned featured as heresy.

"There was pressure from a lot of people not to do this," Bennett says. "Not the least of whom was Roddenberry. I don't think there was any question that the self-interest of the supporting cast was not served by it. Their jobs and their livelihoods were jeopardized. You have to understand there's good news and bad news for these people. They are the principal bearers of the *Star Trek* curse. The good news is everybody loves them, and the bad

news is they can't work anywhere else. [But] it was only going to be postponed. There was an equally vigorous *Star Trek VII* that came back with the original cast like farmer's rotate their soil. The intention was to reignite the passion of the franchise by saying you never knew this story. Everyone knows how Superman came to Earth, but no one has ever done the obvious. How did these three characters [Kirk, Spock and McCoy] come to be together? The only one I'm really furious at is Jimmy Doohan, [who] said I was fired. I can't abide lies. My term was up. I was offered $1.5 million to do *Star Trek VI*, and I said, 'Thanks. I don't wish to do that. I want to do the *Academy*.'

"I had wanted to direct, but had no intention of directing the regular cast. That wouldn't have been fun. I'm at an age and an achievement level where all I'm concerned about is doing stuff that I love. I would have loved to have done the *Academy*. The deal was cut for me to direct it if it went forward. The fact is that not going forward coincided with the end of my term. I was then presented with the choice of doing a *Star Trek VI* in 11 months. I didn't want to do a conventional one and I didn't believe I could do it in that time. The fact that they have done it in a little more than that is a tribute to all my buddies, and they are good buddies. Nicholas Meyer is the fastest writer in the world, Ralph Winter is the most ethical and perfect producer of special effects movies anywhere, and one of the nicest men I've ever known. It wasn't easy to walk away from that, but if your heart is not in something and you've earned the right not to have to do things that cause you pain, then you don't do them.

"My last words to [Frank] Mancuso before he was asked to leave [by the then recently installed head of Paramount, Stanley Jaffe] was if it was a question of anyone's concerns about my directing, I'd back off on that," points out Bennett. "They then offered me *Star Trek VI* and gave me a pay or play commitment to direct and produce *Starfleet*

Academy afterwards. My position was, and I think it was correct, that they would pay me to do *VI* and make the movie — which would have been a real big, fat check for me — and never make *Starfleet Academy.* To be paid off because the movie I might have done, which is being done by others, would close the franchise was not my intention. I had a life, it's not like I hadn't done anything else before *Star Trek.*

"*Starfleet Academy,* like *Star Trek IV,* would have reached beyond the cult. It would have interested people who had never seen a *Star Trek* film. It did not exclude the regulars, but it simply said, if you don't understand what it's all about, come see how it all began."

For his part, Bennett came to see how it all ended. "I saw it because it was my family and my friends," he explains. "The picture for me was okay. It validated my decision to leave, not because it was bad or because it was a failure, but because it was the third day of turkey soup after Thanksgiving, and that was what I feared. I was there and said I've already done this banquet so many times — what are we going to serve the guests today? The answer is three day old turkey soup. If you never had it before or love it to death, you're going to love the picture."

For Bennett, the film's biggest flaws were lapses in the rigorous internal logic of the *Star Trek* universe. "The only serious problem that I would have never allowed if I were king," he says, "was that for the first time in the *Star Trek* movies they violated the rules of some of the characters. They did not behave in character and the reason for that is Nick always wanted to do that and I was always there to say no. That's my personal response and he knows that. I would have never had Spock do some of the things he did in that movie and I would have never allowed Shatner to be in drag and fight with himself and to do all that stuff, because those things in the series did not appeal to me. It was like, 'Look at

Like Enterprise: The First Adventure, *Bennett's* Starfleet Academy *would have been a prequel to the original series (photo courtesy Science Fiction Book Club).*

me, I'm Bill Shatner.' So there was Spock's human behavior, narcissism by Kirk.

"The final thing," he continues, "and Nick surprised me on this, is that in *Star Trek II* we got away with quoting *Moby Dick* and *A Tale of Two Cities* because it worked. Khan never quoted *Moby Dick* in the original, but it worked

and Nick had a blinding vision that this was like *Moby Dick* and the whole picture became a metaphor and it was a very good metaphor. It was kind of theatrical. But Christopher Plummer plumbing the depths of Shakespeare and coming up with 'to be or not to be' because he ran out of other quotes, came to me like a punching bag and that pulled me out of the picture."

Upon leaving the *Star Trek* universe, Bennett decided he would spend some time exploring the world of computers when, much to his surprise, a series of writing assignments came his way. One of them, *Crashlanding: The Story of Flight 232* (originally titled *A Thousand Heroes*), was the story of the crashlanding of a jetliner in a cornfield in Sioux City, Iowa. The TV film starred James Coburn, Richard Thomas and Charlton Heston.

"It was not an airplane crash story but a story about an incredible town effort," says Bennett. "I began to realize after writing it that I like to write, this is what I want to do now. I don't have to worry about actors' egos and craziness and schedules. Then I got a call from a guy who had given me the most creative freedom and support I could ever want. He was the guy who was my blocking back instead of my supervisor who had run Paramount television when I went there in 1980. It's where I had gone to do television and suddenly I was making feature pictures."

That "guy" was Gary Nardino, the former Paramount executive who had worked with Bennett on the second and third *Star Trek* films. He was informed by Nardino that the organization that had produced *A Woman Called Golda*, the Consortium, wanted to produce a television series. Among the lures that attracted Bennett to the project was the fact that Warner Bros. was committed to producing an entire year of 22 episodes as opposed to a traditional network order which only guarantees 13 episodes or, with the advent of the limited series, sometimes as little as six episodes.

"Need I tell you what that means in the television series business?" asks Bennett rhetorically. "What it means to the filmmaker is time to think and economize effectively, to shoot things in their proper place and order, and time to cast properly. All those good things instead of what are we shooting

Monday, which is a nightmare I would never go back to again. So I asked Gary what he wanted me to do and he said, 'Give us a concept and write the pilot.'"

Based on an idea hatched by Grant Rosenberg and refined by the new partnership, Bennett drafted a presentation to the Consortium in which a detective from the future comes back into the 20th century to pursue criminals who have escaped from his time period.

"I did the presentation which we then presented to the Consortium, which is now the Prime Time Network," says Bennett. "They are the owners of the stations and they're sitting in a boardroom and we walk in. I knew five or six of them, so when you walk into a room like that it's a lot nicer than walking into a network office and saying hi to a 23-year-old kid who says, 'What have you done?' All of a sudden, I'm dealing with people who know who I am or at least know what I'm capable of doing. It was a verbal pitch, I don't think they even opened their written presentation. Basically speaking, they liked the idea enormously."

In the two-hour premiere, police officer Darien Lambert (Dale Midkiff) discovers that a brilliant physicist, Mor Sambi (Peter Donat), is sending criminals back in time to the 20th century to elude capture. When Darien tracks him down, Sambi returns himself to the 20th century and is pursed by Lambert.

Not surprisingly, one of the aspects of *Time Trax* which held fascination for Bennett was the fish out of water premise, in which a man from the future would find himself trying to cope with contemporary society. It was a similar premise that had resulted in his most critically and financially rewarding *Star Trek* feature, *The Voyage Home*.

"The reason I shined to this premise was I had so much fun on *Star Trek IV*," he concedes. "The reason it was a success was because all of us were having a ball with the implications of bringing someone back who knows what's going to happen and won't tell and at the same time can't drive a stick-

shift car. In *Star Trek IV* there's a line that Nick Meyer wrote, and silly little things stick out as being your favorite, where Kirk and Spock get on a bus and the door opens and they get off the bus. Spock says, 'What is it, exact change?' and they don't know. That's the fun side of this picture."

In addition to the comedic attraction that *Time Trax* offered Bennett, he believes that *Star Trek*'s influence can be felt in another way as well. "What made *Star Trek IV* subliminally very successful is we live in a time that's very troubled, and this has been true for all times. It just seems ours is more troubled," Bennett emphasizes. "It's comforting to know things we're worrying about will be solved, and the world will be a better place. Most science-fiction of the past up until *Star Trek* was very pessimistic. *Blade Runner* is a classic bleak science fiction picture and there were many others. *Star Trek* came along and is a major television series and it says it's going to be great in the 23rd century. That's why I did *Star Trek* because I think that's true. I think Rick Berman, who does *Next Generation*, thinks that's true.

"I can remember when I was a kid during World War II. It was, 'How much worse can it be?' It's always how much worse can it be. The future always looks troubled, so it's very comforting to know that 200 years from now it's going to be okay. But it's not a free lunch, you have to worry first in order to solve the problems. My final analysis of it is here's a guy who left a very good world that your grandchildren are going to live in, because he has an ethical and personal need to catch bad guys. He is a marshall, he's a loner in a strange land trying to find people who have transgressed. Then he becomes, in most cases even though he doesn't wish to be, a kind of judge and jury. He becomes Roy Bean because he may walk into circumstances where the situation has altered dramatically for better or worse."

When it entered the first-run syndication sweepstakes, *Time Trax*'s pri-

Dale Midkiff portrayed future police officer Darien Lambert, who pursues criminals that have escaped into our time period, in the Bennett produced Time Trax (photo copyright ©1993 Warner Bros Television Distribution).

mary competition was Paramount's *Star Trek*. Since its premiere, the market has grown increasingly crowded with such genre programming as *RoboCop: The Series*, *Babylon 5*, *Kung Fu: The Legend Continues* and *Star Trek: Deep Space Nine*, *Forever Knight* and *Star Trek: Voyager*. As they say, *something* had to give. Unfortunately, it was *Time Trax*, which was canceled at the completion of its second season. Although clearly disappointed, Great Bird Harve Bennett remains philosophical.

"It's not like I haven't done anything else," he notes wryly. "The *Star Trek* curse is something that the poor supporting actors have to live with, but I don't. While I was doing *Star Trek*, I won an Emmy, I won a NAACP Image Award. I had a lot more fun doing *A Woman Called Golda* with a great 20th Century actress than doing any *Star Trek*.

"But," he admits matter of factly, "I'm not remembered for that because *Star Trek* is what it is. It's a pop phenomenon."

NICHOLAS MEYER
"Trek After Trek"

Despite unleashing Victorian serial killer Jack the Ripper on modern day San Francisco in *Time After Time* and subsequently destroying the world in *The Day After*, it seems likely that director Nicholas Meyer will be remembered primarily as the man who saved *Star Trek*....twice. Not bad for a guy who became fascinated with the idea of "telling stories" when he was five years old.

The fact that *Star Trek* needed saving at all is the ultimate irony. The show, which had been canceled in 1969 due to low ratings, had engendered a fervent following which had given birth to the animated series, an aborted '70s television revival and then —in the post-*Star Wars* era where science-fiction was equated with mega box-office — a $44 million big budget silver screen voyage, *Star Trek: The Motion Picture*. Yet despite it's nearly $175 million world-wide gross, *Trek* was considered a failure. Its cost overruns and scathing critical reception seemed to preclude the possibility of another Enterprise voyage.

Yet Paramount realized the golden goose that was *Star Trek* still had a few eggs to lay, some of which *could* be golden. However, this time they were intent on reigning in costs. This process began when they brought in an experienced producer, Harve Bennett, who ultimately guided the motion picture series through four missions, and was intelligent enough to hire Nicholas Meyer as director. The production was being handled by the company's television division, less anyone doubted the studio's determination to keep costs low.

"I chiefly see myself as a story-teller," reflects the director. "I liked to tell stories, I liked to hear stories. My daddy used to read me stories at bedtime, and round about that time I started making them up and I've been making them up ever since."

Meyer's career in show business began in Captain Kirk's old (or future) stomping ground, Iowa. The fledgling storyteller sharpened his skills in play-wrighting and screenwriting by taking classes at the University of Iowa. Upon matriculating, his choice was to go back east to Manhattan — which is where Meyer is from — or head west to Hollywood.

"I was frightened," he admits, having realized that many young and overly optimistic writers have headed west in the hopes of making it in Tinseltown, only to realize that dreams didn't always become reality in la-la land. Meyer, who didn't have family connections or friends, realized the odds were against him. "I didn't know a soul. Also, if you live in Manhattan you'll never hear anything good about Los Angeles for the simple reason that people who don't like it go back to Manhattan, shake their heads and say, 'How awful.' All you were going to meet in Manhattan were the California rejects."

Meyer-the-reject went back to Manhattan, and became an associate publicist for Paramount Pictures, where he had to translate press releases filled with words like boffo and grosses "into English" from "Hollywoodese so they could be read by civilians." Nine months later, Meyer became unit publicist for the film *Love Story*. He was present for the entire production, while continuing to write original screenplays. From there he segued to the story department of Warner Brothers.

"I did that for a while and then I figured that I really had to write something that would sell so I could call myself a writer instead of someone who's always wanted to be a writer," Meyer says. "I had written novels that weren't very good so I couldn't show them, and I'd written screenplays, but I couldn't seem to get a screenplay off the ground in New York. So I thought, 'Non-fiction sells. What could I write that would be non-fiction?' The only thing I knew which was true was how they

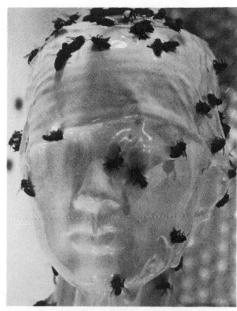

Nicholas Meyer's first produced screenplay was The Honey Factor, *ultimately released as* Invasion of the Bee Girls *(photo copyright ©1973 Sequoia Pictures).*

made *Love Story*, because I was there for the whole shoot. So I wrote a book which was originally titled *What Can You Say about a 25-Year-Old Girl Who Died? The Love Story.*"

Avon Books published the effort as *The Love Story*, paying Meyer $3,000, which he converted to traveler's checks and drove west on. Quite amazingly, he was able to secure an agent to represent him based on his unproduced screenplays, found an apartment and got to work immediately.

"Eventually little assignments began to travel in," he reflects. "The first movie I ever wrote was what they call an exploitation picture for two producers named Fred Weintraub and Paul Heller. When I wrote it, it was called *The Honey Factor*, and when it was eventually made, having been rewritten, it was called *The Invasion of the Bee Girls*." TV film critic Roger Ebert has hailed the film as one of his most enjoyable "guilty pleasures".

"It was an interesting experience," says Meyer. "I had written this script and it was really a good script. It was a script that could have played in an art house or a drive-in. It had something to say to everybody — and it really

Director-Writer Nicholas Meyer, cigar in hand as always. He is essentially credited as being the man who saved Star Trek (photo courtesy Anderson Archives).

Meyer recreated Orson Welles' War of the Worlds *radiocast in* The Night That Panicked America *(photo courtesy ABC).*

worked on a number of levels, which is the kind of thing I usually look for. Right before it started production I went to visit my parents on Christmas vacation. When I got back, Paul Heller said, 'Well, you know, we had to make a few adjustments. A script is like a blueprint, isn't it? There are a few changes that we had to make for the director and so forth.' And I said, 'Oh, yeah, I understand. Could I see the script?' He said, 'Sure,' and I looked inside and it said 'Screenplay by Nicholas Meyer and Sylvia Snebley.' I thought, 'Who is Sylvia Snebley?'"

Meyer was so disappointed that his name was even included in the rewrite that he tried to get it removed, but through Writer's Guild arbitration, Sylvia's name was removed instead. He followed with the TV movies *Judge Dee and the Haunted Monastery* and *The Night That Panicked America,* a vivid retelling of Orson Welles' famous *War of the Worlds* radio broadcast. In between there was a Writer's Guild strike and he decided to write a novel during the interim. This time, Meyer returned to one of his most passionate loves, Sherlock Holmes, and came up with a book entitled *The Seven Percent Solution.*

"I suppose I first got the idea of

doing my own Sherlock Holmes story when I was fifteen," he recalls. "Right about the same time I was trying to do that, a producer named Alexander Cohen produced something called *Baker Street on Broadway* with Fritz Weaver and Inga Svenson and Martin Gabel, which was all about Sherlock Holmes. That sort of killed it for a while, but Sherlock Holmes stayed in my mind and when I was 23 I re-read all his stories and I really loved them."

The novel was a critical and commercial success, leading Meyer to write a second Holmes adventure, *The West End Horror.* In between, *The Seven Percent Solution* was adapted to a film, featuring Nicol (*Excalibur*) Williamson as Holmes.

"I was involved in [the film] all the way," he explains. "I really liked the film a lot. My major complaint is with the editing, which I had the least to do with. We had some strong points and some weak points. The strong point, I think, from the psychological point of view, is that the film is edited beautifully. You always are where you want to be. But from the point of view of pace, it isn't very musical. It proceeds along, always at the same kind of stately way, whereas I think a drama should have more movement. By the time you reach the climax, you should be spinning off the deep end, or something should get wilder."

Meyer's next film project was *Time After Time,* his first directorial effort, in which H.G. Wells (Malcolm McDowell, who went on to star in the feature film, *Star Trek: Generations*), utilizing a time machine of his own design, pursues Jack the Ripper (David Warner) into the 20th Century, and must remove this terror from what he perceives to be a future utopian world.

"*Time After Time* is a story of good and evil," he says, "very generalized things. Wells in the movie is not so much based, except in a very superficial sense, on H.G. Wells, but is really much more representative of a civilized human being who rationally expects to

approach problems and solve them. He represents the constructive side of the human race. And the Ripper....who's interested in the Ripper anyway? Small potatoes. It's just representative of something for me in the movie, which is evil — the destructive, flip-side of that thing. It may be true that the actors and the writing make them somehow become three dimensional, but at least originally, as conceived by me, that was the way I was thinking of them as characters.

"In general," Meyer elaborates, "if you are writing about people who really lived, you owe them some dignity. I tried to make Wells' character true to him intellectually and philosophically, if not always personally, so that he was a social utopianist as a young man and at the end of his life he wanted to put on his grave, 'God Damn you all, I told you so!' In some sense, the movie tries to explain the transitional disillusionment that bridges these two extremes, so that he could literally come back to the 19th century and say, 'I've seen the future and it doesn't work.' In that sense, I think I was true to him."

Time After Time, as previously mentioned, marked Meyer's directorial

Meyer's somewhat pessimistic view of the future was given the opportunity to be captured on film in The Day After *(photo courtesy ABC).*

Based on Meyer's novel and screenplay, The Seven Per-Cent Solution *cast Nicol Williamson as Sherlock Holmes and Alan Arkin as Watson. Meyer's fasci-nation with Holmes would carry over to his handling of the Spock character, particularly in* Star Trek VI *(photo copyright ©1976 Universal Pictures).*

Meyer directs Mary Steenburgen and Malcolm McDowell on the set of Time After Time *(photo copyright ©1979 Warner Bros Inc.).*

debut, a feat carefully orchestrated by him. "I optioned the material with my own money," he smiles, "I wrote the screenplay I wanted and brought in my producer and that was the deal. If you wanted to make the movie, I would have to direct. It's the same way Stallone got to be in *Rocky*. He wouldn't sell them the script unless he got the part."

Of course, that's not to say sitting in the director's chair was always the easiest task he could have assumed. "I had strengths and weaknesses," Meyer admits. "What many people don't know is that I started out being an actor many, many years ago. Then I was a stage director. I directed plays and I also directed radio plays, which was great fun if I could play a week on the radio. So I had done some directing before and was good at it. That's what I wanted to do; that was always my goal. The writing thing is some incredible tangent that I got into."

Working with actors was something he felt familiar with, and since he had a background in music, that aspect of production was easy to grasp. As far as editing was concerned, "I took to it like a duck to water, because editing is like writing." The most difficult aspect of directing was working with the camera. "I

have no background in it at all, and the camera-work in *Time After Time* was extremely simple and crude, and lots of times just plain wrong because I hadn't even directed a television show," he notes. "I was at my best when I was really bold and inventive, and at my most inane and absurd when I just plunked it down and didn't really do anything. Lots of shots I did from hunger. How do I shoot this? Well, I'll put it over there and then it will all be in the picture, and things like that. Sometimes it's a matter of angle."

Unlike many directors, Meyer welcomed the suggestions of his cast and crew. "You betcha," he laughs. "There are some directors who don't want to get suggestions from anybody. You can't walk up and suggest things to them. They get angry. They have it all in their head and they know. But I was very receptive, not only because I was ignorant and hadn't had a good deal of experience, but because I know that theater and film have one thing in common — they are collaborative efforts. They are team efforts. I assembled the best possible team that I could get, and I made the same speech to everybody who came in to interview with me. I said, 'Look, I don't know what I am doing. I have never done this before.

You will have to teach me. You will have to not mind teaching me. You will also have to not mind if having heard what you have to say, I go off and do it my own way.' I took advantage of all the suggestions, and there were many. At one point the focus-puller on the camera said, 'Wouldn't it be great if when he took his glasses off, the picture went out of focus?' I said, 'Great, we'll do that.' My cameraman, who was excellent, would suggest moves. And some of the better moves in the picture I'm sure were suggested by him. You're a fool if you hire wonderful people and don't stimulate them to do their best. That's like hiring Renoir and telling him what colors to paint. That's stupid."

Queried as to the social commentary he was trying to bring forth in the film, Meyer responds, "I think the film deals with a lot of implicit social commentary, and that is that....if you want to say something about television. That's what I loved about the story. All I had to do was show Wells watching a television set. I didn't have to say anything about television, anything about the age we live in, no editorializing necessary. It was all implicit. Everything about our age was suddenly seen or intended to be seen from the point of view of a Martian.

Whether it was a Coke bottle or a 'Gimme a ring' language and so on, and the social implications of the story appeal to me almost the most. But what I really like is that I fundamentally think that theater and film are supposed to entertain.

"Entertainment, however, is a word which has become debased," he adds. "It has become a synonym for 'mindlessness.' *Smokey & The Bandit* is entertaining, meaning you don't have to think, but entertainment can be thought provoking. All entertainment must be moving. It doesn't have to be mindless. What I liked about this film is that I'm not interested in being preached at nor am I interested in preaching. If I want to be preached at, I'll go to church or something like that. But the best art, it seems to me, is art that makes you feel first and think later. And what I like is art whose meaning evolves organically from the premise without having to be troweled on with an overview. Nothing that Wells says about love or life is foreign to the plot. It's all integral to his experience and you never get the feeling that a little beeper is going on that says, 'Author's Message! Author's Message!' That's what appeals to me. That's what I love about Conrad. That's what I love about Herman Melville, is that on one level it's a story about a man who goes after a whale that took off his leg, but on another level there's a whole bunch of meanings and suggestions, implied meanings, even if you never boil them down to literally what they are. Not everything has to be literal. Not everything has to be answered at the back of the book. Not everything has to be a summary like a sentence for *TV Guide*. If you could reduce the meaning of *Wuthering Heights* to a paragraph, I'm sure it would not be necessary nor advisable to read the book, but obviously not all art is or should be reducable."

After writing the novel *Black Orchard*, Meyer next hit the cinematic decks of the starship Enterprise in *Star Trek II: The Wrath of Khan*. While the hiring of the much-lauded Robert Wise was seen as a major coup for *Star Trek: The Motion Picture*, the resulting film was a major disappointment and there was a need for the director of the sequel to get *Trek* back on track.

"A friend of mine, named Karen Moore, who at the time was working for Paramount, was visiting me one night," relates Meyer. "I had done nothing since *Time After Time*. I had turned down a lot of stuff, trying to get my own script for a movie called *Conjuring* made — with no success, I might add. So I wrote the book, *Confessions of a Homing Pigeon*, which came out in October of 1981. This was just before that. Karen said to me, 'You know, if you want to learn how to direct movies, you should direct!' She suggested the *Star Trek II* movie and said that the two guys producing it were very nice. They sent me the script, which I loved. I met Harve [Bennett] and Bob [Sallin] and I thought they were wonderful, and I haven't changed my views since. As far as the film was concerned, I could not have been better partnered to not look like a fool because of the expertise and support I was given. The miracle of it was that we were all making the same movie. Everything really could have come unstuck if we had started going off in different directions. But there was never a substantive disagreement about the tone or the action. Details, yes."

Meyer admits to not having seen an episode of the series at the time, noting that he didn't particularly like the science-fiction genre. "I'm interested in good stories first," he states. "I loved *Star Wars* and *The Empire Strikes Back*, which I thought were very exciting and a lot of fun. I saw some *Star Trek* stuff after the film was offered to me, and they also ran the first movie for me. I didn't like it very much. I thought that it was spectacular in some ways, but it didn't fulfill what it was supposed to, or could be improved upon. I looked at the first film and thought that there was no way that we were going to make a movie as filled with ennui as that one. I also knew

we could do it for a quarter of the cost, so we would probably look like heroes!

"Adding dimension to the characters was definitely the aim. I have always thought, to the extent that I've had any clear thoughts about *Star Trek*, that it was something that for one reason or another never quite fulfilled its promise. Either because in terms of a television show they couldn't afford the sets or the effects, or because in the first movie they dropped the ball somewhere. This was an opportunity to make something right that had never quite been on the nose before. The more specific you get, the better. It was not necessary for me to see Admiral Kirk go to the bathroom, but I said why couldn't he read a book? At which point, I grabbed the first book off my shelf, which was *A Tale of Two Cities*, and for some reason or another, I just stuck with that, which was interesting because it's the one book that everybody knows the first line and the last line to. That became the bracket of the movie and it also somehow became the theme of the movie. Leonard and Shatner got excited because they always felt in some way that they had the Sidney Carlton-Charles Darnay relationship going on between them. That's very specific, and from the book we got the glasses, which was specific too, and real! From all of that came age. Interestingly enough, *Star Trek II* is not very much about science-fiction, the Genesis Planet aside. Its themes are entirely earthbound — death, aging, friendship."

It was these themes that helped make *Star Trek II* such a success and reignite interest among fans who had been disappointed by the lifeless characterizations of their favorite characters in *Star Trek I*. Meyer also strove for a different look in terms of the film's production design, rebuffing the carpeted, recreational Ramada Inn look of the first feature for a more stark nautical look. "I wanted to stretch the nautical analogy," says Meyer. "I said it should be like Captain Horatio Hornblower in outer space. I made everybody on the set watch the movie version of Hornblower. The young midshipman who gets killed....he's stolen right out of the movie. And it was interesting because when I first spoke to Bill Shatner about my idea, he said, 'That was also Gene Roddenberry's original take on it.' So far, so good. But I really wanted to pursue it. I had ship's bells, and boatswain's whistles and all that sort of stuff. And we very much stressed the idea of the ships as galleons in space. There's even that scene where they start pulling up the gratings to fire the photon torpedoes; it's followed through on a lot."

Meyer credits the first film with having shown those crafting the sequel what to avoid in making theirs, which proved an asset to the production. "I think it's fair to say that our movie would not have been as good as it was if it hadn't been for the first picture," he says. "We definitely learned, in the broadest sense, that they had made a picture based on a technical nature with runaway production costs. We said we wouldn't do that. We tended to feel very superior to it, and I think we're right to feel superior. But at the same time, they had their own stuff to work out and they're lucky they got the movie on film."

One of the issues Meyer was pressed with was deciding what elements of the *Star Trek* formula he should maintain and what should be discarded. "Very simple," he muses. "I kept what was good and changed what was bad. I decided that I owed an allegiance to what was good in either the first movie or, more importantly, the television series, and that I owed no allegiance and no respect to things that were bad. What that really boiled down to was the characters. I had to keep the characters as they were, but at the same time I had to redesign everything that I could — the uniforms, the sets, etc. Again, it was in the context of what they were, the overall shapes, I couldn't do anything about. But I could add twinkling lights whenever possible. I tried to get away from that

BASED ON THE PARAMOUNT PICTURES FILM

STAR TREK II
THE WRATH OF KHAN

A NOVEL BY VONDA N. McINTYRE
BASED ON A SCREENPLAY BY JACK B. SOWARDS
STORY BY HARVE BENNETT AND JACK B. SOWARDS

The novelization of Star Trek II: The Wrath of Khan, *the filmed version of which was co-written and directed by Meyer (photo courtesy Science Fiction Book Club).*

gray look. Philosophically, I said that I was simply going to take these characters more seriously and more literally than anyone has ever taken them before.

"The humor in *Star Trek* is the tragicomical view of life, that of people talking, real people. It seemed very difficult for me to do the movie without including a lot of that. It's a fine line to walk. I didn't want to be camp. I wanted to be affectionate and real. By saying I was taking them seriously, I didn't mean that they had no humor. I meant that I took them seriously, as if they were real people. At the very beginning, I said I'd do the picture under one condition: 'Let's make it real, because everything else is either camp or bland. Let's play it up to the armpit and if we're going to kill Spock, kill him.' Because the unforgivable thing is to fake it, to rip people off that way, to manipulate them. That is tasteless."

The cast had an overwhelming enthusiasm for Meyer, though this did not preclude their giving this newcomer a bit of a hard time during the early days of shooting. "Leonard and Bill kidded me a lot," reflects the director. ""They used to test me in the first couple of weeks. No one ever pulled rank. No one ever said, 'Well, we used to do it differently in the old days.' They understood up front that it was going to be completely different, that's how I got them to do it, but during the first two weeks they tested me in a lot of little ways. I remember we shot a scene where Uhura had a line which I don't remember, and she had to deliver it a certain way. While this was going on, they would mutter back and forth to themselves. They had me so nervous by the time they were finished, the pair of them talking about how this was wrong, that they effectively had me convinced that the whole picture had just gone down the toilet, based on this one line, which I'm not even sure is in the finished movie anyway. They ragged me a lot like that."

According to Meyer, it was the filming of Spock's death scene which finally made him comprehend the true power of *Star Trek*. "The scenes which were the most difficult, or at least the most wrenching to do, were the death of Spock," he said. "Everybody stood around on the stage in tears, which was very surprising to me because I [was] not that experienced as a movie director and I was amazed at how moved they were. The next day at the dailies, same thing. Everybody cried. I come from the 'less is

more' school of thinking. You can have somebody point to something and say, 'Look at that,' and you don't have to cut to what he is pointing to. In fact, you can raise considerable tension by *not* showing the audience what the character sees. For example, once Spock enters the reactor room I deliberately didn't cut back to him for a long time. After hearing, 'You can't go in there, you can't go....', you gotta be wondering, 'What's happening to him?' You want to see what's going on there. It's a matter of choice, of taste. I would rather underplay and let the audience's imagination rise to meet something halfway. From what I've seen of the series, I tend to think they overacted or showed too much. "

However, Meyer admits that when he's watched Spock since the dailies, he experiences his own twinge of remorse. "My attitude has changed perceptively. I don't know whether it was the actors themselves or the characters, but I finally thought, when I was watching the death scene and I realized that I was choked up, I thought, well, we have now transcended the subject matter. This is no longer simply about a man with pointy ears, which is how I felt because I didn't know it that well."

As has been well documented, the fans protested the death of Spock, though Meyer disputes the notion that they had any influence on the ultimate ending of the film. After a screening at a science fiction convention in Kansas, a high-placed Paramount official indicated that other endings had been considered, perhaps filmed, and that the one used would depend on fan reaction. Meyer firmly denies this.

"My job," he relates, "is not to find out what the public wants and give it to them. My job is to make the public want what I want. If you take a vote on things before the fact, you will never do anything. Nobody wanted Spock to die. There were threatening letters from fans: 'If Spock dies, you die.' The question in my mind was not whether he died, but whether he died well. His death needed

some organic relationship to the rest of the movie, and a plausible connection to whatever else was going on. If we did that, I don't think anyone would question it. On the other hand, if the movie suddenly turned around a corner on two wheels and we 'fulfill Leonard Nimoy's contract by bumping off this character which he has grown tired of playing', if indeed that was the scenario, which I have never heard, that wouldn't be so good. That stuff that we were going to have more than one ending, that we were going to let the audience decide....that was all bullshit. Art is not made by committee and it's not made by voting."

Meyer rebuffs the notion that another ending had ever been considered for the close of the film. "I don't think it was ever seriously considered," he says. "I never had any pressure about it. The closest thing that happened was that we were under great pains to keep the whole movie under wraps. We succeeded until a month before it opened, when Paramount insisted on previewing the movie in Kansas City. The next night, Johnny Carson was on television. He said, 'Well, it's out, he dies.' And I thought, they must be crazy. Here we tried so hard to keep this under wraps and then they insist on doing this. And then the Paramount publicity department started cranking out this stuff about whether there was actually more than one ending or not. They were trying to convince people that there was more than one ending to keep the suspense going. I said, 'I'm not going along with this.' I'd just look stupid. I have enough trouble not doing that anyway. So that was the only time there was any attempt to convey the illusion that the thing wasn't locked up. They were just trying to backpedal."

Meyer's next directorial effort was ABC's controversial drama about nuclear war, *The Day After*, which chronicled the results of the unthinkable: World War III. "It's a story about people in the center of the United States, minding their own business — doctors, lawyers, Indian chiefs — who all get blown to kingdom come. The movie concentrates on those people who are not fortunate enough to be at ground zero," Meyer recounts. "I was interested in *The Day After* because of my commitment to trying to stop the arms race, my support of the nuclear freeze, or my trying to stop us from installing the Pershing IIs in Europe. They don't work. The Pershing II doesn't even fly. You launch them and they blow up. The MX doesn't work. A four-stage rocket, and it doesn't work. It's a waste of money. Meanwhile, from a purely social point of view, this country is going down the tubes."

Next up for Meyer was the Tom Hanks/John Candy film *Volunteers*, about two guys who join the Peace Corps, as well as the novel *Confessions of a Homing Pigeon*. Although Meyer chose not to be involved in *Star Trek III: The Search for Spock* — in part, because of the character's inevitable resurrection — he did co-write the series' most financially successful installment, *Star Trek IV: The Voyage Home.*

"I got involved in *Star Trek IV*," he says, "because they had another script they were not happy with. Dawn Steele, who [was] the head of Paramount and has been a friend of mine for many years, called me and said, 'Would you do us an enormous favor?' And I said, 'For Harve and Leonard? Yeah, absolutely.' They had a script written. The script, I guess, was for Eddie Murphy as a guest star. I never read it, so I don't know. But they weren't happy with it. They wanted to go back to their original story and write another script. Harve said, 'We don't have a lot of time, so here's what I want to do. I write the first 20-25% of it and when they get to Earth or when they're about to get to Earth, then you take it, finish the Earth stuff, and I'll do the ending.' And when I heard the story, I said, 'Well, wait a minute, the whole middle of the story is a kind of rip-off of *Time After Time*. I said, 'Do they have to go to San Francisco? I've done that city. Can't they go to Paris?' And

they said, 'No, they have to go to San Francisco.' And I said, 'Well, it's even more of a rip-off then.' So I agreed to do the middle part because, obviously, I've done it before and I'm familiar with it.' In fact, there are scenes in *Star Trek IV* that were cut out of *Time After Time*. There had been a scene in the movie with a punker holding a ghetto blaster. I cut it out of the movie because I didn't shoot it right, but Leonard did so it made it into *Star Trek IV*. [Harve and I] went over each other's stuff. My contribution begins with Spock's crack about 'Judging by the pollution content of the atmosphere, I believe we have arrived at the late 20th Century,' and goes from there to someplace after they get the whales and leave. I didn't read the other script because I just thought it would confuse me, and since they didn't like it, why bother?"

As vehemently as Meyer opposed the suggestion at the close of *Star Trek II* that Spock would come back, he was against marine biologist Gillian Taylor's sojourn through time to the 23rd century with the rest of the Enterprise crew. "In my version of the script," he notes, "when they all leave to go back, she didn't. She said if anyone's going to make sure this kind of disaster doesn't happen, somebody's going to have to stay behind, which I still think is the 'righter' ending. The end in the movie detracts from the importance of people in the present taking responsibility for the ecology and preventing problems of the future by doing something about them today, rather than catering to the fantasy desires of being able to be transported ahead in time to the near-utopian future society of the *Star Trek* era."

In between his voyages into the 23rd century, the writer-director performed an uncredited rewrite on the climax of Paramount's mega-hit *Fatal Attraction* (which had much to do with the film's phenomenal success), and directed Pierce Brosnan in *The Deceivers* and Gene Hackman in *Company Business*. While electing to sit out the next Enterprise voyage, *Star Trek V: The*

Meyer directed **Volunteers**, *a comedy that starred recent Oscar winner Tom Hanks and the late John Candy as a pair of Red Cross workers (photo copyright Tri-Star Pictures).*

Final Frontier, Meyer returned to helm and co-write *Star Trek VI: The Undiscovered Country* at the behest of fellow *Trek* Great Bird, Leonard Nimoy.

"*Star Trek*, in many ways, tends to reflect what's going on in the real world," offers Meyer. "At its best, *Star Trek* appears to function as pop allegory-pop metaphor, taking current events and issues — ecology, war, and racism, for example — and objectifying them for us to contemplate in a science fiction setting. The world it presents may make no sense as either science or fiction, but it is well and truly sufficient for laying out human questions. Removed from our immediate neighborhoods, it is refreshing and even intriguing to consider Earth matters from the distance of a few light years. Like the best science fiction, *Star Trek* does not show us other worlds so meaningfully as it shows us our own — for better or for worse, in sickness and health. In truth, *Star Trek* doesn't even pretend to show us other worlds, only humanity refracted in what is supposed to be a high-tech mirror."

Nimoy, who had worked with writers Mark Rosenthal and Lawrence Konner on devising a glasnost-inspired allegory, approached Meyer on the beach in Cape Cod, where the director was recuperating from the ill-fated shoot for *Company Business*.

"The Cold War idea really originated with Leonard Nimoy, who said to me, 'Let's make a movie about the wall coming down in outer space.' His statement just spoke to me," enthuses Meyer. "What I wanted to do with it, was to widen the world of *Star Trek* before closing out the series, if that's indeed what's happening. The thing I've learned from these movies is that your only chance of succeeding is not to repeat yourself, not to try the same exact thing. I didn't want to go mano-a-mano because I had done that with *II*; I didn't want to make a comedy because I felt *IV* was the most broadly comedic of any of them. So I thought, I want to make an ensemble piece and I want it to be a political thriller. Like everybody else, I was fascinated by the events from 1989 on. I had been in Berlin working on another film and I had seen the wall coming down. God, what are the possibilities? What are the potentials for greatness or disaster? Who would have thought it? It's a bright spot, but it's filled with the potential for real disaster, and this is the theme of the movie, because change is real scary. In this film, the intention is certainly to deal with what people do when they are confronted with the prospect of radical change. There are some people who are capable of embracing it, and some who have a lot of trouble with it."

Meyer doesn't mince words when viewing humanity's future, and it's obviously quite different from the one that Gene Roddenberry postulated in creating *Star Trek*.

"I think our future is ashes," he states categorically. "I'm looking at the ozone layer that is now opening up in the summertime and I'll say, 'Jesus, the omens here aren't good.' I didn't say we were going to end up in a nuclear holocaust, I'm merely saying that at the rate we're going, one way or the other we seem bent on a course of self destruc-

tion. I do not share that optimistic view of human affairs taken by Gene Roddenberry that man is a perfectable creature. Show me any evidence of that happening. Show me any difference between 1991 and 1691, or 91 or 91 B.C. Where have we changed? The ultimate proof that we haven't is that we can look at art from any era and perfectly understand and identify with the emotions being depicted. Why would we be performing *Hamlet* if human beings had altered so much that the story was emotionally incomprehensible? Why would we be doing Sophocles if you couldn't understand what was motivating Oedipus? Nothing has changed at all, so why should it change? What you're seeing, if you look at Eastern Europe, is a revival of xenophobia, a revival of prejudice, things that were dormant because they were in a deep freeze."

He compares these points to the events of *Star Trek VI*, in which Kirk and his crew must negotiate a peace with the Klingon Empire, despite their — particularly Kirk's — prejudice. "I think the heroic thing about Kirk and the rest of the crew is their effort to acknowledge, to confront and ultimately try to overcome their prejudice," Meyer emphasizes. "If a man leaps into a raging torrent to save a drowning child, he performs an heroic act. If the same man leaps into the same pond to save the same child, and does so with a ball and chain attached to his leg, he must be accounted not less heroic, but more heroic still because he overcomes a handicap. And that's what heroism and drama is about. I think Kirk is more of a hero for being a human being and not less because he's a super human, which I never believed. I think the movie is certainly a reflection of my sensibility. The movie is also funny, which is part of my sensibility. It's a dark funny movie, by which I do not mean to imply that the humor is black, because I don't think that it is. The humor is very sort of weirdly going hand in hand with this very serious thematic material. That is

definitely a reflection of the dichotomy of my own personality."

Over the years, Meyer's vision of *Star Trek* and the tone he set on his maiden voyage — which he feels has been carried through the film series and into *Star Trek: The Next Generation* ("Their uniforms certainly retain the color scheme and the nautical flavor of the film series, and the captain refers to his first officer as 'my Number One'...all that harks back to *II*.") — has been criticized by Roddenberry as being too militaristic. In fact, Meyer's take on the *Star Trek* universe, despite its wide acceptance by fans, had been the object of frequent criticism by Roddenberry, perhaps owing to the series' creator's lack of involvement in shaping the continuing destinies of the characters he crafted two decades before.

Meyer remains philosophical in his view of the first great bird. "The history of human endeavor has frequently comprised itself of certain institutions which are based on two archetypes," he explains. "There's a guy who comes along and with a certain kind of messianic fortitude and charisma conjures up a universe out of nothing, hot air, if you'll pardon the expression. He makes it happen. Usually, he never stays around to run it. The task is always turned over to some can-do type who is distinctly lacking in messianic qualities, but is a very good organizer. You can probably look at various institutions like the children's museum in Los Angeles, MADD, FILMEX and plenty of others that were founded by somebody who was later booted out by his own board of directors or who, for one reason or another, split because of the paperwork, the desk job, the bottom line, the numbers.

"Jesus Christ presumably founded the Christian faith," continues Meyer. "But it seems like it was either Peter or Paul who got the thing rolling as a business. And I think that *Star Trek* would not have existed without Roddenberry. There's no question about that. I have no wish in any shape or form to detract from the magnitude or significance of his accomplishments, but I also think that nothing can stay the same forever. For things to grow, there has to be these Joshua types, of which I suppose I am one, who come in and pick up the burden and carry it. Maybe we carry it clumsily or in the wrong direction, but we carry it."

Meyer believes the *Star Trek* universe has taken on a life of its own and can no longer be considered only the purview of Gene Roddenberry, but that of the many creative talents who have shaped it over the last decade and a half. "At the risk of an absurd parallel, I will say that to me *Star Trek* is no longer any one man's creation, and I think therein lies its richness, its diversity and a lot of its meaning for people. *Star Trek*, for me, is somewhat analogous —here's my strange parallel — to the Catholic Mass, which is to say that everybody knows the text of the Catholic Mass. But the Catholic Mass changes every time a different composer sets it to music. It sounds different in different people's hands. But the same core of something is there. In that sense, I think the different people on *Star Trek* inevitably bring different sensibilities to it, different music, and it's just a question of — to mix metaphors — which different wine you are pouring into the same generally shaped bottle. These particular movies are, to whatever extent you care to take it, representative in whole or in part of my vision of this thing. This is the music I want it set to."

While Meyer seems generally pleased with how the production went, he did have to cope with a problem that has vexed many of *Trek*'s directors both of the tubular and theatrical voyages: spending a great deal of shooting time on the Enterprise bridge, as well as bringing in the highly complex film on an extremely tight budget.

"The bridge scenes are the hardest," he concurs. "I hate that set. It's very confining. It's 360-degrees and it's been done to death. I don't feel that my best work has been done there. My mind just goes numb and I'm grateful less of the film takes place on the bridge [than previously]. I [do] think we made the ships feel more intense in a lot of ways by doing things differently with the sets. We found if we made some of the sets smaller — the corridors of the Enterprise shrank, for example — they did get more intense."

As for budget, "I think every director in the world would say, 'Yeah, I could've used more' and I'm no exception. I came here to make the movie on a certain assumption and when I got here, my assumption was wrong by certain millions of dollars. I didn't have it, and that's the real world. You have to play the game. I think ultimately people may say how come we didn't do this or that, but that's nit-picking. In a way, I was more curious to see how the movie was responded to by non-Trekkers than Trekkers. I could anticipate what the Trekker response would be, but the movie interests me because of its subject matter. The people who seem to get off on it in ways that are very provocative to me, are people who are in no way prepared by previous association."

Considering the fact that the film's stars, William Shatner and Leonard Nimoy, are also directors, rumors ran rampant that Meyer had his hands full. "I don't think you could distinguish that Shatner and Nimoy were directors from the fact that they were actors working with a director and we were all trying to make a movie," he differs. "Shatner and Nimoy, and all the original cast members, had been involved in the series with these characters for so long. They didn't always agree that certain lines would be said by their characters. I had a great deal of fun working with them. I find them individually and collectively charming. They're real pros. There's a lot of give and take, but I don't think it's because they're directors. I found this easier than *II*. On that film I was an unknown quantity. On this one, I've been around. I've known them very well and they trust me. I think it was much easier."

And what are the differences between directing two *Star Trek* films a decade apart? "There is no difference between the two projects," Meyer replies. "The mechanics of moviemaking, aside from the progress that has been made in special effects, are more similar than not. I think what's different is that the two movies are very different. [Personally], the older I get the less I feel I know. This isn't just about directing, it's about my whole life. When you're young you walk along a tightrope over a chasm of rock 900 feet below. You never look down, you dance, you twirl and you're doing fine, and then there comes a point when you look down — maybe you're forty — and you say, 'How can I have been dancing and prancing up here?' It's a scary proposition and you've got to watch that you're not inhibited."

Whether this Great Bird intends to take flight in the *Star Trek* universe again is a mystery, but Meyer is not involved with the seventh feature, *Star Trek: Generations*. "I don't work on the odd-numbered ones," he laughs. Nonetheless, he has some advice for executive producer Rick Berman.

"Have fun, stay loose," Meyer smiles. "The older I get, the more it becomes about process and the less it becomes about result — which doesn't mean you're supposed to slough off what you're doing. But it means how are you spending your life? What are you doing with your life? Are you having any fun? Are you being useful to anybody or are you just sort of jerking off and taking up space, no pun intended? I would hope that the people who do [*Generations*], do it for love and for fun, because, who knows, maybe they'll be able to slide in something along the way that's meaningful."

LEONARD NIMOY
"Director With Ears"

Among the original *Star Trek* cast members there is supposedly something of a curse, which has resulted in those within the phenomenon becoming elevated to something above humanity, while simultaneously denying them the opportunity to work in other roles.

Any doubts? Just ask Walter Koenig, James Doohan, George Takei or Nichelle Nichols, each of whom are forced to make a living for themselves by attending various conventions held throughout the world each year. On the flip side is DeForest Kelley, who could care less one way or the other if he ever worked again; William Shatner, who has

Leonard Nimoy, looking quite un-Spocklike, in Catlow (photo copyright ©1971 MGM).

not only scored as T.J. Hooker but as commercial pitchman, host of *Rescue: 911* and Great Bird of his *TekWar* galaxy; and Leonard Nimoy, who has perhaps lived long and prospered the most from his association with *Star Trek*, seguing into not only a successful post-*Trek* acting career, but an impressive directorial filmography as well.

When *Star Trek* left the airwaves in 1969 following a three year run, it was Nimoy who shifted over to *Mission: Impossible* for two seasons as IMF operative, Paris, before serving as host of the syndicated series *In Search of....* Throughout the 1970s he appeared on stage in *Vincent: The Story of a Hero* (a one-man show he wrote, directed and starred in), *Equus, Full Circle, Oliver!, Fiddler on the Roof* (who would have imagined Nimoy in a musical after his off-key tenor in "Plato's Stepchildren"?) and *Sherlock Holmes*. His big-screen credits included *Deathwatch, Catlow,* the 1978 remake of *Invasion of the Body Snatchers* — directed by Philip Kaufman (originally considered as a potential helmer for *ST: TMP*) — and *Star Trek: The Motion Picture*. More recently he received an Emmy Award nomination for his role in *A Woman Called Golda*, was

featured in *Marco Polo* and starred in TNT's critically acclaimed Holocaust drama, *Never Forget*, on which he also served as executive producer.

Although long a part of the *Star Trek* lore, Leonard Nimoy, who had quietly (and sometimes not so quietly) exerted a great deal of control over the continuing destiny of *Star Trek* along with William Shatner as actors during the series and subsequent movies, took charge as director and shaped the course of *Treks* to come. Ironically, it was *Star Trek* that ultimately led him to his most significant "second" career, that of a motion picture director. This evolution can be traced to Nimoy's disappointment in the first feature film based on the series.

"During the making of *Star Trek I,*" says Nimoy, "there were many days when we felt frustrated with what we were given to do as actors and how the characters were being handled. Most of the time we stood around the bridge of the Enterprise saying, 'What is it?' Then somebody would say, 'I'm not sure.' Ten minutes later, we would say, 'What's it gonna do next?' 'I dunno. We'll have to wait and see.' You know what I'm talking about. So I came in a number of times with suggestions of little pieces of material that I gave to Bob Wise and he said, 'Okay, let's shoot it.' And these were character touches that I felt would help the audience to have some empathy with this feature story. Thus Spock would be experiencing something as a result of V'ger that the audience could relate to, and by understanding true Spock, maybe get some emotional feelings about V'ger. We shot a lot of stuff that was cut out of the movie that was later put back in when we needed a longer version for television [and is, incidentally, included on the pan and scan version of the film's video release, but not the letterboxed versions of the VHS or laserdisc editions]. I have seen in print and have gotten a lot of letters that tell me that people felt they could relate to the picture better as a result of that material.

"There have been times when

Nimoy as seen in the television mini-series, Marco Polo (photo copyright NBC).

I've been concerned about the future of my career because of the identification with the character," he adds. "But I never had a confrontation with the studio in which I said I would never play the part again. My only concern with *Star Trek* has been that if we're going to do it, we do it well. I don't want to do a rip-off just because people will pay to see it. If it's going to be good, I want to be there. I'd hate like hell to see a great *Star Trek* movie hit the screen and not be in it. I'd feel very jealous. [At the time] I really was adamant that I would not work on *Star Trek II* because I had been so frustrated with the first film and I was feeling very negative about the whole thing."

Nimoy began to change his mind when the film's executive producer, Harve Bennett, approached him with the idea of Spock's dying in the film.

"Harve caught me completely by surprise with that one," Nimoy admits. "The more I thought about it, the more I thought, 'Well, maybe that's the honest thing to do. Finish it properly rather than turn your back on it.' Eventually we agreed that Spock would die. There was a lot of controversy over whose idea it was and why. It was even said that it was the only way I would do

A very early publicity photo of Nimoy made up as Spock (photo copyright ©1966 NBC).

it and that it was in my contract that Spock would die. It got to be a messy situation. The only thing I can tell you is that when Harve and I started to explore the idea, I thought back to the first season of *Star Trek*, when the Spock character had taken root and been widely accepted. The whole concept of his lack of emotionality, his control of emotions, was a very interesting and important part of the character. Dorothy Fontana, who was a writer on the series, came to me on the set one day and said, 'I'm going to write a love story for Spock.' I told her she couldn't do it because it would destroy the character, destroy the whole mystique about whether or not he's emotional. The whole story we'd been telling was that he was completely in control of his emotions. She said, 'I have an idea that might work and I'm going to try it.' She did, and wrote 'This Side of Paradise,' a beautiful episode in which Spock fell in love. At the end of it, there was a bittersweet parting and it was all over. And he had gone through this fantastic experience.

"I learned a big lesson then. That is, if you say you can't do it, it won't work. If you say let's not try it, you're mistaken. Particularly in science fiction and with characters like these, you must try interesting and daring ideas. If they're well-executed, they can work. Now there are an awful lot of people, I'm sure, who said that to kill Spock would not work. Audiences won't accept it, they won't want to see it, whatever....I think people who've said that and who have now seen the picture, are agreeing that they were wrong, that it really does work, that they were terribly moved and excited by it. Suddenly you find that a whole new creative possibility comes out of that because you've taken a chance. And if I might use the word 'art' in this process, I think that's what art is all about. When you venture past the obvious, when you reach into the unknown and try something daring. If it works, it opens up all kinds of new creative possibilities. That's

why I was willing to take a chance."

Nimoy probably hoped that the death of Spock would lead his career in other directions. But he had to know that the film would only spur on the *Star Trek* fever; that the fans would demand his return; that some way would be found to bring Spock back and that he would be the one to reprise the role. What he never expected, and what made his career move to temporarily get away from Spock all the more successful, was that he ended up taking the directorial chair on *Star Trek III: The Search for Spock*. Getting the job was, to some degree, an accident. Prior to *Trek III*, Nimoy still wanted his contract with Paramount to include projects other than periodic voyages aboard the starship Enterprise, but they did not have anything specific for him to do in the future.

"For many years," he explains, "my concern has been to try to build a career outside of *Star Trek* so that it wasn't that single straight line. So there was nothing for us to discuss. I said to [then Paramount executive] Gary Nardino — I was being arrogant — with all due respect to Bob Wise, who directed the first picture, a top notch filmmaker; and all due respect to Nick Meyer, an extremely talented writer/director who directed *Trek II*; I know more about *Star Trek* than either of them and I said I could direct *Star Trek III* successfully. When I first presented the idea of my directing to Paramount, the response was very good — but there were certain trepidations. We had to talk them through. My position during those discussions was, 'I don't want you to perceive me as a problem. I don't want you to think I'm an actor trying to build a directing career on the strength of my leverage. I want you to see me as the solution to your problem. You need a director, and I know this material. I will bring you a movie that will satisfy the *Star Trek* audience.' I didn't want to take the posture with the studio of, 'You want me to act in *Star Trek III*? Then I'm the director. Period.' Instead, we worked on what

A pensive looking Spock at his station (photo copyright ©1966 NBC).

I felt was a constructive approach.

"Basically, I told them, 'Promote from within.',", recalls Nimoy. "Michael Eisner [then Paramount President] got very excited about it and said, 'Great idea! Leonard Nimoy directs the search for Spock!' It went downhill from there. At one point they said, 'No, we're not going to do it.' Harve and I kept operating on the assumption that it was going to work out and I kept talking story ideas. In April of '83, I started my prep on the picture, reported on the lot and immediately went to work with Harve."

It may be hard to believe coming from someone who had been a part of the industry since the '50s and a former Zombie of the Stratosphere, but Nimoy insists he honestly felt that moving out of the cast and taking over the film would not be a major concern to his fellow cast members. It was only a matter of time before he discovered that he was wrong.

Says Nimoy, "I must be really naive about this. I really must. I was surprised that there was so much interest and so much concern about that. The interests and concerns are valid. I just didn't perceive the potential problems or friction that other people perceive.

William Shatner and Leonard Nimoy at the 1979 Academy Awards.

My fellow actors were concerned about it before we started doing the picture. I simply took it as fact that I had their best interests at heart. That I would know their characters well, and I certainly knew their potential well and would try to explore it. That was one of the things I argued in that period of time when I was asking for the job. I said, 'I know these people. I know these characters. I know what can be done with them.' So it was ironic for me and kind of startling that the very thing I thought I would have the greatest success with was the cast, and that was the major question that people were more concerned about. I didn't have anybody say, 'What do you know about shooting a $16 million movie with spaceships and planets exploding, fire scenes and fights and people falling off cliffs and stuff like that?' Nobody asked me about that. They said, 'What about the actors?'

"I discussed it later, after the fact, with some of the cast, and they admitted to me that they had been concerned. I think the concern grew out of a potential competitiveness. I discovered that there was more of a sense of competition between the actors than I have ever been aware of. That's a strange

thing to say. I'm an actor, have been in television and films since 1950. This was the first time that I had it really enunciated to me that some of the actors in the cast were concerned. I think we got over that very quickly. Generally they saw that I was well prepared, that I was well intended where they were concerned, and that they were given the opportunity to develop and have some fun in their performances. I see each of the cast as individuals. I don't see them as simply 'the chorus.' I understand their potential as actors, and I understand the potential of their characters. I wanted to have their contribution in the movie. It wasn't something I reluctantly felt obligated to do. It was something I intended to do from the start."

Once the problem of dealing with his fellow actors was overcome, the big risk in the script was the loss of the starship Enterprise, which would be destroyed by Captain Kirk in his battle against the Klingons. Word of the vessel's destruction leaked to the fans and campaigns — not unlike the ones to save Spock — were begun to save the Enterprise from its demise.

Explains Nimoy, "I understand how they [felt]. I sympathize completely. But my feeling was that it was not arbitrary. It was well-built into the story. I've had people say, 'Gee, why did you do that?' My response is, 'What else would you have had Kirk do under those circumstances?' It seems to me that the script laid itself out that it was the only thing to do. I can understand the emotion connected with it, but nevertheless it was a dramatic event. I think it was played very successfully as a dramatic event. Frankly, I thought it was well executed. We didn't destroy the Enterprise for cheap or inflammatory reasons, but because therein lay drama. It was a certain kind of drama which you can do in motion pictures, but you can't do on television. It was drama that I think we're mandated to do, because we're not doing television anymore. As Nicholas Meyer said about killing Spock

in *Star Trek II*, 'We're not playing games here. This isn't a red herring, like they do on TV. Spock is really dead.' Destroying the Enterprise was the same. It was a valid dramatic choice, not a transparent TV plot."

Since Leonard Nimoy's directorial credits were limited to such episodic television fare as *The Powers of Matthew Star, Night Gallery* and *T.J. Hooker*, the challenge of getting Harve Bennett's script on film was a difficult yet exhilarating experience, from the filming of scenes to the actual editing of the movie. His love for *Star Trek* and his obsession for perfection drove him through the arduous shoot. However, that kind of dedication has a price.

"The shooting began on August 15, 1983," Nimoy states, revealing what his workload as director was like. "It was 49 days of shooting during which the biggest problem I had was lack of sleep. I went to bed at 9:00 or 9:30, set the alarm for 5:00 or 5:30 and would be up at 3:00, the head going with ideas. I was just so super-charged and wired. It was a constant tiredness of the best kind."

There were many things Nimoy learned on this project while honing his craft, such as how frustrating it can be to

Nimoy directs actor Ted Danson on the set of the box office hit, **Three Men & A Baby** *(photo copyright Touchstone Pictures).*

direct oneself. "There is no question in directing yourself that you need help," Nimoy says. He relied quite heavily on Harve Bennett, William Shatner, director of photography Charles Correll and others for that help. They are the "people off-camera I've come to trust. I cannot emphasize enough that you don't make these pictures alone. You sure need an awful lot of talented support. In some cases, there is simply the fact that there are things going on behind you that you cannot see as an actor. The biggest problem I had, and this is really silly, but it happens that it was the scene in the sick bay of the Bird of Prey. Spock is unconscious and McCoy is talking to him. Now, not only am I in the scene, but I have to play the scene with my eyes closed. So I can't even look to see if the actor I am playing the scene with is looking anything like I think he should look. It drove De Kelley crazy. He swears that I was trying to direct him with the movement and flutter of my eyelids. It was very difficult. In a sense, I was very pleased and relieved that the design of the story allowed me to do a minimal amount of performing."

As a stylistic director, Nimoy has given himself time and room to grow, noting, "I'm probably somewhere in between Bob Wise and Nicholas Meyer. Not as precise as Bob, not as imaginative or rough-edged as Nick. I think the major difference, and for me the most important difference, is my attitude toward the story and the actors. [Wise and Meyer] are looking for a different kind of final product than I am."

An intriguing part of the directing for Nimoy involved editing. "In the editing process, specifically, the most interesting challenge was how to tell the story and in what sequence. Having seen it on the screen in its rough cut form, we all came to the conclusion that there was something about the juxtaposition, scene to scene, idea to idea, character to character; it wasn't quite in its proper order. The jigsaw puzzle hadn't quite fallen into place. Gradually we worked

our way towards it and discovered what the picture turned out to be. The flow just didn't want to come to life until we repositioned certain of the opening scenes. For example, what we came to call the caper, which was the gathering of the Samurai to steal the Enterprise. In its original form, it was scattered in pieces throughout the first third of the film and they were all wonderful, fun pieces. But somehow, when you cut away from each of the happenings, it was always as though the fun was being interrupted. When you came back to it, you had to get geared up to have fun again. And suddenly that little piece would be over and you were being interrupted and taken away from the story again.

"The one major reconstruction that took place in editing was to put much, if not all, that caper together as a piece so that once we start with the idea of Bill Shatner walking up and saying, 'The answer is no, I am therefore going anyway,' it starts. So that piece became a trump within itself whereas it had been originally constructed as several pieces. I think 14 minutes from the time we first started looking at cuts of the film were cut down to its present condition. Perhaps two or three minutes were cut after the picture went to preview audiences. So we were pretty close to what we had planned to put on the screen. I think that's due in great part to very successful writing and producing for the film.

"I wasn't making a personal statement," Nimoy notes. "The major theme in this film is about friendship. What should a person do to help a friend? How deeply should a friendship commitment go? What price should people be willing to pay? And what sacrifices, what obstacles, will these people endure? That's the emotion line of the film. For me, that's its reason for existence."

Having performed beyond expectation on the film, Nimoy was asked back as director of the fourth entry in the series, *The Voyage Home*. This

Nimoy as a Holocaust survivor who comes up against Neo-Nazis in Ted Turner's Never Forget *(photo copyright ©1994 Turner Pictures).*

time he was invited to develop the storyline along with Harve Bennett. Notes Nimoy, "We decided early on that we wanted to do a time travel story. When I say we, I'm talking about Harve Bennett and I. We were asked by the studio to come up with a story, and our very first conversation was about doing time travel, which we both agreed was a good idea. We also felt that we should lighten up. The picture should be fun in comparison to the previous three. The first movie had no comedy at all. That was intentional. It was intended to be a serious study of a problem. The second film had a little. The third film had a little. But there we were dealing with a lot of serious drama. There was a lot of life and death going on. In [*Star Trek*] *II* Spock died. In [*Star Trek*] *III* Kirk's son died, the Enterprise was blown up and people were being killed and planets were disintegrating. I just felt it was time to lighten up and have some fun. That meant that if we were going to do time travel, the best thing we could do was come back to contemporary Earth, where we could have some fun with our people. They would more or less be a fish out of water on the streets.

"Now the next question

becomes, why are they coming back in time? Is it accidental? We knew we wanted them to come home and face trial for all that had happened in *Star Trek III*, rules being broken, the Enterprise destroyed and all that. It would have been out of character for them not to at least try to come home and deal with their obligations. So we figured we would start them on their way home in this Klingon Bird of Prey. Does something go wrong? Do they find themselves going through a time travel accidentally, or was it intentional? For a number of reasons, we chose that it would be intentional. If they're coming back to the 20th Century, what are they coming back for? Is it something they need, something they want? That led us to the idea that there's a problem in the 23rd Century, which can only be solved by something that's now gone, extinct. I have had a lot of good conversations with scientists. Some of the things I have learned from them have been technical, some philosophical. I think the most pertinent to what is happening in this film is that there are scientists who are deeply concerned, because of the prevalent attitude that we don't have to worry about what we do on this planet. The attitude is whatever problems we create, science will fix. They are afraid that something will go terribly wrong and someone will turn around and say, 'Fix it,' and they will have to say, 'We can't. It's gone too far and it's something we can't control.'

"We experimented with a lot of different ideas on that subject, including the idea that certain crafts and techniques might be lost by the 23rd Century. Maybe there's nobody who knows how to make a violin anymore. Probably by that time we won't have anybody who knows how to crack oil anymore, because it won't be necessary. Cracking oil will be an extinct process by then. Suppose we needed to start an oil refinery in the 23rd Century, it might be useful to find someone in the 20th Century who would know how to do it."

Shortly thereafter, Nimoy had

Who loves ya, Baby? Spock does. A moment from the Star Trek *blooper reel.*

numerous conversations with members of M.I.T. regarding communication with other species. "We were talking about the idea that if alien intelligence was trying to contact us, it would probably take quite a long time for us to know what it is saying, and for us to communicate with it," Nimoy states. "I became intrigued with the idea that there was some lack of communication that was causing the problem. [I was] aware that humpback whales sing this unusual kind of song, which we don't understand but which obviously means something to them. They communicate it to each other, they pass it on one to the other, they repeat it. It has a form, lasting anywhere from six to 30 minutes in cycles, and they sing it again and again. Then they cease periodically, and they change the song. It's quite a complex structure, and that's very interesting. We don't

know, and we may never know, what the communication is all about, so supposing that something in the 23rd Century is trying to communicate with them and they're gone. That's how it all happened, and it's a hell of a lot more interesting and challenging to pick up a pair of whales than it is to pick up a plant or insect.

"I did some homework and researched different scientific concerns of modern day. I started looking into the problem of endangered species. I had read a book by a Harvard biologist named Edward O. Wilson called *Biophilia*. In the book, it said that in the 1990s we'll be losing 10,000 species per year off the Earth at the rate we're going now. A lot of those species we may not even know exist but, nevertheless, they'll be gone before scientists and biologists even have a chance to research them

Nimoy directing The Good Mother *(photo copyright Touchstone Pictures).*

and understand them. So there's many different forms of life facing extinction and one of the most well-known are the whales. Wilson states in his book that there are certain 'keystone species.' That means, for example, if you build a house of cards, you can pull out so many cards without the house falling down. But there are particular 'keystone' cards, that if you pull them out, the whole house crumbles. So we may not even know which species on this planet are the 'keystone' cards, so to speak, for our ecological system. If we were to wipe out one species, it could start the whole thing crumbling."

Nimoy certainly felt the challenge of co-starring in a film that he was directing as well. "It was hard physically," he says. "But I had a good time doing it because I really enjoyed playing the Spock character in this picture. He's a very different Spock. A Spock who's evolving, who's confused. He's trying to figure out who he's supposed to be and how he's supposed to function. It was great fun to play but, physically, very tough because it's a long day. If you just direct the picture, it's a tough job. If you act in it as well, it's tougher. Then you have to add on a two hour make-up job every day, which means that you have to

be in at 5:00 every morning. [But] this is a funny Spock. He's also very touching. I think it's a very touching moment when Spock discovers his identity. It happens at the moment when Kirk and McCoy are talking about what to do about Chekov in the hospital, and Spock says, 'We must help Chekov.' Kirk says, 'Is that the logical thing to do, Spock?' Spock replies, 'No, but it is the human thing to do.' I hope audiences [were] touched by that. It's the kind of moment when you say, 'Ah, Spock is there. He found his way.'"

As a director, Nimoy felt that *Star Trek IV* was much more ambitious and exciting than the previous films. "We were off the soundstages for the first time," he enthuses. "The first three pictures were almost exclusively on the soundstages. In *Star Trek I*, we were off the soundstage for a couple of days; on *Star Trek III* we were off for a couple of nights for the Vulcan exterior scenes. To get off the soundstages on this one was very invigorating. It gave a lot more energy to me and the cast of the picture, and I had a little bit more time. I shot *Star Trek III* in 49 days and on this one I had 53. Actually, I had 57, and I came in four days early."

Interestingly, the majority of the on-location material was achieved via a

hidden camera on the streets of San Francisco. A moment that comes to Nimoy's mind is the one in which Uhura and Chekov search for "nuclear wessels."

"I covered the scene exactly as it was written," he notes, "but once I had that, then I began to improvise and explore to see if there was more to be had. The scene as written was, he finishes looking at the phone book and she says to him, 'Did you find it?' and he says, 'Yes, now all we need is directions,' and he turns to a passerby and says, 'Excuse me, can you tell me the way to Alameda where they keep the nuclear wessels?' Cut. So we got that. Then there was a police officer with a motorcycle who was part of our unit helping to control traffic, and I had him moved into that spot and said to him, 'You just stand here and stare at the guy,' and we dropped the camera a ways back so that people would not be self-conscious about the fact that they were being photographed. We were about 30 or 40 feet back, almost like a hidden camera kind of feeling, and we just sat and watched the people come through and said react to whatever happens here. And the two of them, Walter and Nichelle, did this wonderful thing about these people going by. And sometimes you get really lucky. A lady who was not even on the job with us that day, asked to be hired as an extra to walk through the scene. I said thank God they did, because she walked through and they stopped her and she said, 'I don't know, I think it's across the bay in Alameda.' And I said, 'We've got it! We've brought the whole thing full circle.' Then I got a close-up of the cop just to have something to cut off to; to have a reaction to cut away to, and we walked away from it. But I knew I had the scene at least as written before I started experimenting."

Summarizing his feelings regarding the film, Nimoy notes, "[The feeling on the first film] was that we had to do a 'motion picture.' Nick Meyer brought a jauntiness back to it. I tried in *Star Trek III* to do a dignified job of resurrection, and do it with a sense of mysticism, a sense of wonder and, above all, to really capture the loyalty of these people for each other; their willingness to sacrifice themselves and their careers for the purpose of helping Spock. Having done that, I really wanted to have a good time on this one. Somebody had been constantly dying in the films, and this time I said, 'Nobody's going to die. I don't want anybody hitting anybody, I don't want anybody shooting anybody,' or any of that stuff. If anybody was going to be injured, it was going to be accidental.

"I insisted that there be no bad guy. We had done two pictures in a row with black-hat heavies, and I didn't want a bad guy anywhere. Circumstances would be the problem. Lack of awareness, lack of concern. Ignorance would be the problem. Not a person. With this one we really come full circle and come home, which is why, in a sense, [it's called] *The Voyage Home*. We're saying, 'Enjoy yourself, have a good time, and don't mind us as we drop off a few ideas along the way.'"

As *Star Trek IV* went on to become the most successful in the series, it also managed to touch the non-Trekker audience. The result was that Nimoy was taken very seriously as a director, and was offered a variety of follow-up projects. He chose *Three Men & A Baby* — a remake of the French film *Three Men & A Cradle* — which starred Tom Selleck, Steve Guttenberg and Ted Danson as a trio of bachelors who are suddenly thrust into a position of fatherhood when one of Danson's girlfriends [Nancy Travis] drops off their child at the high-rise they live in. The film was a smash financial success, grossing over $100 million at the box-office. According to Nimoy, the chemistry between the three leads was there from the get-go and the director managed to whip it all into a highly commercial project. Nimoy, who expressed passion for the film, refused to shoot the sequel, feeling that the script wasn't ready. Apparently he was right, as *Three Men &*

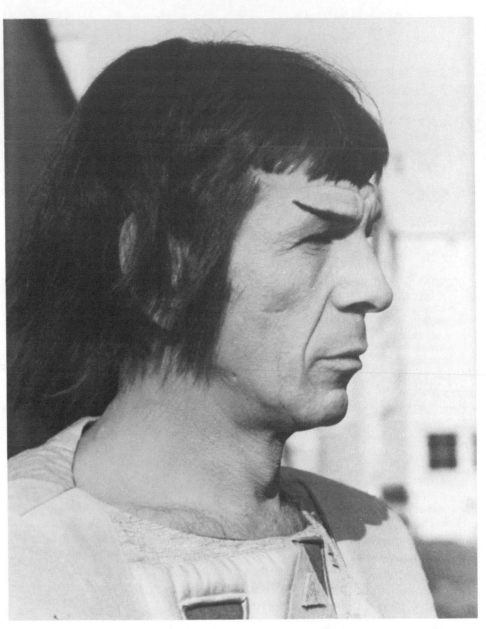

A candid photo of Nimoy made up as Spock on the Paramount lot during production of **Star Trek: The Motion Picture** (photo courtesy Jon Povill).

A Little Lady only grossed about a third of its predecessor and was trounced at the box-office by John Hughes' *Home Alone*. Instead, Nimoy went on to direct Diane Keaton in *The Good Mother*, based on Sue Miller's bestselling book, as part of his three picture deal with Touchstone Films. While far from the commercial success of *Three Men*, the film nonetheless garnered some impressive critical acclaim. He followed with the Gene Wilder/Christine Lahti comedy,

Funny About Love (originally *New York Times*), which was neither critically nor commercially noticed. The failure of the latter he chalks up to the same reason that *Star Trek V*, which he starred in but did not direct, failed to ignite the box office: the script.

"Bill worked very, very hard, and he directed it as well and as capably as any of our other films," offers Nimoy. "He was not riding on a good script, and if you're not riding on a good script, then you're the person people point fingers at. And he was responsible. It was his story. I've had that experience. *Funny About Love* didn't work at all. I wasn't successful with the script. Sometimes things bubble together and sometimes they don't, even though you've got well paid and professional people doing their job. Sometimes it works and sometimes it doesn't, and that's why some pictures succeed and some pictures fail."

Reportedly Nimoy had considered directing *Star Trek VI*, but ultimately decided that playing Spock and directing was too difficult. Still, he is credited with coming up with the film's storyline along with Lawrence Konner and Mark Rosenthal. In their final mission, the Enterprise is attempting to establish a peace treaty with the Klingons, despite racial prejudice on both sides. "My idea was to do a closure to the Klingons," he says. "That was exactly what I suggested. It was clear that there were Klingon characters on the Enterprise in *The Next Generation*. And it was clear to me that what Ronald Reagan referred to as the Evil Empire was coming apart, and we would have to reach out and make some kind of détente. The Berlin Wall was coming down. I had been in Russia and seen glasnost in action. I thought there would be a new kind of dialogue; a new thinking of these relationships; a whole new military vision and a whole new vision of hardware. I thought what an ideal way for us to have closure too, because the Klingons for us have always been the Communist Block, the Evil Empire. It just made sense to do that story."

After 25 years, Nimoy still holds a soft spot for *Star Trek*, and by the time of Gene Roddenberry's death, it had become evident that Nimoy was the new caretaker of Gene's "classic" cast and Great Bird of the Enterprise-A. With the exception of *Star Trek V*, Nimoy's imprint can be found on each film from *Star Trek III* on, and when former Paramount president Frank Mancuso decided to jumpstart production on a *Star Trek* feature for the show's 25th anniversary, it was Nimoy whom he turned to for help.

The Undiscovered Country has proven itself to be the final voyage of the original *Star Trek* crew, although William Shatner, James Doohan and Walter Koenig do appear in *Star Trek: Generations*. Nimoy, who declined to appear in the theatrical debut of *The Next Generation*, siting script problems, remains proud of the fact that the "classic" feature series went out in style. He emphasizes that he has never grown tired of playing Spock.

"The whole experience has been very satisfying, very fulfilling," he notes. "If we were not doing interesting stories, it would be a bore. Just to put on the clothes again, put on the ears again and trudge in and trudge out. As long as the mind is engaged, you can't get sick of it. I feel a great sense of accomplishment. Overall, we've done some sincere work. I hope that I haven't taken myself too seriously too often. I hope that the general fallout is positive — I think that it is. I'm very pleased when I hear that people's lives have been affected positively in one way or the other because of *Star Trek*. Without throwing any stones at anyone in particular, I would rather be associated with *Star Trek* than a lot of the other stuff I've seen on television over the past twenty five years. I have often said that if I had to choose between characters that I would have to be identified with, I would choose Spock. In general, I've had very good, positive feelings about it."

WILLIAM SHATNER
From Trek to Tek

It's easy to confuse the forceful, heroic and promiscuous persona of James T. Kirk with the man who personifies him, William Shatner. But over the years it has become clear that while there exists many similarities between actor and character, the differences are startling.

Shatner, who is the first to proclaim "I Am Not Kirk," can actually be quite shy, which he often overcompensates for by acting like a clown. Anyone who's seen Shatner squirm through a talk show appearance has to pause a moment to reconcile the actor with the starship captain he has so perfectly etched onto the collective pop consciousness. In fact, parodying Shatner

Early in his career, Shatner starred in TV's The Defenders pilot.

has become a regular cottage industry, with comedians across the country all taking their shot at imitating the actor's famous over enunciated recitations and jerky motions. However, there's little doubt that no one parodies William Shatner better than William Shatner.

In both *Airplane II: The Sequel* and his infamous *Saturday Night Live* appearance — in which the actor tells the pimply, overweight *Star Trek* set to "get a life" — the actor acknowledges the perception that people have of him. Yet behind the pompous veneer lies a thoughtful and contemplative individual, whose career has spanned several decades. It has been his behind-the-scenes involvement with every line of dialogue over *Star Trek*'s near-30 years and his involvement in the genesis and filming of *Star Trek V* that easily qualify him for Great Bird honors.

Without Shatner, it's highly unlikely *Star Trek* would be the "classic" it is today. In addition to the science-fiction series, Shatner has starred in *T.J. Hooker, Barbary Coast,* narrated the Emmy Award winning documentary *Universe* and hosted the CBS-TV reality based program *Rescue: 911,* while serving as executive producer, story consultant, occasional director and one of the

stars of *TekWar,* based on his series of bestselling novels. He's starred in stage productions of *Cat on a Hot Tin Roof* and on Broadway as the leading man in *The World of Suzie Wong,* as well as in *A Shot in the Dark* and the hit comedy *L'Idiote.* The McGill University graduate was, additionally, a familiar staple of television's Golden Age.

Born in Canada, Shatner developed an early interest in acting and started working professionally at the Canadian Broadcasting Company. After graduating with a business degree from McGill University, he took the job of assistant manager at the Mountain Playhouse in Montreal. "I was a disaster,

Shatner serves as host of the top-rated CBS series, Rescue: 911 (photo copyright ©1994 MTM).

forever losing tickets and such," he recalls. Abandoning the business end of the profession, he performed for three years with the Canadian Repertory Company in Ottawa, and joined the famous Stratford, Ontario Shakespeare Festival as an understudy, where he worked with such distinguished actors as Sir Alec Guinness, James Mason, Anthony Quayle and, ironically (given the casting of *Star Trek VI*), Christopher Plummer.

A performance as the second male lead in "Tamburlaine" brought him to the attention of New York critics, and Shatner was soon playing important roles on American television, including *Playhouse 90, The Twilight Zone* and *The*

Outer Limits. His motion picture debut was in the film adaptation of Dostyevsky's *The Brothers Karamazov,* and was followed by a number of Westerns and Stanley Kramer's milestone film, *Judgment at Nuremberg.* Since replacing Jeffrey Hunter as the Captain of the Enterprise, Shatner has starred in the feature films *Kingdom of the Spiders, Visiting Hours, The Kidnapping of the President, Airplane II: The Sequel* and *Loaded Weapon 1.*

For Shatner, whose Kirk is the most memorable role of a long career in television and film, *Star Trek* has been a very pleasant association. "I was offered the part in a rather peculiar fashion," Shatner recalled in the English press. "They had made a pilot of *Star Trek* with an actor who is now deceased, Jeffrey Hunter, and NBC did not like the pilot but they liked the idea. They said change the cast, change the story but give us another pilot for *Star Trek* and we'll pay a certain amount of money. So they showed me the first pilot and said, 'Would you like to play the part and here are some of the storylines that we plan to go with; you can see the kind of production we have in mind. Would you care to

William Shatner was frequently a guest star on the best of television's anthology series. Here he is seen in Rod Serling's The Twilight Zone (photo copyright ©1962 CBS).

Captain James Tiberius Kirk and his stoic first officer Mr. Spock lose it in this moment from the Star Trek blooper reel. Bones, as usual, looks kind of serious.

play it?' I thought it was an interesting gamble for myself as an actor to take, because I've always been fascinated by science fiction. I liked the production; I liked the people involved with the production and so I decided to do it. But it was under these peculiar circumstances of having a first pilot made that I did it.

"I talked at great length with Gene Roddenberry about the objectives we hoped to achieve," he continued. "One of those objectives was serious drama as well as science fiction. His reputation and ability, which I knew first hand, was such that I did not think he would do *Lost in Space*. And I was too expensive an actor, with what special or particular abilities I have, to warrant being put in something that somebody else could walk through. So I felt confident that *Star Trek* would keep those serious objectives for the most part — and it did.

Says Bob Justman, associate producer of the original *Star Trek* series, "Gene was very happy that we were able to get Bill Shatner who was highly thought of in the industry. I had worked with Bill on *Outer Limits* and he had a good reputation in television and entertainment industries even at the time, well before the second pilot of *Star Trek*. He was someone to be reckoned with and we certainly understood that he was a more accomplished actor than Jeff Hunter was, and he gave us more dimension. The network seemed to feel that Jeff Hunter was rather wooden. He was a nice person, everyone liked him. But he didn't run the gamut of emotions that Bill Shatner could do. Shatner was classically trained. He had enormous technical abilities to do different things and he gave the captain a terrific personality. He embodied what Gene had in mind, which was the flawed hero. Or the hero who considers himself to be flawed." John D.F. Black, who story edited the series in its early days, recalls a pensive Shatner contemplating the future of the series, not imagining the phenomena they were creating at the time. "The show was meaningful for many people back then," says Black. "Billy had just done *Alexander the Great* [a TV pilot]. He was good but it was not a hit. On that night of the first shoot, I left the office and found Bill leaning against my car. He had a look of enormous innocence on his face. I said, 'How's it going, Billy?' And he said, 'Fine'. I figured there was something going on. He just looked at me and said, 'It's so damned important to us'. And I said, 'Yeah, we've got a hit'. That's what you say to everybody when it's in the fan and you don't know what's going to happen next, particularly to actors who are vulnerable. He said 'I hope so,' and walked away. The sense I had was that we were all doing the best we could and giving it everything we had."

Noted Shatner, "*Everybody* was making contributions —including the head of the studio, Herb Solow. There was a great deal of excitement. It seemed to catch people's imaginations. I mean, creative people often try to contribute to something new, even if it's not their job. Actors write, and so forth. But this was almost as if people were designing the real future. I felt it myself."

However, that feeling of innocence that typified the early start-up of the show has long since been lost in the ego clashes that ensued, and the subsequent transformation of *Trek* from a well-regarded, low-rated network science-fiction series to an international money-machine of a major entertainment conglomerate. By the time *Star Trek* was closing the logbook on its first season, it became apparent that Shatner and Nimoy — despite their protestations of personal friendship — were engaged in some major league professional friction.

"During the first season, *Saturday Review* did this article about *Star Trek* that said Spock was much more interesting than Kirk and that Spock should be Captain," says *Trek* scholar, "Trouble With Tribbles" scenarist and science-fiction author David Gerrold. "Well, nobody was near Shatner for days. He was furious. You've got to look at it from his point of view. He had been hired to be the star of the show. It was, 'Starring

On the set of Star Trek: The Motion Picture, *from top-left: Leonard Nimoy, DeForest Kelley, Stephen Collins, Persis Khambatta and William Shatner (photo copyright ©1994 Globe Photos).*

William Shatner, *with DeForest Kelley and Leonard Nimoy.'* All of a sudden, all the writers are writing all this great stuff for Spock, and Spock, who's supposed to be a subordinate character, suddenly starts becoming the equal of Kirk. The show that started out about Kirk is now about Kirk and Spock. Bill definitely feels that he was lessened by that. On the other hand, Leonard is a very shrewd businessman, a very smart actor, and recognized that this Spock business was a way to be more important than an 'also ran' and he pushed."

Shatner noted, "I've always felt that the cast had a typical actor's sense of competition. We weren't saints, and we had actor's needs. But it was a good, healthy sense of competition, mostly focused on doing a good job, mostly good for the show."

Whatever form of rivalry may have taken place off-screen, on the bridge of the Enterprise things positively sparked between Spock and Kirk.

"All of the movies and all of the episodes hold together because Shatner holds it together," points out David Gerrold. "Spock is only good when he has someone to play off of. The scenes where Spock doesn't have Shatner to play off of are not interesting. If you look at Spock with his mom or dad, it's very ponderous. But Spock working with Kirk has the magic and it plays very well, and people give all of the credit to Nimoy and not to Shatner."

Surprisingly, Nimoy himself agrees with this observation. "During the series," says Nimoy, "we had a failure — I experienced it as a failure — in an episode called 'The Galileo Seven.' The Spock character had been so successful that somebody said, 'Let's do a show where Spock takes command of a vessel.' We had this shuttlecraft mission where Spock was in charge. I had a tough time with it. I really appreciated the loss of the Kirk character for me to play against, to comment on. The Bill Shatner Kirk performance was the energetic, driving performance, and Spock could kind of slipstream along and make comment and offer advice, give another point of view. Put into the position of being the driving force, the central character, was very tough for me and I perceived it as a failure."

When *Star Trek* went off the air in 1969, a financially strapped Shatner — who was coming off of a costly divorce — desperately sought out any work that would come his way, ranging from Promise margarine commercials, to college lecture tours and such low-budget oddities as *Impulse, Big Bad Mama* and *The Devil's Rain.* Many of these roles, he would explain, were things he would never have taken in his younger days, but he had to survive — *that* was the bottom line.

Of course, throughout the 1970s he remained attached to *Star Trek* via supplying his voice to the animated spin-off, appearing at conventions around the country, and signing to reprise his role as Captain James T. Kirk for the proposed syndicated series *Star Trek II,* which fell apart one week before filming began. Instead, he took the helm of the Enterprise in the $44 million extravaganza, *Star Trek: The Motion Picture,* a journey many felt not quite

worth the trip.

"We had no idea that the first film would be a disaster," he admitted in 1982. "We never knew it was falling apart while we were shooting. We didn't have an ending to the script when we started, but we had months to play around with solving it. With all the high-priced talent around, we were sure that someone would come up with a corker of a finale. Somebody would certainly create something which made sense. [But] we never got it together....Nobody connected with the film ever sat in a theater and saw the movie with an audience *before* it opened. After you've spent nearly two years on a project, that's essential. By that point, you're just too close to a movie to judge it objectively.

"The finished *Star Trek: The Motion Picture* was really two movies: one about *Star Trek,* one about special effects. Had 15 minutes been trimmed out of the released version, I think it would have been a different, stronger film. I also felt that the characters weren't as fully realized as they could have been. We certainly were dwarfed by the special effects. It was a very confusing time for me. One felt helpless. I remember having lunch with the studio head, who asked me, 'What made *Star Trek* so successful?' I couldn't tell him anything. What was I going to say, 'Character development and story'? If I told him that, he would have said, 'Yeah, but we need big effects to compete with *Star Wars.'* As a result, you wound up with a weak movie."

Despite his reservations regarding the first film, Shatner nonetheless warped into the sequel — *The Wrath of Khan* — and delivered what is probably his best performance *ever* as Kirk.

"I was nervous about the film," he pointed out. "Especially after the first film. The success of your performance, essentially, rests in the words. Everything rises and falls on the script. When a script is good, it takes a heroic effort to ruin it. As this script developed, I swung wildly from awful lows to exalted highs. I began to realize that the movie might be good. By the time we were ready to shoot, I knew *The Wrath of Khan* would be great. I knew we had ILM for the effects, so the movie couldn't *look* bad. We also had a very human, *Star Trek*ian script. It was a wonderful working experience. It was as if the years between this film and the old show never existed."

At the outset of *Star Trek III: The Search for Spock*, the "experience" might have shifted for Shatner when he heard that Leonard Nimoy had been signed to serve as the film's director. As Shatner himself explained it: "Leonard and I are the dearest of old friends. We had shared a mutual struggle with the management in various stages, whether it was a script, a thought, a concept or a dressing room and asked each other what we thought. We'd have a plan! Whenever we were to deal with management, we'd plan it out together. Now, suddenly, my 'brother' was saying, 'Well, you should do this and I think you should do that.' There was an awkward period of time for me, although I don't think for Leonard, when I felt alone in anything I might have objected to. From my point of view, it was more awkward in the beginning than with either of the other two directors [Robert Wise, Nicholas Meyer]. But that slowly erased itself."

Once again *Star Trek* was a theatrical hit, and 1986 saw the release of *Star Trek IV: The Voyage Home*, in which the Enterprise crew comes back to our time in search of a pair of humpback whales which will be used to save earth in the future. As such, this was the first *Trek* cross-over film; the only film in the series to appeal to the general movie going audience.

"We discovered something in *Star Trek IV* that we hadn't pinpointed in any of the other movies," said Shatner, "and it just shows how the obvious can escape you. There is a texture to the best *Star Trek* hours that verges on tongue-in-cheek, but isn't. There's a line that we all have to walk that is reality. It's as though the characters within the play have a great deal of joy about themselves, a joy of liv-

ing. That energy, that 'joie de vivre' about the characters seems to be tongue-in-cheek but isn't, because you play it with the reality [that] you would in a kitchen-sink drama written for today's life."

Star Trek IV became — and remains — the most successful film in the series, and effectively launched Leonard Nimoy's directing career (which has included *Three Men & A Baby*, *The Good Mother* and *Funny About Love*).

Based on the friendly, and at times fiery, rivalry that existed between Shatner and Nimoy on the series and during the filming of *Star Trek: The Motion Picture*, it should have come as little surprise that after Nimoy directed two successful and well-regarded installments of the *Star Trek* feature film voyages, Shatner would clamor for his chance behind the camera. Actually, this desire should not have caught anyone off-guard, as Shatner had been intimately involved with the development of new *Star Trek* right from his first appearance in "Where No Man Has Gone Before."

"I made some very definite contributions to the script," he said in his biography, *Shatner: Where No Man*. "We tried to get as much lightness in it as possible. Gene [Roddenberry] and the writer, Sam Peeples, were writing all the time, and the new drafts were coming in and they were giving me the pages to read — which was good of them to do. I got involved with the writing, then and later, not in terms of 'I want more for *me*' but in terms of 'I think the script has a problem here. Here's an idea how we could solve it.' Or, 'I don't think this is right. This dialogue isn't right. Could we do this?' Sometimes it worked, sometimes not. Sometimes it sparked somebody to have a better idea."

Contractually, Paramount Pictures had little choice but to allow Shatner to follow in Nimoy's footsteps.

"Somewhere along the line," Shatner detailed in *Captain's Log*, "Leonard's lawyers and my lawyers had gotten together and drawn up a favored nations clause, which meant everything

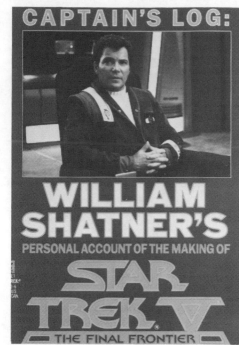

he got, I got and vice versa. Well, in the beginning I was commanding more money, so that any raises I was getting, Leonard would get also. So I made Leonard a great deal of money on my lawyers bringing him up to the salary I was getting. We used to joke about that, how that clause had benefited him so much. But in the end, the fact that Leonard directed a picture, which meant that I would get to direct one, was by far the most important consequence of that clause.

"Directing has been a lifelong dream," Shatner enthused elsewhere. "My business is to entertain people, and to communicate my feelings to them, so I find the best way is to direct. Directing is the pinnacle of our business. A really good director has a point of view on his film and all his other skills emanate from that spine. I've always wanted to entertain, and I think I can do that with my point of view, so I'm under the impression that I can gather all my skills around me to make people laugh and cry. I wanted to do more. I haven't done it to the extent that I wanted to. I think the movies have matured beyond the series and we have to give our audience that maturity. I'd like to think that's what I've done."

In addition to directing the film, Shatner's contract allowed him to develop the storyline, and he had one in mind. It began with the fascination he had always had for television evangelists who claim that God is speaking through them rather than someone else.

"I took the TV evangelist persona and created a holy man who thought God had spoken to him," said Shatner. "He believed God had told him, 'I need many followers, and I need a vehicle to spread my word throughout the universe.' That vehicle he needed became a starship which the holy man would capture when it came to rescuing some hostages he had taken....Finally the Enterprise arrives at the planet where God supposedly resides, in the center of the universe....Kirk, Spock, McCoy and the holy man are beamed down to the planet. It's like the drawings of Dante's *Inferno*, like a flaming hell. When God appears, he seems like God....but gradually, in a conversation between God and the holy man, Kirk perceives that something is wrong and begins to challenge God. God gets angrier and angrier, and begins to show his true colors, which are those of the devil....So essentially that was my story: that man conceives of God in his own image, but those images change from generation to generation, therefore he appears in all these different guises as man-made Gods. But in essence, if the devil exists, God exists by inference. This is the lesson that the *Star Trek* group learns. The lesson being that God is within our hearts, not something we conjure up, invent and then worship."

Screenwriter David Loughery, who turned Shatner's story into a screenplay, explains, "Paramount liked Bill's outline, but they thought that it was a little too dark. After the success of *Star Trek IV*, they wanted to make sure that we retained as much humor and fun as possible, because they felt that was one of the reasons for the big success of that film. They wanted us to inject a spirit of fun and adventure into the story. I think they just wanted a balance between the

Captain Kirk scales new heights in Star Trek V: The Final Frontier, *which marked Shatner's feature diretorial debut (photo copyright ©1989 Globe Photos).*

darker elements and some of the lighter stuff. I think everybody felt they'd sort of had their romp and now they were getting a little more serious again, but let's keep that spark alive.

"The idea of God and the Devil was reflected in the script's earlier drafts. Those drafts were much more comprehensible in terms of the idea that you think you're going to Heaven, but you turn out to have found Hell. We weren't literally saying Heaven and Hell, but we were suggesting the idea that it was like, 'Wait a minute, is this God or the Devil?', without saying specifically that it's either, but instead is an alien entity that has tapped into our perceptions about where they're going. We did, however, run into problems, one with Gene Roddenberry."

Roddenberry believed that Shatner's story was all wrong. He rejected the notion of the Enterprise encountering God, believing that *Star Trek* should avoid such specific religious themes.

"I didn't object to it being an alien claiming to be God," Roddenberry said in *Captain's Log*, "but there was too much in it that an audience could have thought was really God or really the

devil, and I very strongly resist believing in either. I do not perceive this as a universe that's divided between good and evil. I see it as a universe that is divided between many ideas of what is."

This stance seemed particularly ironic since, in 1975, Roddenberry himself penned a proposed *Star Trek* movie script entitled *The God Thing*, which dealt with similar themes.

"Maybe Gene turned around and figured that it didn't work, and wouldn't work the way we were doing it either," Loughery muses. "I just don't know. I think we managed to pull off something that is able to tread the line. I don't think it was too controversial and I don't think anyone was too radically upset by what we did, although it seems to me that *Star Trek* was always meeting God in some way or another. That idea permeated many of the old episodes, and it certainly played a part in the first movie.

"To me," adds Loughery, "God was never the most important part of the script. Yes, it was part of the story, but my focus and concentration was on the relationships. The whole God idea was a subplot. We had to tread a fine line, because we could really become very pretentious and pretend that we're saying something infinitely important. What I think we're really saying is something that's very simple, which is that if there is a God, he's not a place you go to in terms of outer space. He's a place you go to inside yourself. We also wanted to challenge the audience's imagination and expectations when they realized that this is what Sybok's divine mission was. We really wanted the audience to stir around, look at each other and say, 'Are they serious? Can they possibly mean that we're going to see God?' Because, for me, *Star Trek* is probably the only arena in which you might actually try to do that. *Star Trek* has always been big enough to encompass almost any kind of concept, so we thought when we dropped the bomb and said, 'Oh, by the way, we're going to see God,' it would be something the audience would be excited about and say, 'Gee, maybe they will....who knows?'

Of Roddenberry's protestations, Shatner admits, "He did come down strongly against the story and set up circumstances that were negative and unfortunate. There's nothing wrong with a good story about the search for the meaning of life, that's basic to any great storytelling no matter what form it takes, whether it's *The Bible* or a myth or a fairy tale, and I was hoping to be able to accomplish that."

Leonard Nimoy and DeForest Kelley also had certain problems with the screenplay, the alterations of which both Shatner and Loughery felt weakened the overall product.

"One of the smart things we did early on," says Loughery, "was bring Leonard and De in to go over the script, because we wanted their input. These guys have lived with these characters for more than 20 years, and have very strong opinions on what their characters would and wouldn't do. There were problems with this too, however. As originally conceived, only Kirk held out against Sybok, which gives you more of a one man stands alone kind of thing, betrayed by

his best friends. Leonard and De objected and it was changed. Suddenly there were three guys against Sybok. When you start doing that kind of stuff, bit by bit you remove and dilute the real strength of the original vision and finally you end up with a bit of a mish-mash. It would have been great for Kirk to have squared off against Spock in some way. But you find the script beginning to accommodate the needs of the actors who know their characters and say, 'Spock wouldn't do that.' It's kind of indefensible. You don't really have an argument that can turn them around on something like that."

Shatner's collaborator on the film was long-time film series producer Harve Bennett, who, subsequent to the film's release, has been critical of his star-director, whom he said showed a lack of awareness of the limitations of the medium.

"Well, he's right," says a surprisingly self-effacing Shatner. "But it's like youth. I wish I were able to say it's because of my youth, but it *is* like youth. A youthful or first-time person knows no boundaries and it's in not knowing them that you shatter them. Rather than accepting the status quo, I have tried to break the boundaries and make the camera do things that it wasn't supposed to. Not because I didn't know how, but I thought that by standing firm and by being as adamant as possible, it would happen. But there came a point where I had to compromise. I was rushing around trying to save what I thought was my movie. I had spent days and weeks with Harve telling him the story and him telling me his version of the story, and going over and over and over as we built the story and the script. We worked in a very close and intimate way and got to a point where we were talking about the death and birth of people close to us, and there were times when tears passed between us in the intimacy of his office. Those moments are part of making *Star Trek V* for me. If anybody else is doing another trip, that's their problem. For me,

I dealt and met with a series of people and made a film. Sure I asked for more than what could be expected and tried to get people to do more work for the money than they would ordinarily have done, and many people did it because I asked them to. Yes, the cast loved Leonard, and why not? He's a very lovable person. I don't know why, a couple of people of the cast — and they've never said it to my face — didn't enjoy making the film with me."

One of Shatner's biggest dilemmas to contend with were budgetary constraints. Despite being the highest priced installment since the budget-busting *Star Trek: The Motion Picture*, most of the film's budget went to paying the inflated above the line costs which included the costly star salaries, leaving little room to pay for expensive special effects and set pieces.

"The problem when I was required to reduce the budget was that I kept slicing away at the ending," Shatner says. "I didn't realize until we got there how much of the ending I had lost and what a disservice I had done to the film. That was lesson number one. I made compromises on *Star Trek V* thinking I had to do that, that's the nature of the business and it is the nature of the business to compromise. But the line where you do not compromise I couldn't tread because of a number of factors, not the least of which is my own nature. I got to learn when it's time to stand and when it's time to turn, and that's really — for a knowledgeable person in the business — where the camera is and how to play a scene and what your establishing shot is....those mechanics of making a film no longer become a point of discussion, it's automatic, it's there creatively. The political point of a director is a constant learning process because the interpersonal relationship between the director and the rest of the people — the cast and crew and management — is constantly changing from day to day and moment to moment, depending on how confident you feel and how confidently you express that feeling. And it changes from job to job, because you come to a job with more or less prestige and perceived prestige."

In *Star Trek V*'s lost ending, Kirk stands alone. As he races back towards the shuttlecraft, a horde of gargoyles are unleashed by the god-creature intent on devouring him. They pursue Kirk relentlessly while Scotty desperately tries to repair the damaged transporter —disabled by a phaser blast when the Chief Engineer accidentally beamed a gargoyle on board the ship and vaporized it.

This epic ending in which Kirk faces the Devil's minions was never filmed, but can be found in early drafts of the script. It was one of Shatner's grand ideas for capping his installment in the *Star Trek* mythos and was considered a fitting end for what many perceived as the last Enterprise silver screen voyage.

Explains David Loughery, "When the torpedo came down and explodes the hole, it's like the bottle is uncapped and all the imps spill out, free, and chase our characters back to the shuttle. That was our original concept. A movie, especially a movie like this one, goes through so many transformations from original story to final film. Because of all the hands involved in the making of these movies, it sometimes starts to take on a committee atmosphere to movie making. Things don't turn out exactly the way you originally wanted them to, but there are reasons for that. We certainly wish we could have hung on to some of that concept. The area of the movie that has always been in flux is *how* we represent the god-being. That sequence got lost when it became financially impossible for us to create the gargoyle creatures. You're always sorry to see those things go, because your imagination is one thing and the budget is something else. In various places, we had to make certain cuts and rearrangements based on how much we could afford."

Despite some of the critical barbs as well as cool Trekkie reaction

that greeted the film upon its release, Shatner is proud of the finished product.

"What the final result was, was the final result. I have certain regrets, but I feel in total that a lot of the vision was there," he says. "I made one major compromise at the beginning when, if the one line idea was *Star Trek* goes in search of god — which in itself was a wonderful one-line idea — then to mitigate that idea by saying *Star Trek* goes in search of god and finds an alien pretending to be god, you've eviscerated the enormous thrust of the first idea. That was my first compromise, and it seemed that was a necessary one due to the fact everybody was very apprehensive about the obvious problem. Then I faced budgetary problems on the expense of the end, and I didn't have the sense to horde my money for the grand finale. I was busy spending wonderful dollars fighting for effects in the opening. I'm not that much of a neophyte not to know that you don't need a good opening, and I hurt my finale by not having enough money. Nothing I could do to the studio would make them say here's another $3 million for more gargoyles and special effects, which it needed."

"In retrospect," offers David Loughery, "you look back from the distance of a couple of years, and I've always felt — it was always in the back of my head — that one of the problems is that it's a reactive story rather than an active one. What I mean by that is that our guys are kind of required to stand by and be dragged along on somebody else's quest. In this case, Sybok's. It's sort of *his* quest and *his* passion, and Kirk, Spock and McCoy and the rest of the crew are dragged along almost as though they were a supporting cast to this guy. If it had been Kirk who suddenly had this vision of God and hijacked his own ship and turned against the Federation, *then* you've got this much more active, passionate kind of story."

Shatner is diplomatic in addressing the film's botched visual effects, which were also decried by afi-

cionados and critics of the self-styled auteur. "We had problems that we might not have had if we had had different personnel. I did not have first-hand knowledge of these things and I was in on the decision, so I make no excuse for that, but there, again, my lack of experience showed."

After having captained *Star Trek V* from the director's chair, Shatner was asked to simply sit in it for the following feature film voyage, *The Undiscovered Country*.

"On one hand, it was a tremendous relief," laughs Shatner about not directing the film. "I was only too aware of the pressures on [director] Nick Meyer both from a production point of view and a political point of view from the studio." For the actor turned director, the problems which typified *Star Trek VI*, including a tight shooting schedule and last minute slashing of the budget by nervous studio execs, was deja vu.

Few actors can claim, as can Shatner with the role of Captain Kirk, to have indelibly etched a character of near mythological proportions onto the American pop consciousness.

"Having done a quick course with Joseph Campbell, I've realized that the magic of *Star Trek* is to provide a mythology that this culture doesn't have. As he pointed out, mythology relates man to his environment and tries to explain some of the inexplicable dilemmas and the dichotomies that face us. Because of the construction of our culture, we don't have time for that because all of us are busy solving these problems with science. I think mythology is best served by an individual, along with his hearty band of brothers, as was done so many times, so well by the Greeks."

It is for this reason that Shatner maintains *Star Trek*'s triumvirate of classic archetypes have become "classics" and the reason he believes its successor, *The Next Generation*, is less satisfying. "My perception is that it's more interesting storytelling to have passion and have one person in a dilemma. It's a more person-

The stars of the feature film Star Trek: Generations, *Patrick Stewart and William Shatner, seen here at Creation's "Two Captains" convention (photo copyright ©1994 Karen Witkowski).*

ally effective way of telling a story. A story told by committee is not as exciting. There's more distance between you and the audience. But from what I can see, *The Next Generation*'s very popular, has achieved an audience and that's good."

Shatner resents those who would accuse the original series of being dated and sociologically irrelevant. "In every moment in time there is an exciting historical event that takes place, some of which we hear of immediately — like we're hearing now — and some that we don't hear of because it may only concern 10 people in a cave on the Seregetti plane. To the people of the Seregetti plane where the event happened in the '70s, that was a very exciting time. I think storytelling is a universally continuous thing, from the beginning of recorded time and stories of personal adventures and heroics and dilemmas, and the conventions of telling the story as written down with the Greeks. For my taste, following those conventions of antagonist, protagonist — that's tells me a more satisfying story than anything else. The fact that our show was a '60s show, I don't think holds up. I think it's the point of

view of the people who made the early shows, who had a different point of view than the people who are making *Star Trek: The Next Generation.*"

Despite his scant praise for the competition, Shatner claims to be a fan of Patrick Stewart, his opposite number aboard the Enterprise 1701-D. When the actors appeared together on stage at a *Star Trek* convention, dubbed "The Two Captain's Con" by fans, Shatner took notice of his fellow thespian.

"To me, Patrick Stewart is not the captain. He's just a wonderful actor. It was a pleasure to be in his company. He seemed, in person, to be a little straight, matter of fact, but certainly very admirable before we got on stage. However, when we got on stage, he was wild, funny, with a quip for everything and very quick on his feet. I enjoyed him very much and had a wonderful time."

Regarding a *TV Guide* cover story in which viewers preferred Captain Kirk to Picard as their savior if our planet was in peril, he adds, "I'm sorry that they perceive it as competition. It's not — but wouldn't it have been awful if I had lost?"

After living with *Star Trek* for over 25 years, Shatner has developed strong opinions, and found it gratifying that *Star Trek VI* showcased a side of Kirk's persona rarely evidenced.

"I think that a topical issue is very much a part of the movie storytelling genre and therefore many of our successful movies were cold war spying, which was very much in vogue and very much part of our consciousness during the Cold War," he says. "In *Star Trek VI* we grasped an opportunity to tell a *peristroika* story. We made the movie at the time it took place, yet we are offering it as it happened 200 years from now as a futuristic history. That being the case, we can comment with some objectivity even though it hasn't happened yet. I'd like to think that this movie does that and provides an added element of entertainment and interest.

"The portrayal of Kirk attempts to show a right wing....no, that's the wrong

term....a man who has spent a lifetime imbued with the idea that his mission in life is to subdue and subvert and make the enemy submit to his nation's or his Federation's view. That's his whole training, and that is the military training. He then learns differently, and that is the classic dilemma that *Star Trek* has sought to do in its most successful shows."

A fan of the series format, Shatner feels — and tried to accomplish this with *Star Trek V* — that the films should essentially be an episode on a much larger scale. Perhaps in that sense he succeeded. Like Nimoy, much of Shatner's creative contributions to *Star Trek* over the years have gone unnoticed.

"*Star Trek* is certainly a star vehicle," says Walter Koenig. "Those two guys [Leonard & Bill] were always the ones who went in to petition the producers for changes in dialogue and emphasis on the scenes. We didn't do that. We were never led to believe that was a way to go."

James Doohan, who sees Shatner as nothing more than a great side-of-ham of the galaxy, blames the actor for the diminished role of the regular ensemble in the original show as well as the subsequent features.

Shatner is not surprised to be the butt of criticism and is diplomatic in responding to it. "If the original concept of the show was still in effect and the series was still going today, the situation would be exactly the same," he offers. "There are people whose names and parts are above the title and people who aren't. That's the nature of the business and that's the way these stories are told. Certain people and certain characters lose sight of the overall larger issues and are totally involved in their own world. That's good for an actor, because he takes care of his own business and traditionally actors are totally self-involved. There's no reason for them to see where does this scene fit in and where does the character fit in. When the actor who came in during the last five minutes of Tennesee Williams' play *Streetcar Named Desire*, who plays

The faces are familiar, but the uniforms are not. Leonard Nimoy and William Shatner reunite on T.J. Hooker (photo copyright ©1994 Columbia Pictures).

the doctor and who has the last five lines of the play, is asked what the play was about and answers it's a play about a doctor who comes in, that's okay. That syndrome has always been part of an actor's make-up. I can't fault Jimmy Doohan for thinking what he does".

As for the criticism he has received on the convention circuit and in the press, from not only Doohan and Koenig but other members of the *Trek* ensemble, Shatner is puzzled. "It's coming from a couple of people," he says. "I don't understand that. I'm not even aware of it, quite frankly. Occasionally I'll hear something from an ardent fan of mine who'll say so and so said this about you, and it bewilders me because I have had no trouble with them. Nothing certainly bad, nothing particularly good either. We have done our job and gone on and I have never had bad words with anyone. I don't know what vitriol is spilling out. The people who I see a lot of — Leonard, DeForest, the people in management and the directors, I've heard nothing bad from.

"Regarding *Star Trek* itself," adds Shatner, "I'd like to be connected in any

way I can. It's been a wonderful story-telling form and I enjoy the people very, very much. Anything I could do, I'd be willing to do."

In fact, there is one particular idea he would still love to see brought to life. "The Spock/Kirk interrelationship is really key to so much of the way the stories are told and Leonard and I are playing off each other better and better all the time. I would love to see if there was any chance of doing a future *Star Trek*, which seems hardly likely....a great story between these two characters who love each other and fall out would be wonderful."

Assessing his association with a character named James T. Kirk, Shatner doesn't even have to pause before recalling the most pleasant memory of his involvement with the series.

"My greatest moment in *Star Trek* was *Star Trek V*, the anticipation about the release and some of the notices we got. As much as we got blasted, we got lauded. In Los Angeles, we got a wonderful review in the *Los Angeles Times* and a mention from Gary Franklin on KABC. Mr. Ten. Well, it's hard

to get a 10 plus — and we did. It was gratifying that the notices I read were positive — and I try not to read them. But the whole experience, good, bad and indifferent, was a high-water mark for me."

Another positive aspect of *Star Trek V* is that it had stretched Shatner's imagination in such a way that it served as the impetus for the creation of his own universe. The result was the science-fiction novel *TekWar*, which has led to several bestselling sequels, four TV movies, comic books and a weekly series for the USA cable network.

TekWar was an attempt to blend elements from two of Shatner's most popular television series, *Star Trek* and *T.J. Hooker*, resulting in a unique science fiction adventure. Shatner does, however, admit that he may have been influenced just a little too much by *Star Trek* in terms of his creation's futuristic setting.

"When I sat down to write the novel," he explains, "I followed my instincts rather than any conscious desire. It was almost as though I didn't believe anything more would come of it

Shatner enters the newest phase of his career: that of science fiction novelist. TekWar is his first effort, and has resulted in several sequels and a new TV series.

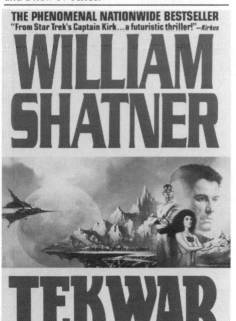

THE PHENOMENAL NATIONWIDE BESTSELLER
"From Star Trek's Captain Kirk...a futuristic thriller!"—*Kirkus*

WILLIAM SHATNER

TEKWAR

than my doodling around with the story. As a result, I wasn't too careful about where I set it. Since I was working on a *Star Trek* movie at the time, I set it instinctively, almost, in the general time of *Star Trek*. So the novels are set 200 years from now and the world that I imagined was a world that I probably had absorbed from various contacts, pictures, paintings and covers of magazines and other science fiction that I had read from the multitude of sources that one gets their imagination from. I had a generalized feeling of the world of *Tek*, but what I was concentrating mostly on was this policeman whose life was torn asunder by the various things that had happened to him."

TekWar introduced ex-police officer Jake Cardigan, accused of murdering his partners while under the influence of Tek, a drug-like virtual reality experience that is oftentimes fatal in its addiction. As a result of this supposed crime, Cardigan is placed in cryogenic freeze for a 15-year sentence, but freed after four by the influential Bascom, who wants him to work for the Cosmos Detective Agency. Partnered with Sid Gomez, Cardigan goes up against one TekLord after another in each subsequent adventure while simultaneously trying to repair the rifts between he and his wife and son, clearing his name and getting on with his own life.

The basic concept of the Tek "drug" came about, Shatner says, "by the fact that I put a television set in a wall in my bedroom and used it — and use it — as a means of going to sleep. In the middle of the night when the dark hangs heavy, to light a candle was to open the television set so that the television, in a way, is something I've become accustomed to using both for information, of course, but to sleep as well. It's almost something I try to not do because I do it so often. As a result, I extended that drug effect into a totality of drug, in that the television miniaturized can then become your fantasy and your fantasy becomes real. In that case, it would

become difficult to even leave your house, which is what happens to a Tek user in addition to getting their neurons scrambled. That's the lure of Tek, that your fantasy world can be better than your real world."

Although Tek was a creation Shatner was satisfied with, he still wanted the opportunity to alter the premise's time frame. That opportunity came in the form of Marvel Comics, which approached him with the idea of using the novels as a springboard for a comic book series.

"I then began to think more consciously of what I wanted to do," Shatner admits. "By now I had stuck myself in the extreme futuristic world and when I had gone out to sell *TekWar* as a potential vehicle, people said, 'It's going to be too expensive,' and it's then that I began to realize that I shouldn't have gone so far in the future. So I had another shot when Marvel Comics came at it. We granted them the rights, but with the admonition that it be set 50 years from now, fantasizing again that the comic books could serve as storyboards for a potential movie. Some part of my mind was cunningly aware of that. Then, when the movie people came and said, 'Let's make a film,' I was prepared by that time to say, 'This story takes place 50 years from now, so we can use the architecture of today and just talk about a new building being kind of creaky and old and needing refurbishing.' That's what worked for me. So that's the world of *TekWar* that slowly evolved from *Star Trek* into something more meaningful."

Shatner and his production company, Lemli, was approached by a variety of studios interested in producing *TekWar*, but he finally opted for Atlantis Films and together they struck a deal with Universal. "We went together to three or four people who were bidding on it," he says. "We ended up in a strange position of having more than one person who wanted to do the project, which was wonderful. It was the first time that's ever happened to me in a life-

time of striving."

As *TekWar* moved toward production, William Shatner and those involved made the decision that their future would be decidedly upbeat.

"We held a symposium with about eight or 10 so-called futuristic experts in their fields," says Shatner, "who felt they knew what will transpire 50 years from now, which, as I've said, is the setting of *TekWar*. And there's a duality in everybody's mind — knowledgeable people's minds — and that is that there is the possibility of Doomsday around the corner, and that isn't very entertaining. It's a reality, but it's not something people want to see.

"It's human nature to be optimistic," he continues, "so everybody at the symposium, including myself, chooses and chose to be optimistic, believing that the problems of today can be solved with courage, wisdom, intelligence and rapidity. And they'll only be replaced by other problems, which in turn need to be solved. But that's the history of mankind. The only question is, can we solve the present-day problems in time so that our children and our children's children can live? We choose to think that they can."

Among those bringing *TekWar* to life are cast members Greg Evigan and Eugene Clark, respectively Jake Cardigan and Sid Gomez, Shatner himself, who oversees the scripts, serves as executive producer, co-stars as the enigmatic Bascom and even directed the first telefilm; former *Next Generation* producer Hans Beimler, who is developing scripts for the weekly series, and producer/production designer Stephen Roloff, who virtually everyone connected with the show credits with giving the future its distinct look.

Enthuses Shatner, "Stephen has captured my vision and enhanced it. He's a real artist in that he has set up certain rules for his/our universe, and when you come against the rules that need to be bent for the exigencies of production, it's very difficult for him to

Jake Cardigan meets his maker. On the set of *TekWar* is Greg Evigan (right) and William Shatner.

let go of it because he has created something implacable in his mind. And it's wonderful."

Probably the most difficult aspect of creating the world of *TekWar* was its fiscal limitations, which one assumes would have been rather stunning to Shatner, who had gone from directing the $30 million *Star Trek V* to the first TV movie in the series.

"As for working with a different budget," he points out, "it's like nature abhorring a vacuum. Movies seem to fill the budget that they have. Even at $30 million there was never enough money [for *Star Trek V*]. And certainly at $4 million, we were scraping along. It never seems to be enough. I've got a better idea, we can do this, we can do that — sorry, we don't have the money for it. That's always the plaintive cry."

Another problem facing *TekWar* beyond budgets is the fact that there is a long history of failed science fiction television shows. "But," Shatner offers, "there's a history of sci-fi working on television as well. The key to great science fiction is the human story and my earnest attempt will be to keep the stories human and let the technicalities take care of themselves. In point of fact, if you identity with the characters and are intrigued by the story, it matters little how good

the technological stuff is. The audience will forgive a lot, even if the techniques aren't as adroit as they might be."

So far, audiences haven't had to be too forgiving, as the films feature state-of-the-art computer effects and intriguing science-fiction storylines. Shatner emphasizes that this will continue in the weekly series as well.

"There's no question the audience will be entertained," he smiles. "There are elements of Cyber-Punk and Cybernetics. The world of *Tek* is much closer to our world of today. The problems that we'll deal with are problems that we haven't solved yet or are extensions of the problems we know of. One of the shows deals with the deposed king of England in exile in the United States, striving to get back to an England taken over by the TekLords. That's a typical story of today where the monarchy is in trouble. The contention is that the monarchy is deposed. So there is, I hope, a vivid mixture of fact and fun drama of today with the technology of tomorrow."

Interestingly, Shatner is now Great Bird of his own galaxy, a role Gene Roddenberry had filled with *Star Trek* — one which reportedly resulted in conflict between producer and star, both of whom felt things should go a certain way.

"The conflicts have been emphasized for dramatic reasons only," says Shatner. "The word conflict suggests to somebody who isn't in the film world that there was great warfare going on, but in fact if somebody says, 'This is the way I think it should go,' and you say, 'Wait a minute, what about this way?' and there's a discussion, somebody on the sidelines will say, 'Oh, they're having a war,' whereas in fact it may just be a disagreement about something. Gene Roddenberry had his own world and I was just a part of it."

But isn't Shatner now in Roddenberry's position of having to turn to co-workers and say, "This is my universe, and this is the way it's going to be"?

"You have to be that way and so

was Gene Roddenberry, let's make no mistake about that," he points out. "If somebody comes up with a good idea, you don't eliminate a good idea. But at a certain point when there's a disagreement and it's not going anywhere, you say, 'Hey, wait a minute, this is my world,' and that would happen on occasion. But there's no animosity involved. Somebody has to judicate two divergent opinions.

"It's a democracy up to a point," Shatner laughs, "and then it becomes a totalitarian situation."

Despite his success in *Tek*, Shatner hasn't quite left the world of *Trek* behind him. He recently co-authored his best selling biography *Star Trek Memories* and has inked a deal to write a follow-up, *Star Trek Movie Memories*. Additionally, he assumes the role of Captain James T. Kirk for the final time in the first *Next Generation* feature film, *Star Trek: Generations*, in which Kirk sacrifices himself to save the life of Captain Jean Luc Picard and the galaxy itself.

It's difficult to fathom, but Shatner's near 30-year love affair with *Star Trek* and its fans will actually be coming to an end.

"How do I feel?" Shatner muses, regarding this penultimate moment. "I'm feeling great nostalgia, great sadness. I feel a sense of loss. It's a wonderful character and another setting in which to place the character. I love action films with some kind of conflict, so the human conflict is told in action-adventure rather than a sedate tone. A picture should move, and *Star Trek* lends itself to that genre."

Shatner pauses for a moment. "I leave it with great reluctance and great sorrow."

He's not alone.

RICK BERMAN
"Great Bird of The Next Generation"

While Gene Roddenberry was the force that shaped *Star Trek: The Next Generation* throughout its fitful first two seasons, in the years since Roddenberry's death, Rick Berman's role as the new great bird of the *Star Trek* galaxy has become abundantly clear.

Certainly, Paramount acknowledged this fact when they asked Berman to produce their first *Star Trek: The Next Generation* feature film (*Generations*) and shepherd a new TV series to the screen, *Star Trek: Voyager*.

As *Star Trek*'s Executive Producer, Rick Berman has not only adhered to the strictures laid down by Roddenberry during the show's genesis, but also created and maintained his own set of rigid guidelines which have helped define *The Next Generation* throughout its seven year run.

"I'm handed a 35-page script and my job is to turn into a movie, which is what I do 26 times a year," says Berman of his responsibilities then and now for *The Next Generation, Deep Space Nine* and *Voyager*.

Berman was a Paramount Pictures television executive who had been brought in by the studio to ride shotgun with Roddenberry during the series' earliest days to keep costs [and Roddenberry] under control. Berman, who joined Paramount in 1984 as director of current programming, overseeing *Cheers, Family Ties* and *Webster*, had come to the studio with a wealth of producing experience, including *The Big Blue Marble* and the PBS special *The Primal Mind,* as well as serving as director of dramatic development for Warner Bros. Within a year of joining Paramount, he was named executive director of dramatic programming, overseeing the miniseries *Space, Wallenberg: A Hero's Story* and ABC's *MacGyver*. In 1986, Berman was promoted to vice president of long-form and special projects where he oversaw the development of telefilms, miniseries and specials. In 1987, he joined the behind-the-scenes crew of *The Next Generation* and witnessed first-hand the difficulties in obtaining appropriate teleplays.

"*Star Trek* is a problem in that it's very easy for a writer to script an episode which would cost four times what we have to spend," he says. "Our writers must be able to watch their work get pulled down in terms of scope so that it's producable. There are some writers who were successful at this and some who were not. Because of the complexity and difficulty of writing a show like *Star Trek,* it was wrought with a little more problems than most television series early on."

Creating a *Next Generation* was a difficult chore rife with potential haz-ards, and several ideas were bandied about by Roddenberry who had been put in the captain's chair by Paramount to guide the sequel series.

"They needed Gene's involvement which at that point entailed conceiving and creating the premise of the new show," says Berman. "There were many ideas that were discussed, including making it a prequel to the original *Star Trek* and thoughts of it being set on a starship that was run by cadets in Starfleet Academy. Some suggestions were made by the studio, some by others. Gene's idea was to create an entirely new cast of characters and set it eighty years further into the future, to continue the premise and philosophy of *Star Trek,* but to do it with a new Enterprise and a new generation of Enterprise characters. I had spent almost all of my career as a producer and writer. I was serving as Vice President of Special Projects for network television at Paramount when I was asked to get involved with the new series, which at that point was no more than something Mr. Roddenberry was playing around with."

Berman acknowledges that "the aura of the old show" was both *The Next Generation's* greatest asset and its biggest drawback. "We tried to bring back the magic of a television show that had been off the air for twenty years, yet had continued to grow in popularity. The fans we had been in touch with felt you can't go home again. There's no way you can give us a new Enterprise with a new crew with a bald English actor as captain and no Vulcan on board. Their attitude was one of great skepticism. It was a great challenge in that sense. I think if we had tried to recreate younger or older versions of Kirk or Spock or had we tried to make characters who were extremely similar to characters on the old show, we would probably have failed. What we got was the essence of *Star Trek* as opposed to the specifics of what the show was about.

"I think the people who survived on this show are the people who are comfortable with the concept of what it's all about," adds Berman, alluding to the infamous "revolving door" policy at *Next Generation* in its early seasons, which saw myriad writer/producers signed on to the show and shortly thereafter depart over the rampant rewriting that they felt were degrading their scripts. Roddenberry was the subject of several grievances filed with the Writer's Guild early on. Later, Maurice Hurley came under fire from disgruntled writers who disparaged Hurley's "Machiavellian" running of the show. Even Executive Producer Michael Piller, who has shepherded *Next Generation's* most successful episodes into production, has received his fair share of criticism from a number of writers who have toiled briefly on the show. However, Berman has, for the most part, remained above the fray and has been with the series since the beginning.

"First season there were a group of writers who had friction with Gene, but it was not personal. It was over how people wrote the show. There were some personality conflicts, but no more than there are on most television series. It was all blown a little more out of proportion than I thought it deserved to be."

In describing his day-to-day responsibilities producing a *Star Trek* series, Berman details, "My life is involved in a lot of different things. My fingers are in a lot of different pies and the two things I spend most of my time doing are working on scripts and working in the cutting rooms. I get very involved with the scripts once they're into the first draft stage; I'm involved with the concepts but the beating out of the stories and the getting them to the first draft stage is something I'm less involved with than the various drafts of the scripts. I put a lot of work in subsequent meetings with the writers and reworking scripts from the first draft to the final shooting drafts. That takes a lot of my time and I spend a lot of time in the cutting room. I spend about 30 hours a week with the scripts and another 30 in the cutting room. There are a lot of other post-production elements: the opticals, I spot the music and the sound effects for the show, I go to the sound effects dubs. I also select the directors and work with the directors, and cast the shows.

"What happens at any given time is I'm working on four or five shows at once. I'll be reading and working on two or three scripts," continues Berman. "I will have a show in prep and there's a director working, and we're having production meetings and casting sessions and working out prosthetics and costuming and all of those things, I'll have another show on the stage and I'll be involved with screening dailies everyday and talking with the directors and the actors on that, and then I'll have shows in two or three different stages of post production."

Throughout the course of the several production meetings prior to the commencement of photography on an episode, Berman is very involved with every phase of the production. "We'll discuss parameters of casting and prototypes of the people we're looking for and how he [the director] plans on covering different elements of the show. Invariably, the directors want things that you don't let them have, toys that are expensive and time-consuming on the stage and problems with interpretations and specific actors and how they're gong to react to various situations. I get very personally involved with our department heads in the make-up prosthetics and in costumes and props and all that, and that happens in drips and drabs all day."

Over his seven year tenure on *Next Generation*, Berman received accolades for giving many members of the production team a chance to take charge behind the camera, including former assistant directors Les Landau and Chip Chalmers, editor Tom Benko, actors Patrick Stewart and Jonathan Frakes.

"I got the reputation as a producer who's willing to give people who I thought were ready to direct their first shot, which is something that doesn't

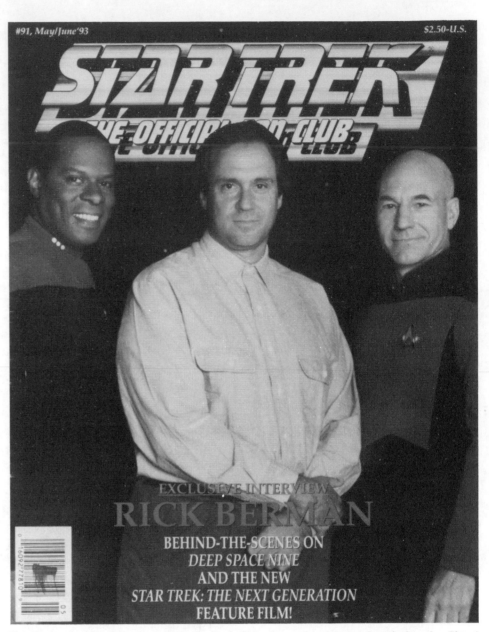

#91, May/June '93 $2.50-U.S.

STAR TREK
THE OFFICIAL FAN CLUB

EXCLUSIVE INTERVIEW
RICK BERMAN

BEHIND-THE-SCENES ON
DEEP SPACE NINE
AND THE NEW
STAR TREK: THE NEXT GENERATION
FEATURE FILM!

Rick Berman is flanked by Commander Benjamin Sisko (Avery Brooks) and Captain Jean Luc Picard (Patrick Stewart).

happen very often in this town," says Berman. "The studio trusts me enough that they tend to corroborate my choices."

He has continued providing directorial opportunities to aspiring talent on *Deep Space Nine,* allowing Avery Brooks to take the directorial reins of "Tribunal" during the show's second season.

In terms of writing, Berman notes that the creative staff on the *Trek* shows don't start with an agenda at the beginning of a season — they're just intent on presenting the best treks possible. "We don't really set a season goal," he says. "We know which characters we want to focus on and what kind of stories we want to do in very broad strokes. For instance, fourth season of *Next Generation,* we knew that Wesley was going to be leaving, and we had to start off with a show that finished up the Borg experience; and Michael and I each had a script we wanted to write. But our ultimate goal is to do good episodes as opposed to work on a seasonal arc of some sort."

Berman got to flex his scriptwriting muscles for the first time on "Brothers", his fourth season episode in which Data once again must face-off against his evil twin, Lore.

"I had spent a lot of time pencil-in-hand over the previous three years and one of the main reasons I hadn't written any scripts myself is because I didn't have time to," Berman recalls, "and during the fourth season hiatus I said enough already, I'm going to do a story. There were a number of things I wanted to say and they came out in the script. I also dealt with Brent and Dr. Soong, which was a story I wanted told."

One of Next Generation's most unique episodes was the fourth season follow-up to the 'Best of Both Worlds' conclusion — "Family" — in which Picard must deal with the emotional consequences of his abduction by the Borg. It was up to Berman to greenlight such an atypical installment.

"Ron Moore really wanted to do a story on Picard having to work out the emotional problems and results of the two Borg episodes. I was hesitant at first because I didn't want to turn a two-parter into a trilogy, but we got the script going so it sort of stood on its own," offers Berman. "We worked a long time on it because there were three separate stories: the story of Picard going home; the story of Worf with his parents onboard and the story of Wesley getting his little video from his father from years before. It ended up being a very unique show. It's not exactly what we would call a typical Star Trek episode. But we've done a number of those."

Berman enjoyed the chance to expand the characters' backstories in the show's final seasons as well. "It's nice to bring the characters a little bit more to life," he opines. "As a series gets older, the characters get richer because they've got more backstory. We were also able to make characters that existed in the background stronger."

For Berman, Star Trek's enduring popularity is what he labels his most important achievement on the show. "The show got better each year," he beams. "There was an incredibly small turnover after the first season writing turmoil. It is a family and we all take it extremely seriously. That's the only way you can do it, because it's such hard work and the second you start getting sloppy, the audience sees it instantly. The fact we kept up the quality and integrity of the show and simultaneously the audience kept getting bigger, is a wonderful achievement. It's not just an achievement, it's wonderfully good luck as well."

One aspect of the continuing Trek saga that irked the seasoned producer is the constant comparisons to the old series, which continued to plague Next Generation right through the end of its run.

"I don't like comparing the two, it's like father and son. There's no reason to compare them," says Berman. "It's like if your father died at 65 and you got to 66, you wouldn't feel cocky about it, you would just feel a little luckier than him and that's the way I feel."

However, whether justifiably or not, Berman feels his Trek is superior to its predecessor, if only due to the times in which it was produced. "Television has changed dramatically," believes Berman. "TV in the 60s was quite different than television in the 90s. If one looked at some of the greatest dramatic efforts that were done in the 1950s and 1960s, I'm talking about things like Playhouse 90, if you look at kinescopes of those old shows, the production values, the style of acting, the technical elements of the show are almost silly in today's world. What was considered adventurous or groundbreaking 30 years or 25 years ago is quite different now. Television has grown up a lot; the technical end of TV, the cynical element of TV, has grown up a lot. I think our show is much more believable than the old show was, and that's due in large part to the creator of the old show too because it was Roddenberry, who was very vehement when we created Star Trek: The Next Generation regarding the need for it to be believable and not to deal with swords and sorcerers and not to be melodramatic. The old Star Trek had people who looked like Greeks, and people who wore togas and stood under arches. Our Star Trek is much more contemporary and believable. I think we've dealt with issues in certain respects, but there have been so many groundbreaking television shows over the last 25 years. If you really think about when Star Trek began, television was relatively young, especially one hour dramatic television. I think it's a whole different medium today, so it's very hard to compare the two shows. The most important elements of the shows we have retained, I think. A family of positive, strong people who are going off where no one has gone before, and stories that deal with issues and ideas and people who are better than people are today. I think that was very important then and it's important now, and it does have a magical quality to it. It's the kind of thing that gives people a positive and strong sense of themselves and the future."

In fact, it is because of the show's idealistic and utopian view of the future that Berman suggests Next Generation had had such extraordinary turnover of its writing staff throughout the years.

"We had to manufacture our conflict from other than interpersonal conflict among our characters, and that does make it very difficult to write. The language has to be stylized, we don't know how people are going to speak in the 24th century and so we have them speak in a sort of stylized generic fashion. It's not 24th century, it's not contemporary and on the other hand its not medieval either.

"[Next Generation had] to deal

with science fiction and a lot of people don't understand what SF is. A lot of people are interested in dealing with fantasy and the writers have to deal with a lot of technical elements. Any dramatic television show has a set of rules that you've got to follow. If you're writing *St. Elsewhere,* you've got to know about medicine. If you're writing for *LA Law,* you've got to know about juris prudence in the state of California. On the other hand, with *Star Trek* you've got two sets of rules. A set of rules dealing with physics and astrophysics and astronomy that we follow or try to follow as accurately as we can. Then you've got a set of rules that have to do with *Star Trek,* which are made up rules, they're not real. There's no such thing as a dilithium crystal or people transporting. There's no such thing as warp drive and Romulans and Ferengi and Klingons. These things don't exist and as a result it's fantasy, but its 25 years worth of established rules that have to be followed. So you've got the rules of science and the rules of *Star Trek* and writers have to be willing and able to follow both sets of rules, and it's difficult."

However, Berman is the first to admit that although he may be at the forefront of staying true to Roddenberry's vision of the future, it is not one he personally shares. "I believe that for the purpose of our shows, Gene's vision of the 24th century is dramatically correct and it works for us. I don't think we're going to be living in a *Blade Runner* society, but I think we'll be living in a future which will be very, very similar to the world we're living in now. Then again, this show has nothing to do with *my* vision of the future. I have become an expert in Gene Roddenberry's future. It's like learning a language and I'm fluent in it now and I can protect it and police it and nurture it in the same way that Gene did."

And while Roddenberry's vision continues to serve as the conceptual template which shapes the underlying philosophy of all three spin-offs of the original series, it is Rick Berman who has

Patrick Stewart and William Shatner were brought together a couple of years prior to Generations *on the cover of this magazine.*

been most responsible for the success of *Trek* in the 90s, translating the idealism of Roddenberry and Gene L. Coon into a palatable formula for jaded modern day television viewers.

In addition to having overseen the production of *Star Trek: The Next Generation* for seven years and more recently co-creating *Deep Space Nine* and *Voyager,* Berman is now shepherding the *Next Generation* movie,

Generations, to the screen as its Executive Producer.

One of the attractions of working on the motion picture for Berman is his involvement with the movie's storyline, having co-written the original premise.

"I think that one of the things that I miss the most about *Star Trek: The Next Generation* was being involved with story work," says Berman. "I think it's something I'm pretty good at. The people I work with enjoy my input as much as I enjoy theirs. It's something I find very rewarding and something I don't get a chance to do too much now that the two television shows are in production. I don't have the luxury to get involved with conceptual matters and with story as much as I used to and I missed that very much.

"It's a very long process," says Berman of working on the development of the feature film script with, first, Maurice Hurley and, then, the writing team of Ron Moore and Brannon Braga. "When Michael and I were working on the story for *Deep Space Nine*, it was months of work."

Berman is particularly pleased with *Next Generation*'s final seasons, years defined by riskier, more atypical storytelling. He admits he was reluctant to deviate too dramatically from traditional format. "I tended to be the most conservative member of trying not to break format too often," says Berman. "I think that when a show gets into its 140, 150th episode, you obviously need to expand the envelope a little bit to get fresh ideas and keep everybody working productively and creatively. I think you're a little bit more prone to break the rules in the sixth season than you are in the third, but I don't think we've broken them too severely nor too often. I try not to be supportive of breaking format to a point where it's unbelievable. I believe that in a show like 'A Fistful of Datas' or even a show like 'The Nagus,' you're dealing with episodes that have a lot of humor in them. But if you look at the core of the show, the characters have not really broken character. We still stay true to both *Star Treks* and the rules of what we do. We break rules all the time. I don't like to do it too extremely nor do I like to do it too often."

Director David Carson, who worked closely with Berman on the *Deep Space Nine* pilot, "Emissary" and *Generations*, says of Berman, "Rick has always encouraged very individualistic

approaches from the directors. That's why you don't constantly see the bridge looking the same and you try to find different ways of doing it. Rick's idea is to have directors with different viewpoints creating different looks and different styles, which gives the director far more freedom than you normally find in episodic television. You're allowed the freedom to create and, quite frankly, such directing is not encouraged on other shows."

Berman finds it difficult to compare *The Next Generation* to *Deep Space Nine* and *Voyager*, both of which he co-created. "It's like the difference between asking me how I felt about my first kid compared to my second kid," says Berman. "*The Next Generation* was my first year with *Star Trek*. It was a learning experience, it was a mess. It was chaotic, there were a lot of conflicts on the writing staff and no one knew what was going to happen. *Deep Space Nine*'s first season, on the other hand, ran like a fourth season show — it has been smooth and it has been peaceful and I'm much more comfortable with it.

"I think, creativity, *Next Generation* grew greatly from 'Encounter At Farpoint' to the end of the season," continues Berman. "I think *Deep Space* has perhaps grown more. When you're living in a world of chaos as we were in the first season of *Next Generation*, it's hard to be reflective, it's hard for everybody to work smoothly. Everybody was new to it. Here we managed to have such a smooth running machine both in terms of the production and experienced directors and writers. I think it gave us all more of an opportunity to sit back and fine tune and try and make *Deep Space Nine* better. First season of *Next Generation* was more like treading water and getting through it, but they both have evolved in their own ways."

Is Berman concerned that there may be too much *Trek* in the creative cosmos with a *TNG* film franchise and two *Star Trek* TV series, plus reruns of the original series and *Next Generation*?

"I don't yet," he says. "People are always asking me can you take too many trips to the well. I think the answer is yes, but we've been very careful to make *Voyager* different. I think it is not only good for the audience, but good for us, the writers and producers. As long as we can keep it interesting to us and keep challenging ourselves, I think it will work with the audience. Once we starting getting bored, I think it will show in the ratings as well."

A TV Guide *ad announcing the final episode of* **Star Trek: The Next Generation.**

MAURICE HURLEY
"Equalizing the 24th Century"

"The rules of *Star Trek* were basically in the head of Gene Roddenberry, and you just can't fight it. You either go along with it or you don't, and if you can't go along with it, you're going to get rewritten," Maurice Hurley, former co-executive producer of *Star Trek: The Next Generation*'s first two seasons, explains. "That's just the way it is. *Star Trek* is not like any other show, because it is one unique vision, and if you agree with Gene Roddenberry's vision of the future, you should be locked up somewhere. It's wacky doodle, but it's his wacky doodle. If you can't deal with that, you can't do the show. There are rules on top of rules on top of rules. There are some people who have a deep history with Gene, whose egos are bruised easily. People get confused about who really is *Star Trek*, and that messes people's heads up. *Star Trek* is Gene Roddenberry and nobody else."

Hurley, whose credits include staff positions during the first —and best —year of both *Miami Vice* and *The Equalizer*, pauses for a moment when queried for the definition of the term he used to describe the 24th Century of Gene Roddenberry's imagination: "wacky doodle."

"Gene sees this pollyanish view of the future where everything is going to be fine," he notes. "If we keep going in this world the way we're going, there is no future, and the idea that humanity is going to go from its infancy to its adolescence in the next 400 years, I don't believe. But he does, and that's why *Star Trek* is a success. It gives the audience a sense of hope. I don't believe it, but you have to suppress all that and put it aside. You suspend your own feelings and your own beliefs, and you get with his vision or you get rewritten."

There is an emphasis on the last word, and for good reason. From the announcement of the series in October

Maurice Hurley held the most influence on Next Generation's *second season, which featured Diana Muldaur as Dr. Katherine Pulaski.*

of 1986, much had been made of the fact that many writers during the first two seasons arrived and departed from the staff, all complaining about the same thing: that Gene Roddenberry and his executive producers were rewriting their scripts, taking — they felt — the creative heart out of them and resulting in mediocrity, rather than greatness.

"As I said, *Star Trek* has absolute rules than cannot be broken, and

nobody knows that until they get into it," says Hurley. "It's a problem that all writers have had for the most part. My ability comes from character and action, so what I thought they wanted from me was characters and action. They didn't want that. They wanted writers who could take the *Star Trek* parameters — Gene's vision — and put a shine on it, buff it and not change anything. That's a hard lesson for writers to learn, especially those writers coming in with bonafide credentials and a lot of ego. Some people thought they had better ideas and, God love 'em, they may have, but that's not the point.

"If you have a form and it works, you have parameters and you must paint within the lines," he adds. "If you start to go outside the lines, the show loses its definition and people lose interest in it. *Miami Vice* went out of the lines, and after the first year it broke its own rules and started to fall apart. That's a lesson I'll never forget. *Star Trek*, to me, was like trying to paint a landscape on a postage stamp, and you have to be able to see a boat in the middle of the lake, and a man fishing in it. Now if you can paint that landscape on a postage stamp, you can do the show. That's the kind of mentality you have to have. When I became co-executive producer, I became more Catholic than the Pope and I refused to allow any rules to be broken. If somebody said, 'The captain of the Enterprise does this,' I would say, 'No he doesn't.' 'But I need it for the drama.' 'Sorry, he doesn't do that.' I just refused and [co-executive producer] Rick Berman was the same way. Even Gene on occasion would want to break the rules, and we wouldn't let him."

It's suggested that such strict devotion to certain parameters can result in a restricted creativity that makes its presence known on the air. Surprisingly, Hurley agrees with this assessment, although he does attribute part of the problem to the modern television audience.

"One of the things that the old *Star Trek* did that the new show can't do as well, was make comments on issues," he points out. "Back then, opinions were changing, things were changing, times were changing and it was very volatile and dynamic. Now, we're into a period where it's stagnant; there's no dynamic change happening. People have settled in to opinions and problems that have no real clear cut solution. What's the solution to AIDS? How do you encapsulate, in a word, the solution? There isn't any.

Hurley was creatively involved with Miami Vice during the shows early, and best, years (photo copyright ©1994 MCA).

"Now you take a show like 'A Matter of Honor' and say, 'We're going to do a little culture swapping,' so we explore what it must be like to be the only black face in a room of 40 people all white. That must be kind of tough. That's what Worf, in a sense, is doing. He's the only Klingon on a basically human ship. So we said, 'Let's spin it. Let's put somebody on an all Klingon vessel and see how that works; what it's like to be a fish out of water. What is it like to be the only white face in a meeting in Harlem?' That's got to be a little bit funny, a little different and a little tense. That's how that show started. It was a way to look at a contemporary social problem and give it a spin. At the same time, when you watch that show there are wonderful things in it. When Riker is sitting with the Klingons and one of them says he's surprised that Riker has a sense of humor, Riker looks at him and says, 'Son of a gun, I was thinking the same thing.' If Riker had said, 'I'm surprised

you guys have a sense of humor,' it wouldn't have meant anything. But spin it, and all of a sudden it became the whole point of the show. When *Star Trek* is hitting its stride and doing what it's supposed to do, it can be very provocative, but because it's reaching so high and trying to live up to its own expectations, it fails more than most other shows. Mediocrity in *Star Trek* is a failure. It's a tough show, and a bitch to write."

One episode that did try to deal with a prominent issue was "Symbiosis," an anti-drug show that went so far as to have one of the characters, Tasha Yar, deliver a "just say no" speech to Wesley Crusher. Needless to say, that moment has been heavily criticized.

"That was Hurley who forced that one in there," he admits. "I take the blame for that. I jammed that in over everybody's objections. They were screaming on the set, the actors were screaming, they were puking and they were yelling 'We can't do this.' I said,

'No, there are kids out there. If we're going to make the message, let's make the message. If it offends the adults or bothers some adults but it hits home with a couple of the kids, then by God we're going to do it.' Part of it was to maybe open up dialogue in a living room somewhere. You see something on the show that maybe somebody uses later on with their kids. That's one of the responsibilities you have when you do episodic television. The important thing is that some six or seven year old is going to hear this, and they're going to hear it coming from one of their heroes. It may sink in and help. I'll take the heat on that one, but I'd probably do it again the same way for the same reasons."

A social conscience was raised again in "Justice," which had the Enterprise encountering a society where the punishment for any crime is death. "That, again, was a part of the contemporary culture we're talking about," says Hurley. "If you want to start controlling crime, maybe the answer is, 'Listen, if you commit a crime at a certain level, it's the death penalty.' And where does that level start? Where does it stop? Why not any crime? Get rid of all the criminals, get rid of the criminal genes. Let's whack them down and let's go. You can make that argument and if a culture like our culture keeps going the way it's going, it's an argument that people may start pushing toward. There's a resurgence of people saying, 'We're not using the death penalty as much as we should be.' You hear that every day, and when you hear the arguments it's hard at some level not to buy them. You say, 'Wait a minute, maybe there are some machines that are flawed at the factory and should be recalled.' Then you take it to its logical absurdity, and you have a society like the one in 'Justice.' I thought the idea of that show was wonderful. It got too fanciful, sexual and there was an innocence that was missing. It got loonie tunes for me."

Hurley had been in a development deal at Universal Pictures, which he says consisted of lots of talking and very little writing, and was looking for something that would get him back in the "trenches." Someone mentioned his name to Gene Roddenberry.

"When they called," he reflected, "my first reaction was, 'God, there must be another Maurice Hurley around here,' because I do hard action. In my stuff, twelve people are killed by the end of the teaser. But I was intrigued by the request to talk to them, because *Star Trek* has such a legend attached to it. You can't think of many shows that have that kind of legendary quality, so I went over there and had a meeting with Gene. In that meeting, I told him that I didn't think I could do a science fiction show because it wasn't something I was steeped in at all, but if they wanted to hire me on that basis, I'd take a chance and see how badly I could fail.

"As a writer," Hurley elaborates, "you have to have that kind of attitude, otherwise you don't have a chance to stretch. You get into situations on a show like that where you're looking at the typewriter or computer with a whole set of problems that you've never faced before. The Enterprise has flown to the end of the universe. What the hell is the end of the universe? What goes on there? Is there an end to the universe, or is it the threshold of something else? I've never had those questions in my mind before, so that part of it was fun. Another thing that was appealing to me, from a purely financial point of view, is that they had fourteen scripts in development when I came on, and there would be a total of 26 shows. I get paid by the show, and when I saw 14 scripts in development, my salary for each episode doubled. At least it should have, if in fact they do develop 14 scripts which are going to work, which they did not. Surprise number one."

In describing the atmosphere on the show when he first joined the staff, Hurley notes that any time there is a series being put together, it's a difficult situation because people want it to succeed very badly. "And that means everybody is paying as much attention as they can, and everybody has an idea of how any show should go to be successful," he says. "So you have a lot of strong minds, opinions and egos that are at work on any show. Sometimes that makes for a great show, but a lot of times that makes for a camel. Things don't work out unless somebody has a strong vision, and on *Star Trek* it was even more so, only because the chance of failure and success were heightened by the spotlight it was under. If the show had been terrible, mediocre, a lot of people were going to be embarrassed, mainly Gene. The stakes were high. Now that causes lots of tensions and lots of problems. That's not personal to anybody, it's just the nature of getting involved with something that has that kind of a risk level. That's all it was. Nothing really more or less than any other show, except in terms of the heat that was under the pot. On every show there's a big turnover in the beginning. It's like a shakedown cruise."

One surprise came in the form of the company's scriptwriting procedure, in which each writer on the staff was instructed to pen a memo critiquing scripts submitted by outsiders as well as their fellow staff members.

"I refused to do that," Hurley says matter of factly, "because that is the most divisive kind of exercise you can possibly imagine. Somebody writes a memo about your script and says something derogatory, and writers being sensitive and having their hearts on their sleeve, are easily offended, hurt and intimidated. It forces people to stop being vulnerable, and as a writer you must be vulnerable; you must be willing to put the most ludicrous thing on the table and have people around you say, 'It's pretty ludicrous, but within it there's something. I know what to do, let's make it even more ludicrous.' But if you don't have the comfort of knowing that the people around you are supportive, you go into a shell and start writing from a very safe position, which is very boring and very flat. Also, if somebody writes

Prior to guiding the voyages of the Enterprise, Hurley equalized the streets of New York with Edward Woodward's The Equalizer *(photo copyright ©1994 CBS).*

something derogatory about your script, what are you going to do when you see something in their script? You're going to take a shot. You're going to be sitting there, spending more time worrying about your memos than you are about your scripts. The time factor, wasting so much time with negativity...I hated it, and I refused to participate."

If not for a contract that guaranteed him a place on the show, he believes he would not have participated with the series at all once he tackled his first rewrite.

"I came on about a month before they started shooting the pilot," Hurley details. "I was vilified for the first four or five months of my job on *Star Trek*. I was treated like the worst stepchild you've ever seen. At one point,

Rick Berman, who became the co-executive producer with me, said he didn't think I could possibly go through airport security because of all the metal I had stuck in my back. I was coming in with big credentials. I was coming in from the first year of *Miami Vice* and the first year of *The Equalizer*. I had credentials that others didn't have. I don't know if David Gerrold has those kinds of credits or Dorothy Fontana either. Herb Wright kind of flowed in and out, and Bob Lewin had a lot of old credits, but nothing recent. And I had the heat. I guess I was viewed as a possible threat or something.

"I did a page one rewrite of 'Where None Have Gone Before,'" he explains, "and they absolutely hated it. I said, 'Wait a minute, I'm used to writing from the point of view of vulnerability. I

just write the most outrageous shit in the world, and then we all sit down and work it out, but don't attack it and don't attack me.' And that's what happened, so I took it and started rewriting it some more, and it eventually turned out to be what you saw on the screen, and a show I liked a lot. But it was during the process of doing two or three rewrites on that script that I started to understand what *Star Trek* was all about; that's where I really learned what the show was. After 14 episodes, I was given control of the scripts and the stories and was moved from the corners into the lights. The first thing I said was, 'No memos.' Once they made me co-executive producer, that whole system changed. If anybody had something to say about a script, they could come into my office, sit down like a human being and we talked. We dealt with it as fellows, not as adversaries and it changed. As a result, the show itself changed."

Turning his attention to the first season of *Star Trek: The Next Generation*, Hurley recalls the episodes he was deeply involved with, although, as he's pointed out, he was involved in most of the scripts, his first on-air credit as a writer was "Hide and Q," in which Q endows Riker with his unique powers. A rewrite by Gene Roddenberry caused him to use the pen name, C.J. Holland.

"That was a turning point script, and now I'm talking about personalities," he admits, refusing to elaborate in detail. "I wrote that script, Gene rewrote it and I took my name off of it. That was where Gene and I had a little talk about the future. My version was more action-oriented and less philosophical, if I can say that. It was more direct, a little more playful. I didn't think it was necessarily a better version, because that's a subjective choice, but it was a matter of procedure of how the show was being done. When you have people on a show who are your staff writers, you don't take work away from them. You get them to modify it closer to what you want, rather than you just doing a rewrite. It was really a misunderstanding between Gene and I, because the last thing he would do is hurt my feelings or do it in an arbitrary way."

"Datalore," which Hurley wrote with then producer Robert Lewin, had the Enterprise encountering an evil android double of Data, named Lore. "The sets, the design and the look of that show was brilliant," he notes. "I thought that might have been the best looking show of the first season. There were, however, some things back and forth in there that I didn't like in terms of the characterizations, but basically it was an alright episode."

Up next for the Hurley/Lewin team was "11001101," in which the Binars steal the Enterprise to utilize the ship's computers to bring life back to their computer planet, which is near death. "Loved it," Hurley smiles. "There were some things in there that came off so well. When Riker and Picard are sitting in the bar and talking about love and how you fall in love with the image and the illusion. Patrick was great, and so was Jonathan. In fact, it may have been the first time he had been given a chance in the series to do something; to show who he is a little bit as a person and an actor. Also, the Binars were just wonderful science fiction creations, communicating in their binary language with their little buffers. Michael Westmore did some wonderful make-up work on that."

A highlight of year one for Hurley was "Heart of Glory," in which a pair of rescued Klingons attempt to sway Worf over to their side to commandeer the Enterprise. "That's a show where I came as close to putting me on *Star Trek* as I possibly could in terms of philosophy, point of view and position. It all worked together perfectly, and that's where Rick Berman and I were hitting our stride. That's where we were locked at the hip in putting these shows together. When I had a problem, I could go in and we could sit there, close the door, yell and scream, I'd pace and he'd make suggestions. The two of us made stories

work in that room that had to be shot in a couple of days. We were under enormous time pressure, and we were working hand-in-glove. We had a wonderful time, on that show especially."

Next, he co-wrote the story for "Arsenal of Freedom." The Enterprise arrives at a world that has essentially been designed as a place of demonstration for a wide variety of weapon systems which are being offered by a holographic salesman. "If we had another couple of days, we could have made it even better," Hurley points out. "It was an attempt to look at a contemporary problem with a future perspective. If you think about it, we're kind of arms dealers to the world now. We make F-14s and then we go over to the Persian Gulf and have to track our own F-14s on radar, because they're going to attack our own ships with our own missiles. There's some insanity going on here, and if you keep taking it to its ultimate conclusion, you're going to have a society that has finally created the ultimate weapon. 'Step right up, boys, we've got it right here. It only kills people, leaves all the buildings. It's better than a cobalt bomb.' 'How do you know it works?' 'Well, come on, we'll give you a little demo.' Good night. Turn off the light, it's over."

He also penned "The Neutral Zone," the last show of the season, which was written just before the 1988 Writer's Guild strike and dealt with a group of 20th Century survivors preserved in suspended animation who must deal with the world of the 24th Century. "That show was written in about a day and a half," Hurley admits. "The characterizations were good, and I think some nice things were done in the casting of the show. It was an alright episode, but nothing great."

The strike lasted some six months, which threw every television series behind schedule, including *Star Trek: The Next Generation*. According to Hurley, the overall effect on the show was quite profound. "The best time for me was the last half of the first season,"

he explains. "The last eight or 10 shows. We found a rhythm there and the show was really tuning up, but then with the strike, everything came to a stop. Now we had a ship dead in the water and we had to try and get it up again, and it was like restoking the furnace. The second season didn't jump off to the right level the way it should have. We didn't have the chance to have the right kind of meetings with the right kind of writers to get things moving and take that momentum we had after the first season. That was a real killer."

So desperate for material was the crew, that it turned its attention to the teleplays written for the aborted *Star Trek* television series of the mid 1970s, and it was decided that "The Child," dealing with an alien impregnation of one of the crewmembers, would be the most appropriate to adapt to *The Next Generation*. Hurley, who did the rewrite, explains that the show "suffered from being the first episode more than anything else. I never even looked at the original script. I merely worked from the premise."

Next, he penned two scripts in a row, one of which, "Time Squared," is considered to be among the series' most confusing and pointless, and "Q Who," deemed one of the best. In the former, a double of Captain Picard arrives at the Enterprise via shuttlecraft, and the crew eventually learns that he is from six hours in the future, where the starship has been drawn into a cosmic vortex and destroyed. This Picard, it would seem, has been sent back to warn everyone of their impending doom. The latter brings back the ever-popular Q, who wants to join the Enterprise crew, stating that he can be of great help to them. When Picard points out that they don't need his help, he proves that they actually do, when he whisks them to a far off galaxy where they encounter the Borg, a relentless race of cyborgs who thrive on destruction. What fans may find hard to believe is that originally there was a connection between the two shows.

"We've seen a lot of people do time backs and forths and jumps around," details Hurley. "They're always coming back 500 years or 1,000 years. Nobody's ever really come back six hours. The idea of six hours is what fascinated me, and the original concept was that the events of 'Time Squared' were orchestrated by Q. He had manipulated all of them as a way to reintroduce himself. In the next episode the way it was designed, the Enterprise would be going through space when all of a sudden Picard finds himself stuck in a shuttlecraft in a flash, and he sees the vortex, the Enterprise is at the top of the vortex and is falling into the top of it, exploding. He thinks he's lost his mind and he doesn't know what's going on. Then Q appears and says, 'Hey, how ya doing?' Picard says, 'You caused that and all these other things?' Q replies, 'Well, I'm surprised you didn't put it together earlier. Oh well, you *are* slow. Just a kind of calling card; something to do. Interesting, wasn't it?' And now we're into Picard saying, 'What do you want?' 'I want to join you.'

"So the first part, 'Time Squared,' ended, and you're left with the feeling, 'What the hell was that? I can't figure it out. Why would that happen? It's illogical as hell.' But you go through an hour of being driven by this plot and then you solve it, although you don't really solve it, because you don't know what happened. Why would going into the center of it save you? It did, but why? It doesn't make sense. But it does if Q is pulling the strings. Suddenly the whole thing works. Those two were supposed to tie together. The thing that I liked about it comes from the audience's point of view as well. Since people follow the show so closely, the next time they see the vortex they say, 'Wait a minute, here we go again,' and they would connect those two shows instantly. And then to have Q jump in and have Picard make the conclusion at the same time the audience is making the conclusion, I thought was a way to involve them at a level they had-

n't been involved at in the past. They're in on the decision making process with Picard. It's a goofy way to do it, but it's different. The ending of 'Time Squared' was confusing. The rationale behind it was gone. Gene hated the idea of tying up the episodes that way, and we were forced to drop it."

"Q Who" was also designed to introduce an adversary that could really stir things up, and replace the Ferengi as the primary threat to the Federation. The result was the Borg. "The Ferengi were a waste of time," Hurley dismisses. "No bushido involved. It was a joke, and we had lots of arguments about them from the beginning. I was the lone voice screaming in the wilderness. Listen, if somebody's interested in gold, they're not much of an adversary. If we can make gold in our replicator, and we can, then it's like sand at the beach in Santa Monica. They want gold? Here, take a truck load and get lost. By that century, gold is meaningless to us, and so are the Ferengi. But, if you noticed, when Hurley became the co-executive producer, goodbye Ferengi. They're out of here. Bring on the Borg!

"What we really wanted to do, but couldn't because of money, was create a race of insects," he adds. "Insect mentality is great, because it is relentless. The Borg are a variation of an insect mentality. They don't care. They have no mercy, no feelings toward you. They have their own imperative, their own agenda and that's it. If all of them die getting there, they don't care. We needed a villain who could make you dance, and the Borg could do it!"

He concluded his writing stint for the show, as well as the second season itself, with "Shades of Grey," a clip compilation episode in which Riker is dying of a rare disease, and has to recall pleasant memories to fight it off. Pretty much everyone has agreed that it was the weakest episode of the series. "Piece of shit," Hurley concurs. "It was supposed to be a bottle show, and it was

terrible. Just terrible, and a way to save money. I was on the way out the door. I wrote it, and then the story editors did the rewrite."

Overall, he was disappointed with the second season, much of it — and he refuses to go into detail — due to behind the scenes conflicts. "I was very disappointed," he sighs. "With the potential we had at the end of the first season, I thought we were going to do something, but year two just flattened out for me. It became a pancake. I think there were more episodes I liked in the last half of the first season than there were in the entire second season. It takes a lot of effort for a show like *Star Trek* to work. When it does work, it's great fun to be involved with it, but when it doesn't, it's a hassle. In the sense of doing two years over there, I think I probably spent too much time in space. I probably should have left at the end of the first year, because I would have been happier and would have felt it was a great experience. The second season became a hassle where you were hassling for mediocrity. You weren't hassling for excellence, and that's always a debilitating kind of feeling. That's not a lot of fun. I told Gene at the beginning of the second season that I was only doing one more year. Two years in space was more than enough for me. I couldn't carry on, and I started disengaging probably around the middle of the year; just started pulling back. It wasn't going the way I wanted it to go, and there was no point in fighting because I was leaving anyway. There's no real overall umbrella philosophy of what I wanted to do. Just the edges, the surprises. Just the kind of things where there was a little more to it, so that it's not just another mechanical god coming in to manipulate things."

Hurley, who wrote "Galaxy's Child" for the series' fourth season, was involved with various television projects at Universal before joining the staff of *Kung Fu: The Legend Continues*. "That's the fun of the business," he smiles. "If you're willing to move around, every show is different. After this, I'll probably do a soap. I've been involved with shows that when they've worked, they were fun. The first year of *Miami Vice* was as much fun as you could have. It was a rocketship. The first year of *The Equalizer* was also a great show to be involved with. There was a lot of ground-breaking done and there are a lot of shows I'm very proud of."

Maurice Hurley has often been confronted with the various rumors concerning his two years on *Star Trek: The Next Generation;* rumors of massive writer turn-over and of his rewriting pen running rampant over other people's scripts.

"Part of the problem," he starts, "is that at the beginning there were people who were doing that show that really didn't understand other people too well. I'm not saying that I'm a great politician. Usually I say what's on my mind, and as a result I can be a little abrupt and brusque. I'm not talking about that. It's worse to keep people in the dark than it is to turn on the light and tell them they're fired. So how you handle people, and how people were handled that first year, hurt a lot of feelings.

"But there's a thing that happens in Hollywood that is really the truth. Hollywood is a place where, if you can dance, you can make it. Anybody can get a chance to dance. People don't necessarily believe that, but it's true. If you beat on the doors out here, the doors are going to open, you're going to be invited in and they're going to say, 'Okay, can you dance?' And then you dance. If you can dance, they say, 'Okay, stick around.' If you can't, they say good-bye. Now you may bang on some more doors and get another chance. If you can, you move up real quick in this town. If you can't, you're pushed off to the side and become very strange. A lot of things happen to people who are pushed out to the side. But it all comes down to whether or not you can dance. I went from writing my first script as a

Most recently, Hurley put pen to paper on the syndicated series **Kung Fu: The Legend Continues** (photo copyright ©1994 Warner Bros Television)

freelancer on *Miami Vice* to story editor, to supervising producer to co-executive producer in a matter of two and a half years. Those are just title jumps, saying nothing about the money jumps that are involved, which are incredible.

"There's another thing you have to understand. Because of the way I am, I put people's noses in it a lot. That means I can be difficult to work with, so that with the kind of personality I have in a working situation — not in an interview — there's a tendency to look and see if there's a way to get rid of me, which people would, if they could. But since I can put it on the page, they suffer me. No matter how rank your personality may be, if you can dance, they're going to keep you around.

"There's a reality," he says. "If I

leave a show like *Star Trek* and become the executive producer of another series, you have to look at these other people who are bitter about their experiences on the show and say, 'Well, after you left *Star Trek,* what did you do?' And see what the level of success is. Did a studio like Universal come to them and say, 'We're going to pay you an enormous amount of money just to be here?' You have to look at what they did before, and at what level, and what they do after, and at what level. In that way you learn a lot about who they really are."

One other thing that Hurley has done since leaving the series was pen a proposed screenplay for the seventh *Trek* feature film, *Star Trek: Generations,* which is the first to star *The Next Generation.* Although ultimately not chosen, it promised quite a ride for fans of the recently defunct television series.

"There was basically a fold in space," Hurley explains, "and an adversary who had been in a battle was blown through it into our universe. It is trying to get home to save its species, but in order to do that — and in order to get home — it has to basically destroy us."

The analogy he draws is to a parent in a schoolyard with his 2-year-old child, with the parent on one end and the child on the other. The child is in a dangerous situation, about to die.

"You rush across the schoolyard," he proposes, "stepping on toes, knocking down children, breaking bones and smashing heads to get to your baby. Then you save your baby and you look back at all the mayhem and chaos and blood that you have caused among all these other 2-year-old children. You could have killed one of them, but it wouldn't have made a difference to you until after the fact when you looked back and said, 'Oh my God, what did I do? I'm sorry, but I just didn't have a choice.' That's the story. These other people who are here and are about to destroy us are basically saying, 'Sorry, but there's nothing we can do about it. You're all going to have to die.'"

Although the Enterprise is sent out to dispatch this adversary, Picard senses that all is not as it seems with the alien, that the destruction being caused must have a purpose, though that purpose isn't clear.

"Picard senses that there's something else going on here because he finds no subtext for the attack, and all battles have subtext," Hurley points out. "In a battle with a Klingon or Romulan there's a subtext and you can define what the subtext is. Romulans want to kick your ass and in the process of kicking your ass they want you to know how damn smart and superior they are. These people have no subtext and Picard says that's wrong. They have to have one. What is it? That among other things starts him investigating, causing him to veer

one way where, on the surface, it seems he should be veering the other way."

Part of Picard's investigation is to go to the holodeck to call up the image of Captain James T. Kirk (the only classic *Trek* character used in the screenplay), who experienced a similar situation in the original series episode "The Tholian Web," in which the captain, on board the U.S.S. Defiant, is trapped in another dimension.

"It's the only other time on record that it ever happened," Hurley notes, "and the only other person who ever witnessed it was Kirk. So Picard and Kirk have witnessed, separated by time, similar events. Now you want to say, 'Wait a minute, I see it this way, how do you see it? Did it happen to you the same way it happened to me? If it was different, how was it different?' It was Picard's attempt to get an emotional point of view from the Kirk character that differed from what he was getting from pure facts.

"For instance, if you describe an event for me and I read it and you say, 'The sky was red and there was a lot of noise,' well, what does that mean to me? What is red? What red are you talking about? What kind of noise? Relate it to something for me. If you're dead and all I have is your writings, I have no way of knowing that. If I can go back and talk to you, when you say red you absolutely see a color. So do I. Your color red might be fire engine and mine might be maroon. If I know that, that alters how I view what you're saying. Noise also means something. What's noise to me, what's noise to you? You know what those answers are. The computer would just put down noise, but if the computer regenerated you in terms of who you are, how you viewed noise is presumably how you would still view it. So I get the subtlety from the personal interview that I don't get off the page. That's all Picard's after.

"But that's not enough," he continues, "so he started manipulating the image so it basically becomes a couple of bizarre scenes between Picard and

Kirk and it gets confrontational at certain moments. You want to bring back Kirk and not have it get confrontational? Kirk will get confrontational with anyone. In *Star Trek V* he got confrontational with God! So it became way to put those two classic characters and two really great actors together, and then let them bang on each other."

Despite the fact that executive producer Rick Berman has indicated that Hurley's script could be filmed after *Star Trek: Generations*, the writer doesn't think it's likely to happen.

"Everything has its time," points out Great Bird Maurice Hurley, "and it's seldom that somebody goes back to the pot. It's a good idea and a good story that Rick Berman and I worked hard on. But that's just the way it is."

MICHAEL PILLER
"Trek's Steady Hand on the Helm"

When people have pointed to the steadily improving quality of *Star Trek: The Next Generation* over its seven years on the air, it is usually Executive Producer Michael Piller who receives the lion's share of the credit. Since its third and most effective season, the show has consistently been praised for its powerful storylines and moving characterizations — going so far as to get an Emmy nomination for best drama in its final year — pleasing the veteran producer whose favorite shows have included such character-oriented fare as *LA Law*, *Wiseguy* and *thirtysomething*.

Piller, who was brought aboard after the premature departure of his former colleague on the short-lived *Probe*, Michael Wagner, contributed the teleplay for the third-season opener "Evolution," which was hardly an accurate barometer of the dramatic heat the producer would bring to the series over its next four years.

Piller, began his career as a journalist at CBS News in New York, and served as a senior news producer in Chicago before seguing into the volatile world of entertainment television. Piller worked as a censor in the CBS docudrama unit and then spent two years as a programming executive before leaving the network to write full time. His credits as a writer-producer include *Simon & Simon, Cagney & Lacey, Miami Vice* and *Hard Times on Planet Earth*. He also co-created and executive produced the syndicated series *Group One Medical*.

Piller did not do it alone. He put together a team on *Next Generation* which remained largely unchanged over the course of its run, including Jeri Taylor, Ronald D. Moore, Brannon Braga and Rene Echevarria. There was only some small turnover, most notably at the end of year three when Melinda Snodgrass, Hans Beimler and Richard Manning all ankled the series reportedly after stormy confrontations with Piller.

On *Deep Space Nine*, Piller recruited third season producer Ira Steven Behr, whose role on the show has grown substantially over its first two years, resulting in his being named co-executive producer.

"Everybody who works on a show like *Star Trek* brings their own ideas and talents to it," points out Piller. "I would certainly hope that I've brought something to it, as has everybody who worked on the show. I'm basically in charge of scripts. If you liked the stories and scripts, then you can give me credit for directing traffic. I have very strong feelings about what makes a good script and what makes a bad script, although it took me a few shows to learn it. I don't think we do very well when we're dependent on stories that are there for the sake of action; are there for exploring social issues. I'm not saying I'm against social issues, because I think there's definitely room for that, but we must be able to say something new about it or it must be done on a very personal, character level.

"We set out to do a show about terrorists, 'The High Ground'," Piller says of one of *Next Generation*'s first stabs at social commentary under his watchful eye. "How will the 24th Century deal with terrorism? I think ultimately we didn't really solve the question we set out to answer. We told a story that could have been substituted for any Vietnam or Northern Ireland, and basically said that terrorism in the 24th Century is the same as it is in the 20th Century. I hope that it isn't, but we didn't have enough futuristic thinking to really score. I think it cut together well and that the people in post-production did another great job. It was a show that was built on a social issue and designed for action, not our best suit.

"What was the statement we made about terrorism in that show?" asks Piller. "Was it the point where the boy puts down the gun and says, 'Maybe the end of terrorism is when the first child puts down his gun?' It was effective in the context of that show, but is certainly not a statement that provides any great revelation. You must be prepared to say something new about social issues. The danger of starting a show with a concept that is socially motivated is that you better damn well find a personal story to tell and something new to say about that issue, otherwise you're not enlightening anybody. You're retreading old ground, and I think that's what we did in 'The High Ground.'

"The *Star Trek* shows are character shows," Piller emphasizes. "They're not action/adventure. They are as much about characters as *LA Law* is about characters. If you want to write a *Star Trek*, you must know what it's about on a personal level. You must pick a character that you want to explore. If you want to do a war story, that's fine. But you'd bet-

One of Piller's credits prior to coming on board the Enterprise, was Simon & Simon *(photo copyright ©1994 MCA).*

ter have a character in a dilemma so that you're really looking at it from a personal standpoint. I'm not interested in how many Borg ships or Romulan ships are out there. I'm interested in what it ultimately means, what happens, what our characters learn about themselves, about life and so on. My favorite shows are the shows that are intimate in nature. When it comes right down to it, even though there's a lot of action in some of these shows, you'll always find an intimate story at the heart of them. 'Deja Q' was a very intimate story about a man who suddenly has to find what humanity is about. The shows that have worked have had personal intimacy that you could reach out and touch the characters. That's what the show is about."

"I just like to see the characters grow and try to stretch the limits and break the format as often and as logically as I can, without breaking the rules of *Star Trek* in the 24th Century. I like all the characters," Piller says. "'Best of Both Worlds' turned out to be a Riker story. When we started it, it was going to be a Picard story. This is the honest truth. It's going to sound corny, and some people are going to say they don't get it, but the characters almost dictate what happens in a script. You get to a point where you know them so well that you sit around saying, 'What would they do in this circumstance?', and they sort of speak to you and tell you which way they're going to go. In this case, Riker has to face some self-doubt and ultimately make some very difficult decisions for himself. It's very interesting, because while Riker is going through a personal dilemma of whether or not to leave the Enterprise, I was going through the dilemma of whether or not I was leaving *Star Trek*, and a lot of that bled into the script. Riker's musing to himself is sort of like Michael Piller musing to himself. It's interesting how things affect. You get very tied up with the characters, you start talking to them about the problems of the show and they start talking back at you.

"My thinking of leaving had nothing to do with the show at all," he quickly clarifies. "I just have so many other things that I want to do. I felt tired at the end of season [three] and I'd really like to go out and write screenplays and create some of my own projects. But I found it very difficult to walk away from a show that I'd fallen in love with, and a show that mattered. I've worked on quite a few shows that nobody watched. It's nice to be on a show that people care about. I cannot complain about anybody or anything. For whatever reason, I can't tell you why, we found harmony in the 24th Century, and we used that harmony to make better shows."

In terms of his desire to create his own shows, Piller has, of course, gotten the best of both worlds in that he is co-creator of *DS9* and *Voyager*.

Piller considers the notion that some of the criteria intrinsic to *Star Trek* make writing for the various series difficult for freelancers, and has resulted in the expression that on *Trek* you don't "write so much as rewrite scripts."

"You could take out *Star Trek* and put in the word television," he laughs. "That's the way television is. Every once in a while somebody comes in with

a pretty darn good first draft, but I have never been in any circumstance where a script was not rewritten. There's no reason to be ashamed of that. There are some writers who don't like to be rewritten - and I happen to be one of them. That's why I like to be the rewriter. But I hope that the writers who I've rewritten don't feel as though they've been brutalized. I think the responsibility of somebody on staff is to protect the good and working elements of the freelance script, and we bring to them a knowledge of the characters from working with them on a daily basis. I think the freelancer's job is a very, very difficult one.

"Most of the material we get are retreads of things that have already been on the air. It's very hard to come up with concepts that break new ground. There has to be an emotional dilemma that has to be resolved and there has to be a science fiction quotient so you're working on a metaphorical level. And it's got to have one of our people in the center. Ultimately, our job is to keep our characters growing and keep them at the center of the show and do good television."

He feels that the new incarnations of *Star Trek* remain true to the spirit of Gene Roddenberry's view of life in the 24th Century. Unlike many other writers who had worked on *Next Generation*, he does not find it a constricting format in which to deal with humanity.

"I think Gene's view of the future serves an important purpose in a very difficult time of our lives and history," Piller points out. "When our daily lives are filled with smog, gangs and drugs, it's important to see that there is hope, that there are ways to solve our problems, that there is a future we can look forward to. I'm sure there's a fine, wonderful series to be made out of *Blade Runner*, but I wouldn't want to live there. I think it's terribly important on television that you provide an environment that people want to stay in. There are those who would violently disagree with me, but I would love to live in the 24th Century that Gene Roddenberry has created. I

also think it's terribly important that family values on television come through, and that [our characters] represent the working environment, the family environment and living environment that we wish we would have. In a way, it sets a role model for things we can accomplish. I endorse it, I enjoy writing it, writers who have a difficult time with it complain that it's hard to find conflict in characters who are all perfect, who live in a perfect world. All I can say is that it is harder in that you can't just drop back and say, 'Okay, let's do a drug story this week,' but these are different people who come from different places. They approach problems in different ways. There is room for conflict and there are ways to find it. It's a little harder, but I also think it's very important that we endorse this. It's certainly the life I want to have.

"I have been accused of bringing angst to *Star Trek*," he smiles. "I think *Next Generation*, as optimistic as it should be, should not try to solve every problem every week. So when Worf decides that he can't bring himself to save a Romulan's life in 'The Enemy', I think it comes straight out of character. He doesn't come around, but that's Worf. That makes his character grow a foot taller. There will be things that are disturbing in our shows, provocative and thought provoking. I think it's important that we do that, because even in the most optimistic and perfect environment, there are still going to be things that happen that aren't going to make everybody happy.

"We're dealing with better humans here. We've evolved a little bit over the centuries, and so you're not going to have a lot of pettiness. But I do think there's room for genuine, honest conflict. For two people who like each other, who come from legitimate backgrounds and are honorable people, you still can have conflicts. In 'Sarek' we have a huge conflict because he and Picard are the most honorable men this series has known, and they can still have a huge conflict. My background is in journalism and when I was in news, I was accused of bringing a sense of entertainment to the news business, which may or may not have been right in the time or place I was doing it. Here I found myself on the other side, bringing a hard edge to the entertainment and that helps me a great deal with *Star Trek*. It almost makes me feel a very important commitment toward detail, making sure our technical areas are well covered and that we're not creating total fantasy. Our fiction is based on futuristic thinking."

Adds Piller, "You'll always find me praising the shows that had character development." Piller, who is quick to point out that he is not a fan of the original series, says that visits like those from Spock, Scotty (in season six's "Relics") and Sarek don't mean that fans should expect to see the beginning of a gradual inclusion of cast members from Classic Trek, despite the inclusion of classic Klingons Kor, Kang and Koloth in *DS9*'s "Blood Oath" and a second season sequel to "Mirror, Mirror," "Crossover."

"I think the reason for that is a good one," he says matter of factly. "We want our shows to stand on their own merits, on its own creativity. It is in its own origins a one of a kind that has survived all these years because of its quality. We don't want to be, 'And then there was....' We want to be a show that a new generation of fans will appreciate for itself. Yeah, sure, we will pay homage to the original, to our origins, but we don't want to depend on them. It's just too easy to go back and invite....whoever...to appear, or go back to a particular story. That's easy and it's like an inside gag for dedicated *Star Trek* fans. We want a whole new audience to find us and appreciate us for who we are.

"It's very hard for me to comment on the old series, because I don't know it very well," he admits. "I did not come to *Star Trek* as a life long fan. Not that I didn't like it, but I didn't watch it when I was growing up. I discovered *Star Trek: The Next Generation* as a show

This issue of **Starlog** looks at the various incarnations of Gene Roddenberry's creation.

unto itself. I was a fan of this show before I came to work for it. I'd watched it for two years and thought it was fascinating television. When the opportunity came to do this, to work with Rick Berman and Gene Roddenberry, I couldn't say no. It may actually be to my benefit that I didn't know the old series, because I understand one of the complaints about the earlier shows is that they were sort of reminiscent of the

other series."

Despite the contention by some fans that *Next Generation* was nothing more than a glorified soap opera, Piller tried to push the barriers beyond what were perceived as the show's traditional limitations. Looking back at *TNG's* earlier years, he points out, "The biggest decision of the hiatus between third and fourth season was to extend the storyline of Picard's kidnapping into the third episode. That was very controversial and there were a lot of people who were very hesitant about doing a threesome and going down to earth because people felt it was not *Star Trek*, and I have friends who are fans of the show who called and said I hope you never do that again. But I've got to tell you, for my money 'Family' was one of the best pieces of film we did that year. It was also consistently the lowest rated in both the original and reruns, so maybe my friend was right that if you're not out in space, you're not hitting the audience where they want to be hit. The normal objections were that we were not serialized and we don't want to give the audience the idea that we're serialized. We try to tell stories that can be told in one hour and that's what we do very well. I got to the end of 'Best of Both Worlds', we made the decision not to extend it and I called up Rick and said 'Hey listen, next week Picard can be fine but for a show that prides itself on its realistic approach to storytelling, how can you have a guy who's basically been raped be fine next week? Plus, there's a story in a man like Picard who's lost control and delving into the psychological crisis that a man like that has to face and what does he have to do.' Finally I was persuasive enough to talk Gene and Rick into taking the chance and I think everybody is glad we did."

In describing his personal writing style, Piller explains, "I'm a very instinctive writer, it's something that I try to convey to the people that I work with. Many of the people that I don't work well with are the people who need all the answers laid out before they start writing. I'm not saying there's anything wrong with that except that I find the discovery process is what the life of scripts is about. Yes, you need to have the broadstrokes and have a direction so you know where you're going. Television is too expensive and goes too quickly to run all the way down the road to realize you don't have anything when you get to the end/bottom of it. But I do honestly believe that you let the characters take you and just listen to what the voices are saying when you write a script because ultimately you'll find wonderful, wonderful things. Just as an example, when I did my rewrite on 'First Contact' the draft before mine had a technically convoluted way of getting Riker into an escape attempt and it dealt with a typical *Star Trek* make-the-locks-go-away type of thing. I felt it wasn't right and since I'm always coming out of character, I wanted to explore all these facets of the alien culture reaction to it. So I get to that page and I don't know what's going to happen next. I just see somebody come in the room and it's a woman. Suddenly this whole scene came to mind with Lannyl basically saying, 'I've always wanted to have sex with an alien.' But that does not come out of planning, that comes out of writing. The danger in all this is when you get a block and you can't figure out what the hell you're trying to say."

For Piller, who hears the voices of his characters so distinctly, it was a source of constant annoyance to be broached with the subject of the lack of interpersonal conflict in Gene Roddenberry's rose-colored universe of the *Next Generation*.

"That is the reflection of writers who can't write *Star Trek*," Piller asserts. "The bottom line is good people who are good humans and highly civilized entities who come from different places and have different codes of honor and priorities, have to come into conflict. What writers are used to doing on television is having blacks and whites, that it's easily seen why people are in conflict - that one has an alcoholic problem or there's racism. It is much more difficult to find the conflict [on *Star Trek*] because you must get inside those characters and really know what they care about. But if they are real people, they will have natural conflicts because they will have different interests that bring them together."

It is this type of conflict that played an important role in the creation of *Deep Space Nine*, in which Federation officers are placed in command of a space station in orbit around Bajor, home of perhaps the most spiritually-oriented race encountered in the history of *Trek*.

"I don't think that spiritualism goes against Gene's anti-religious beliefs," says Piller. "If he was still with us — and he's still on our shoulders as we think about these conceptual issues — I don't think it would bother him one bit. What he felt very strongly about is that humans, and to some degree Federation members, had a humanist attitude. His humans do not overtly celebrate religious beliefs. What we have simply done in creating an environment [on *Deep Space Nine*] that will bring conflict to our people, which we desperately wanted to do, was to put a group of people with a group of aliens that are different than we are; who had a difference and a conflict with our humanist beliefs. By giving them strong spiritual mystical orbs and prophet worship, it forces our humanist people to deal with another alien race that is as different from us as the Klingons are. They're different in the spirituality of their existence. We're saying if there's a problem here, let's fix the problem and they're saying the Prophets have to be satisfied and that causes conflict.

"Gene would be the first to tell you it doesn't matter what alien race you're talking about, how hideous they seem to be. There are no bad aliens. Each of them have a culture within itself which must be defined, recognized and appreciated for what it is. We've simply created a new alien race with a new set of circumstances and not changing Gene's vision of what humanity is in the 24th century. We're simply showing how we are affected by that conflict with that alien race."

It is because of Piller's feelings about the role of conflict in *Star Trek*, that he feels *TNG's* second season writing team dropped the proverbial ball in developing Diana Muldaur's character, Dr. Katherine Pulaski.

"I watched her and enjoyed her," says Piller. "The only thing I felt was that they worked too hard to make her a source of conflict. By giving her this conflict with Data, of all people, you had this terribly familiar relationship between a doctor and the strange one on the bridge, which I felt really echoed Spock and Bones and I thought that was a mistake. As far as whether or not she could have been popular with the gang, I bet you I could have made that work."

Currently, Piller's imprimatur can be found on both *DS9* and *Voyager*, from their reflection of his feelings about family values to rebuffs of violence and force, as well as the stories' frequent references to baseball, a personal passion of the producer which is reflected in the collection of memorabilia displayed in his office, formerly that of Gene Roddenberry. "I think as I watch and write *Star Trek*, there is no greater responsibility than to continue to tell the message that communication is the way to solve problems," says Piller. "When you see Captain Picard and Commander Sisko decide that logic and reason and discussion are ways to solve problems, we are telling something to our audience that needs to be said on a regular basis.

"The original *Star Trek* was a very Kennedy-esque mission to save the universe. 'Let's get these guys out there and show them what democracy is and educate them and if they don't do it the way we want to, we'll hit a few and get them the way we want them.' I think as Gene had a chance to look at the change in our country and the change in the world, that he felt that what the message of *Star Trek* should really be was that we should be out there exploring to learn more about ourselves, instead of trying to teach everybody else what *our* values are. We were very sure of our values in the early sixties. I think in the last twenty years we've begun to question those values. We have a lot to learn as a civilization and I think the fundamental message of the current *Star Trek* is where can we go and what can we learn from you?"

Ultimately, it is that emphasis on character that has defined Piller's tenure in the *Star Trek* universe. "I was presented with what I thought was a terrific franchise," recalls Piller. "Gene had enormous problems finding writers who could write this show and there was extraordinary political infighting, yet I had been a fan of the show for two years. It was always interesting to watch because you had great performers like Patrick Stewart, Brent Spiner, Marina and the rest of the gang. When I walked in the door, I told Gene and Rick that I don't walk in with a bunch of science-fiction ideas, I don't have a handful of stories, what I am is a character writer. What I can help you do is broaden and explore these characters. I was intimidated as anybody in the world about what it was going to take to do this. I needed a lot of help in understanding storytelling on *Star Trek* and I got that from Rick and I got that from Gene. Once I understood what made the equation work, I structured it in a way that I felt really worked and used character as the centerpiece for every show. If I didn't have character, I didn't feel it was a successful episode."

The dilemma, according to Piller, is avoiding the over 200 stories that have been told in *Star Trek's* first two incarnations.

"The bottom line is that the same kind of stories that work on the *Next Generation* are the same kind of stories that we want to tell on *Deep Space Nine* and *Voyager*," says Piller. "But we'll tell those stories illuminating different characters and different alien groups, but still explore the human condition and use the metaphors that work so well. It's the universe of science-fiction and the universe of Gene Roddenberry. We cannot do stories on *Deep Space Nine* or *Voyager* that wouldn't work on the other two *Star Trek* shows. The problems are the same. We can't repeat ourselves. We can't do stories that they did on *Next Generation*. We have to come up with fresh and orig-

inal material and it's very, very difficult."

Although *Deep Space Nine* was widely publicized during its first year, it has not been able to attract the same vast following as its illustrious predecessor. With *The Next Generation* completing its run, it will be interesting to see if *Deep Space Nine* can make it on its own.

Surprisingly, and ever so subtly, *Deep Space Nine* has become one of the best shows on television. "When we created it, I thought we created a good franchise," says Piller. "The real concern we had at the time was will we be able to do all the stories we do on *Next Generation*. It doesn't fly anywhere, but there are so many stories and so many character plots and so many situations that I can draw from in *Deep Space Nine* to create stories."

Clearly, *Deep Space* is a darker and grittier show than its progenitor, a drama which is, arguably, further removed from the Roddenberry vein than *TNG*. As a result, the show has taken its time finding its space legs, but in its second year established a tone and an identity all its own.

"I think the show has found its voice," says Piller. "I want to continue doing a good mix of science fiction thrillers, social issue stories and mysteries which give our cast an opportunity to really act. I want it to be a show that is fun to watch."

Piller admits that the first season, *DS9* had its own problems, many of which were remedied in its second year. "The first season we did stories that were all over the map, but creating television is just like a five year mission in a starship," he says. "It is an exploration. As viewers, you have the opportunity to get onboard and to search along with the people who are writing and creating and producing the show or you don't accept it right off the bat and say 'Obviously it's not *Star Trek: The Next Generation*' which, unfortunately, happened with a lot of people. However, those people who stayed with us are on a hell of a journey. It's frustrating because we're

CINEFANTASTIQUE

SPECIAL DOUBLE-ISSUE

October 1993
Volume 24 Nos 3/4

$10.95
CAN $13.50
UK £7.60

STAR TREK
THE NEXT GENERATION

ZOOMING
TO A 7TH
SEASON

PLUS: DEEP
SPACE NINE

Captains courageous:
Patrick Stewart and
Avery Brooks, heroes
of the final frontier

Captain Picard and Commander Sisko are brought together on the cover of Cinefantastique magazine.

doing such good work and a lot of people are missing it. There is sort of a cult audience that is attached to *Deep Space Nine* that is very, very dedicated and *that* is very rewarding. It reminds me of when I was playing tennis with one of my friends at the beginning of the year who came back after watching *NYPD Blue* for three weeks and when I said it was a good show, he looked up and said, 'It's not *Hill Street*.'"

Offers Piller, who has been joined by *TNG* writers Ronald D. Moore and Rene Echevarria on the show's third season, "If we had done a pale imitation of *The Next Generation*, those same people who are criticizing us now for doing something different, would have been the first to reject it. We had to find something that had it's own identity."

EXPLORING DEEP SPACE AND BEYOND

By Mark A. Altman and David Ian Solter

JERI TAYLOR
Lady Bird of the Galaxy

Levar Burton enters the office of Jeri Taylor, a large room filled with mementos of the writer/producer's many years in television. He's come to discuss some line changes in his *Next Generation* directorial debut, "Second Chances," in which the Enterprise discovers a duplicate of Riker existing on another world as a result of a transporter malfunction.

Burton is relaxed as he faces Taylor at her desk and discusses the truncating of a long speech by Riker in which the first officer explains why he is content aboard the Enterprise, rebutting accusations by his dopelganger that he has stagnated by allowing his relationship with Troi to falter and failed to earn his own command in the eight years that have passed. Jonathan Frakes wants to truncate the speech and Burton seems to agree with him.

Without missing a beat, Taylor explains to the actor/director why the dialogue is important, detailing how changing only a few lines could adversely impact on Riker's character, making his alter-ego more appealing to the audience. Without making any grand pronouncements, Taylor simply asks Burton to relay her comments to Frakes and to return if he isn't satisfied with her explanation.

"That's the kind of interaction I'm able to have with the actors — and in this case the director," says Taylor. "He comes to me with a legitimate concern and I understand his point of view. I think I also have one and I know he will listen to me because he knows I'm open. If it gets to be a power struggle or a control struggle, it's not the issues that are being dealt with."

Taylor, who was the final arbiter over *Trek* material before it was passed onto Michael Piller and Rick Berman, notes, "Every word in these scripts by the time they come out has been thought about, pared over and lovingly done. We *do* care."

At the end of the fifth season, Taylor was promoted to Co-Executive Producer of *The Next Generation*. While Rick Berman and Michael Piller concentrated on launching *Deep Space Nine*, Taylor quietly made *Star Trek*'s final two seasons among their most compelling. Having worked on the show since its fourth year, Taylor has the distinction of being one of the few people in *Star Trek* history that no one has ever said anything negative about.

"I don't think there is anything you could say that would make me happier than that," says Taylor. "I think my style in terms of management and of relating to people is really to put people first, to be aware that we are all in this together. Everybody is trying to do a job, everybody has feelings. Those feel-ings are important. I feel you get back a lot more from people if you treat them with dignity and respect and understanding and let them know that you care, and that they are as important as an idea, if not more so. It's just the way I work and the way I function, and it's not a calculated kind of thing. It's who I am."

Taylor's management style has obviously proved a boon to the show, although she is reluctant to speculate as to whether she's placed a distinct imprimatur on the show. "I maintain this is not a personality-driven show," says Taylor. "It represents Gene Roddenberry's vision and everyone is true to that. The series comes from the story. It's story driven. What we look for are fascinating, beguiling, interesting stories for our characters. That's everybody's first standard."

"In this contentious room, people's personal feelings definitely rise to the surface," offers Taylor of the break sessions that typify the production of a *Trek* series. "We have some very heated arguments. A lot of the time people feel passionate about things. It would be wrong of me to suggest that my feelings about the disenfranchised, about women, about weaker people, about violence — which are part of me — get very strongly represented and I don't let them get trammeled out of the story. It's also true that the other voices in the room have input too. If there is a contribution I've made, I think that it is in the nurturing of the staff, in making them feel comfortable and allowing them the full expression of their ideas and their creative vision. And the safety for them to say whatever they think and to argue it as long and as hard as they want to until such point as I have to say, 'Okay, we have to move on, we have to come to a decision.' If we're at an impasse, then I make the choice. But it's in just allowing them to grow that may be the most significant thing I've done."

However, the same way that one can see the high-concept science-fiction humanism of Roddenberry in the show's first year and the darker, fatalistic action/drama of Maurice Hurley in the second, culminating in the character-driven family values of Michael Piller's tenure, so can one see a distinct change in the show's themes in the first year that Taylor served as a Co-Exeuctive Producer on the show, including an improved role for the women aboard the Enterprise.

"The one thing that I tried to do, and was marginally successful at doing, was bolstering the characters of the two women," says Taylor. "They had been put in caretaker roles. There is nothing we can do about that. It's harder to find stories that break them out of that mold, and I think we did it more for Troi than for Beverly, although 'Suspicions' was a wonderful vehicle for Dr. Crusher and takes her out of the doctor and caretaker role."

Taylor's contributions can also be felt in more subtle ways as well. When Michael Westmore called her in order to find out the name of an alien race he had created for publicity purposes, Taylor dubbed them the Carvilions after Clinton advisor James Carville. "At that point I was very fascinated by James Carville, who was the advisor in the Clinton campaign. He was such an interesting guy that I just loved listening to him. So when I was casting around for aliens I used his, but I got the name wrong because I thought it was spelled differently at the time."

Taylor began writing for television after a divorce from her first husband. "I was a dilettante," she laughs. "I never expected to have a job or make a living. I came from that generation where you got married and had children and that was your work. I had always been involved with theater and so I continued to stay involved with that and did a number of Equity waiver productions here in L.A. I had my own acting workshop for a number of years and directed a few productions, and really kind of just kept my hand in there. When I got a divorce, suddenly reality hit me in the face and I realized I was going to have to make a living to take care of myself. I had no specific skills for the workplace, so I

Best known for adult dramas, Jeri Taylor cut her writing teeth on the Jack Klugman series Quincy *(photo copyright ©1994 MCA).*

thought having majored in writing in college and having done some newspaper writing, perhaps I could put this together. Now if I had known what I was saying, I would have never done it. It was just an insane notion. There I was, a housewife in Sherman Oaks with two very small children, and I thought if I could write I could be at home and be with my children, so I sat down and started writing screenplays."

Eventually Taylor secured an agent which led to several freelance assignments. "I wrote at home with my small children clamoring around the typewriter," recalls Taylor. "I remember my littlest one was four at the time and he drew a picture of a huge typewriter and me at it. I thought, 'That's his vision of me, mommy always at the typewriter,' but I was able to be there for them and as they began to get older, I began to get staff positions and I was a writer producer on a number of series ranging from *Quincy* in the early 80's until now."

During her tenure as show runner on *Next Generation*, Taylor became deeply involved the various facets of the production, including casting, editing and post-production. Conversely, on her first two years on the show she was exclusively involved with writing.

"My experience before *Star Trek* was much more broad ranging," she says. "Its experience and expertise which I feel I have at my fingertips, which for a couple of years was not utilized because the structure here is very different. I was asked to be a writer and that's what I did, and I was very happy to do that. When *Deep Space Nine* came along and Rick asked me to take over some of those other responsibilities, because he and Michael knew they were going to be so wrapped up in the new show, I was very pleased. Casting is an area where I am probably more comfortable than in any other — including writing. I have had years of experience as an actor, as an acting teacher and a director of stage and screen. What has worked nicely this year is there has been a representative of the writing side — those people who develop the characters and the story points — in the casting sessions. We may also realize some of our ideas are not as clear on the page as we think it is in our own minds, so I realize we have work to do and we have to go back to the page and make sure our original ideas and concepts are being fully realized. There's been a more direct communication with directors than there has been before, and I think it has been a happy combination. I respect the directors and their instincts, but I think by mutuality we have come to a better result."

"I find that quite often we have arguments or differences of opinion between her idea of who a part should be cast with and my idea," says *Star Trek* director Winrich Kolbe. "Sometimes she gives, and most times I give. After all, she is the executive producer. But to be very honest, there are sometimes where I look at this and say, 'Yeah, all right, okay fine. It's going to work,' but I still don't like her choice. Other times I have to say it worked. She is obviously a lot more opinionated about casting than Rick or Michael, which does not mean she does not know how to cast or she is over-casting, or whatever. It just means that she has a certain idea, which is the right of the writer because she has been sitting with that stuff a lot longer than I have."

Kolbe cites "Rightful Heir" as an example of a difference in opinion between he and Taylor in which the result was Kevin Conway being cast as the legendary Klingon, K'ehlest. "My idea of who K'ehlest would be was quite different from Jeri Taylor's and Ron Moore's," he says. "I had somebody who was taller and younger in mind and Jeri Taylor was very adamant and said, 'Absolutely not.' Well, you only get that much time to fight and I withdrew and wasn't quite sure, but then I saw the tape of Kevin Conway and I looked at it and there was something in there. The key word I think that got me to come around was Napoleon. Then when he popped up on the stage, he and I had a talk. We talked about the concept and where we wanted go, and I said 'I want you to come into any room, anyplace on your planet or any other planet, like you own the damn thing.' So he comes in, he's strutting in and he is standing there, and even though he is shorter by a head than anybody else, he is just in charge. I think it worked out very well and my hat is off to Jeri Taylor. Sometimes you say 'Do they have to do this casting like that because it is so out of the ordinary?', but then it works and everybody is very happy."

In addition to working more closely with the directors, Taylor has also proven more accessible to the actors, who have expressed their concerns to her. "I think most of the actors and I have developed a nice relationship," says Taylor. "I know that those things can get out of hand, but I appreciate the input. These are people who have a very strong sense of who they are, who their character is, and they can provide insights and ideas that would never occur to us and I respect them. If they have a problem with a line or with a scene, I listen to that because they've been living in these skins for six years and I think it would be wrong of me just to exclude them. It goes back to my management style, which is to acknowledge that even actors are human and they have feelings and that we can all probably get the richer product if those feelings are acknowledged and responded to."

Jonathan Frakes, who has worked with Taylor as both an actor and director, heartily agrees. "Jeri at the helm has been nothing but delightful and helpful," says Frakes. "She's kept her writing staff intact, which we all benefit from. It's been a great year and it's been a real treat. She's great to work with as a director and an actor and it's been a good year and gone by very fast. She's very bright and cares about actors and writing and all aspects of the show, and she doesn't seem to have a hidden agenda."

Echoes director Cliff Bole, "She's great. She's always available and gets to work real early, which is great because we do. Usually you try to find a writer and he's still sliding in at 10 AM and we've already done three hours of work. But Jeri is an early riser, so she's there for my first question and I probably call her on an average of three times a day for the first four days until we level out. She's always there."

Not surprisingly, *Next Generation*'s final year presented the show's staff with some of its greatest challenges. It also proved one of the most difficult seasons for its writers, who were charged with creating another 26 hours of engaging television viewing while its producers continued to expand the franchise in new directions.

"I'm not sure how everything got done this year," says Taylor, who supervised the writing staff of producers Ronald D. Moore and Brannon Braga, executive story editor Rene Echevarria and story editor Naren Shankar. "Rick Berman not only took on developing a new series, *Voyager*, but also continued the development of a feature film. I think we've all been kind of pushed to our limits and there were several things that made this season uniquely difficult."

Among the biggest challenges

close up

STAR TREK: THE NEXT GENERATION (CC)
8 PM ⑪

ALL GOOD THINGS...

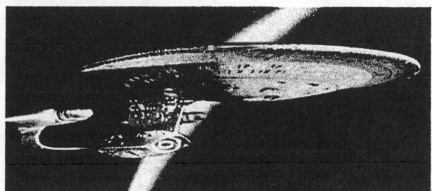

After seven seasons, the sci-fi series warps out of the TV galaxy. As the finale begins, Picard (Patrick Stewart) is hurtling uncontrollably from the past to the present to the future and back again. It seems that a "spatial anomaly" may hold a clue to the time-tripping, and Picard sets off to investigate. But on his way, he encounters his old foe Q (John de Lancie), who informs him that humanity is doomed—and that Picard will be responsible. What Q doesn't tell him is how or why. Tasha Yar: Denise Crosby. O'Brien: Colm Meaney. Tomalak: Andreas Katsulas. (2:00)

TV Guide **highlights the final episode of** Next Generation, *"All Good Things".*

were that the show's senior writers, Moore and Braga, had been hired to write the first *Next Generation* feature film, precluding their full-time involvement early in the season. By the end of the year, Taylor herself was immersed in work on the new spin-off series *Voyager*, which she would co-create with Berman and Piller — who himself was attempting

to streamline the second season of *Deep Space Nine*.

"Rick Berman had been approached by the studio to develop yet another series and he wanted me to be involved, and I was extremely gratified and flattered," says Taylor. "Working with Rick and Michael has been a lovely experience. I can only say that it has been

SCI FI UNIVERSE

STAR TREK
THE NEXT GENERATION
FINAL SEASON

"I CAN'T BELIEVE IT'S OVER!"

$4.99 U.S./Canada • SEPTEMBER 1994

09

0 74369 50225 3

exhilarating and fulfilling and rewarding and my respect and admiration for those two men remains unbounded. They are simply the best at what they do and for me to be included as an equal partner with them is quite an honor."

Taylor was intimately involved with devising the Maquis backstory, which serves as the jumping off point for *Voyager*. Established in "The Maquis" two-parter on *Deep Space Nine* and the "Journey's End" and "Preemptive Strike" episodes of *TNG*, the Maquis were established as disenchanted Federation officers and citizens who found themselves abandoned by the Federation after the signing of a treaty in which their worlds fell under Cardassian jurisdiction in the demilitarized zone between the Federation and Cardassia.

Says Taylor, "The Maquis really existed. That was the name of the French resistance fighters in World War II. My husband, ironically, wrote a teleplay about the real Maquis about thirty years or so ago. They call themselves freedom fighters and the Federation calls them outlaws. They are the people who have taken up arms to defend themselves against Cardassian strikes in the newly created Cardassian de-militarized zone. It is a situation not unlike the West Bank in Israel where people have been displaced. The Cardassians are being supplied secretly by their government because they have a vested interest in keeping the region unstable and trying to drive out the Federation citizens. So the citizens take matters into their own hands and start doing more than defending themselves, making preemptive strikes.

"It's a situation that will quickly get out of hand. Starfleet fears them, so they must control it. These are renegades. They are outlaws. They must be stopped. The Maquis are equally convinced that the Federation has let them down and that they have the right to defend themselves and their families. So it is that mix of people of Starfleet and Maquis who, through circumstances, find themselves aboard the starship Voyager and having to make a long journey home from the far regions of the galaxy."

The only question is can the insatiable hunger for science-fiction programming, and especially *Star Trek*, be quelled? If so, will there be a backlash against the profusion of new genre product in the marketplace? Obviously, nowhere is this concern felt more strongly than behind the hallowed gates of Paramount Pictures.

"We're very aware that there could be a backlash," says Jeri Taylor. "Anything can happen. Somehow, something in me doesn't think that's going to happen. The advance mail that I get and the people that I talk to at conventions are already expressing a great eagerness about *Voyager*. It seems to have excited them, even in advance of knowing anything about it. And perhaps it's knowing there will be a starship show out there that has a 'boldly going' feel to it, makes them even more eager to see it. We can only hope for the best and I don't think that, at the moment, the public or our fans' appetite for these kinds of wondrous, imaginative stories have been jaded."

One thing is certain, though: Taylor has not tired of her *Star Trek* association. "This has been a magical experience," she says. "*Star Trek* is unlike any other television show. It embraces so much more and affects people in such a different way. It has had an enormous impact on my life. I'm extremely grateful for the opportunity that I've had. Who would have thought that when I came here — never having seen any episode of any *Star Trek* — that this would have happened? There's going to be a little stone in the wall of *Star Trek* that will be mine, and it seems remarkable to me that that could happen in four years. I tell people that four years ago I got a phone call that asked if I wanted to do a rewrite on an episode of *The Next Generation* — and that one phone call has irrevocably changed my life."

(Opposite Page) On the cover of Sci-Fi Universe, Jonathan Frakes seems as stunned as anyone that production has ceased on Star Trek: The Next Generation.

HOW TO ORDER YOUR TREK TITLES FROM BOXTREE

1 85283 899 X	Captains' Logs	£13.99
1 85283 399 8	Captains' Logs Supplemental	£ 9.99
1 85293 340 8	Next Generation Technical Manual	£13.99
1 85283 571 0	Exploring Deep Space and Beyond	£ 6.99
1 85283 388 2	The Deep Space Logbook (First Season)	£ 9.99
1 85283 398 X	The Trek Universal Index	£ 9.99

All these books are available at your local bookshop or can be ordered direct from the publisher. Just tick the titles you want and fill in the form below.

Prices and availability subject to change without notice.

Boxtree Cash Sales, P.O. Box 11, Falmouth, Cornwall TR10 9EN

Please send cheque or postal order for the value of the book and add the following for postage and packing:

U.K. including B.F.P.O. £1.00 for one book, plus 50p for the second book, and 30p for each additional book ordered up to a £3.00 maximum.

Overseas including Eire – £2.00 for the first book, plus £1.00 for the second book, and 50p for each additional book ordered.

OR please debit this amount from my Access/Visa Card (delete as appropriate).

Card Number

Amount £ ....

Expiry Date on Card ....

Signed ....

Name ....

Address ....

....